DATE DUE

AG 7 01			

DEMCO 38-296

A scene from the Broadway production of "The Kentucky Cycle." Set design by Michael Olich.

THE KENTUCKY CYCLE

BY ROBERT SCHENKKAN

★

★

DRAMATISTS
PLAY SERVICE
INC.

...rs are hereby warned that THE ...lty. It is fully protected under the ...erica, and of all countries covered ...ncluding the Dominion of Canada ...h), and of all countries covered by ...on and the Universal Copyright ...ch the United States has reciprocal ...g professional, amateur, motion picture, recitation, lecturing, public reading, radio broadcasting, television, video or sound taping, all other forms of mechanical or electronic reproduction, such as information storage and retrieval systems and photocopying, and the rights of translation into foreign languages, are strictly reserved. Particular emphasis is laid upon the question of readings, permission for which must be secured from the author's agent in writing.

The stage performance rights in THE KENTUCKY CYCLE (other than first class rights) are controlled exclusively by the DRAMATISTS PLAY SERVICE, INC., 440 Park Avenue South, New York, N.Y. 10016. No professional or non-professional performance of the play (excluding first class professional performance) may be given without obtaining in advance the written permission of the DRAMATISTS PLAY SERVICE, INC., and paying the requisite fee.

Inquiries concerning all other rights should be addressed to William Craver, c/o Writers & Artists Agency, 19 West 44th Street, New York, N.Y. 10036.

SPECIAL NOTE

All groups receiving permission to produce THE KENTUCKY CYCLE are required (1) to give credit to the author as sole and exclusive author of the play in all programs distributed in connection with performances of the play and in all instances in which the title of the play appears for purposes of advertising, publicizing or otherwise exploiting the play and/or a production thereof; the name of the author must appear on a separate line, in which no other name appears, immediately beneath the title and in size of type equal to 50% of the largest letter used for the title of the play. No person, firm or entity may receive credit larger or more prominent than that accorded the Author. (2) To give the following acknowledgments on the title page in all programs distributed in connection with performances of the play:

THE KENTUCKY CYCLE was produced on Broadway by David Richenthal,
Gene R. Korf, Roger L. Stevens, Jennifer Manocherian,
Annette Niemtzow, Mark Taper Forum/Intiman Theatre Company,
and the John F. Kennedy Center for the Performing Arts,
in association with Benjamin Mordecai,
at the Royale Theatre in New York City, on November 14, 1993

The World Premier of THE KENTUCKY CYCLE
was produced by Intiman Theatre Company, Seattle, Washington,
Elizabeth Huddle, Artistic Director, and subsequently co-produced in
Los Angeles by Center Theatre Group/Mark Taper Forum,
Gordon Davidson, Artistic Director/Producer

THE KENTUCKY CYCLE was originally developed in the
Taper Lab New Work Festival Center Theatre Group/Mark Taper
Forum
The Play was further developed at The Sundance Institute

The Intiman Theatre Company's production of this play was awarded
a major grant from The Fund for New American Plays, a project of the
John F. Kennedy Center for the Performing Arts with support from
American Express in cooperation with the President's Committee
on the Arts and the Humanities

SPECIAL NOTE ON MUSIC

For performance of such music and recordings mentioned in this play as are in copyright, the permission of the copyright owners must be obtained; or other music and recordings in the public domain substituted.

For Mary Anne

THE KENTUCKY CYCLE was produced by David Richenthal, Gene R. Korf, Roger L. Stevens, Jennifer Manocherian, Annette Niemtzow, Mark Taper Forum/Intiman Theatre Company and the John F. Kennedy Center for the Performing Arts in association with Benjamin Mordecai, at the Royale Theatre in New York City, on November 14, 1993. It was directed by Warner Shook; the scene design was by Michael Olich; the costume design was by Frances Kenny; the lighting design was by Peter Maradudin; the composer and sound designer was James Ragland; the dramaturg was Tom Bryant; the fight director was Randy Kovitz and the production stage manager was Joan Toggenburger. The ensemble cast included:

Stephen Lee Anderson
John Aylward
Lillian Garrett-Groag
Gail Grate
Michael Hartman
Katherine Hiler
Ronald Hippe
Gregory Itzin
Stacy Keach
Ronald William Lawrence
Philip Lehl

Scott MacDonald
Tuck Milligan
Randy Oglesby
Patrick Page
Jeanne Paulsen
Susan Pellegrino
James Ragland
Jennifer Rohn
Novel Sholars
Lee Simon, Jr.

THE KENTUCKY CYCLE was produced by Mark Taper Forum (Gordon Davidson, Artistic Director; Charles Dillingham, Managing Director), in Los Angeles, California, on January 18, 1992. It was directed by Warner Shook; the scene design was by Michael Olich; the costume design was by Frances Kenny; the lighting design was by Peter Maradudin; the composer and sound designer was James Ragland; the fight director was Randy Kovitz; the dramaturg was Tom Bryant; the production stage manager was Joan Toggenburger and the stage manager was Cari Norton. The ensemble cast included:

Lillian Garrett-Groag
Martha Hackett
Charles Hallahan
Katherine Hiler
Ronald Hippe
Gregory Itzin
Sheila Renee Johns
Roger Kerns
Erick Kilpatrick
Matthew Kimbrough

Ronald William Lawrence
Scott MacDonald
Vince Melocchi
Tuck Milligan
Randy Oglesby
Jeanne Paulsen
James Ragland
Novel Sholars
Laurie Souza
Michael Winters

THE KENTUCKY CYCLE received its world premiere at Intiman Theatre Company (Elizabeth Huddle, Artistic Director; Peter Davis, Managing Director), in Seattle, Washington, on June 1, 1991. It was directed by Warner Shook; the scene design was by Michael Olich; the costume design was by Frances Kenny; the lighting design was by Peter Maradudin; the composer and sound designer was James Ragland; the dramaturg was Tom Bryant; the fight choreographer was Geoffrey Alm and the stage manager was Joan Toggenburger. The ensemble cast included:

Patrick Broemeling
Amelia Fowler
Lillian Garrett-Groag
Demene Hall
Charles Hallahan
James Hesla
Ronald Hippe
Thomas Hyler
Gregory Itzin

Sonya Anne Joseph
Anthony Lee
Scott MacDonald
Tuck Milligan
Randy Oglesby
Jeanne Paulsen
Novel Sholars
Jillayne Sorenson
Trevelyon Williams
Michael Winters

THE KENTUCKY CYCLE was originally developed in the Taper Lab New Work Festival, and further developed at the Sundance Institute.

ACKNOWLEDGMENTS

The author wishes to acknowledge the assistance and contributions of the following individuals and institutions to the development of THE KENTUCKY CYCLE: Dr. Greg Culley, Harry Caudill, Scott Reiniger, Jessica Teich, New Dramatists, the Ensemble Studio Theatre, Gordon Davidson and the Mark Taper Forum, the Long Wharf Theatre, David Kranes and the Sundance Institute, TheatreWorks, Liz Huddle and the Intiman Theatre, Roger Stevens and the Fund for New American Plays, the Arthur Foundation, the Vogel Foundation, Conal O'Brien, Russell Vandenbrouke, Michael Keys Hall, and Ernie Sabella.

A special thanks to the Seattle, Los Angeles, and New York City acting companies, some members of which have been associated with the play throughout its many years of development.

It is not possible to overpraise the work done by the New York City producer, David Richenthal. David single-handedly brought this play to Broadway and he did so with considerable grace and dignity.

Finally the author is especially grateful to Tom Bryant, dramaturg extraordinare, for his good advice and good cheer; and to the director, Warner Shook, for his unflagging hard work and his brilliant staging, much of which has now been incorporated into this text.

AUTHOR'S NOTE

THE KENTUCKY CYCLE is a series of nine short plays that chronicles the changing fortunes of the Rowen family over two hundred years in that part of Eastern Kentucky known as Appalachia. It is designed to be performed in two parts by an ensemble of twelve principal actors and actresses with an additional chorus of seven on a variable unit set in two consecutive evenings or in a continuous, all-day performance with a single dinner break.

Despite appearances, this text is not strictly speaking, "naturalism." There is a ritual aspect to the entire piece that the audience must never be allowed to forget, and a style of performance that might best be described as "story-telling." This does not mean that actors shouldn't do their normal character exploration or concentrate on playing actions and objectives — they should. What it does mean is that there will also be adjustments to rhythm, tempo, staging, and stage business that are inherently theatrical.

A few examples: The use of a core group of actors to play all the principal roles, each actor creating his or her transformation in full view of the audience with little or no reliance on makeup, wigs, or prosthetics. The use of "off-stage" ensemble members as on-stage "witnesses" throughout the performance. The construction/deconstruction of the set by the entire ensemble in full view of the audience not only between plays but in the scene breaks *within* plays.

The scenic design (scene, costume, property and lights) should flow out of this basic aesthetic of the play and the author would urge future productions to closely adhere to two key principles arrived at for the Broadway production.

One: Everything is seemingly visible to the audience. All the mechanics of the stage and house are in plain view. This is theatre that does not pretend to be anything else.

Two: Nothing must hinder the smooth, forward movement of the action or detract from the story being told. The most important thing here, *always,* is the actor standing in the light speaking the words.

Finally, the "land" is a major, if silent, character in the play and some way must be found to keep its presence alive for the audience. In the Broadway design, this meant starting with an "earthen pit" in the center of the raked stage which was methodically covered over by wooden plugs through the course of the evening as the land falls beneath the axe and the plow until, with the burial of Randall at the end of GOD'S GREAT SUPPER, nothing remains. When the action finally returns to the land for THE WAR ON POVERTY, two central plugs were removed exposing a tiny plot of earth and the infant burial hole.

GENEALOGICAL CHART FOR *THE KENTUCKY CYCLE*

Illustrating the blood relationships of the ROWEN, TALBERT, and BIGGS families

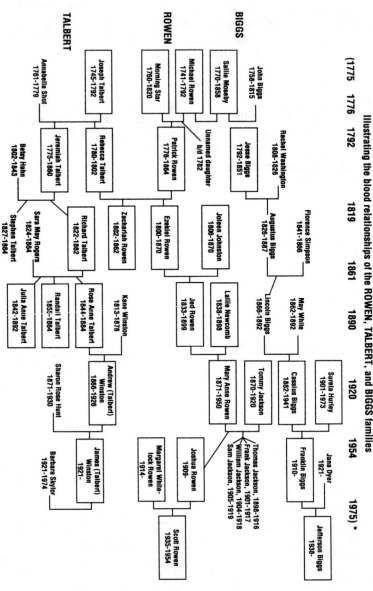

(1775   1776   1792   1819   1861   1890   1920   1954   1975) *

* Dates at top of chart refer to years in which the play takes place

Names in boxes designate characters who appear in the plays.

THE KENTUCKY CYCLE

Part One

*"Ill fares the land, to hastening ills at prey,
when wealth accumulates and men decay."*

— Oliver Goldsmith

PART ONE

MASTERS OF THE TRADE

⟡

Cherokee Translations by
Wes Studi, Levi Carey and Virginia Carey

"It was here on the frontier of the middle and upper South that the Indian Wars rose to their fiercest and cruelest pitch. Here the savage was taught his lessons in perfidy by masters of the trade."

— H. Caudill

CHARACTERS

EARL TOD, a Scottish trapper

MICHAEL ROWEN, age thirty-four, an Irish
    indentured servant

SAM, a Virginia farmer

TASKWAN, a Cherokee

DRAGGING CANOE, a Cherokee

CHEROKEE WARRIORS (non-speaking roles)

PROLOGUE

When the audience enters the theatre, the house lights are on, exposing the entire stage and it's mechanics. When the "curtain" rises, the house lights go out and the actors enter the stage from all four directions. The principal actors surround the earthen pit, facing each other, while the chorus remains stage left and stage right in the waiting areas. The principal actors turn as one and face the audience. A spot singles out one Actor/Actress, the Narrator.*

* The role of the Narrator should shift among the ensemble so that a different Actor or Actress assumes the part each time.

NARRATOR

The Kentucky Cycle.

(Once again, the principal actors turn inwards to face each other. A single actor (Earl Tod) steps into the dirt pit. As he does so, the work lights shift into stage light and the music begins. Chorus members ritually outfit this actor with a hat and a rifle. A large, leather pack is set down beside him. Three wooden "fire" logs are carried on and placed together. As Earl Tod sits down by the "fire," the Narrator again turns to face the audience.)

Masters of the Trade.

The year is 1775. A small clearing in a thick forest somewhere in Eastern Kentucky. A creek flows nearby. "It was here on the frontier of the middle and upper South that the Indian Wars rose to their fiercest and cruelest pitch. Here the savage was taught his lessons in perfidy by masters of the trade."

Masters of the Trade.

(All the actors leave the stage to sit in the waiting areas off-stage left and right where they will remain in full view of the audience. The lights shift, and we are in the forest. The play begins.)

MASTERS OF
THE TRADE

*1775. Early morning, an hour before daybreak. Somewhere in
Eastern Kentucky. A small clearing in a thick forest. A creek
flows nearby.*

*Earl Tod sits hunched over in front of a dying fire. He
dozes, wrapped in a filthy blanket, and cradling a rifle. Forest sounds fade in. Beat. A wolf howls in the distance. Beat.*

*Suddenly, Tod's head snaps upright. Slowly, almost impercep-
tibly, he moves his hands down the stock, locating the trig-
ger. He calls out a greeting in Cherokee:*

TOD.   "O si yo!" *(There is no answer. He swings the gun up.
There is an unmistakable Scottish brogue in his voice as he calls out.)*
You can step out into the light now wi' your hands up and
tell me your name, or I'll put a bullet into ya from here and
you can die unburied and nameless. It's all the same to me.
*(Beat. Out of the dark, a large, squarely built white man in tattered
buckskin limps cautiously forward, his hands up. He speaks with a
heavy Irish accent.)*
MICHAEL.   The name is Rowen. Michael Rowen. And I have
to be tellin' ya, sure but your hospitality is nothin' much to
brag about.
TOD.   What do ye want?
MICHAEL.   A place by the fire. Somethin' to break me fast.
I haven't eatin' for two, mebbe three days now.
TOD.   What happened?
MICHAEL.   Well, after all that terrible trouble at Zion, I said
to meself, "Michael, me boy, it's time you were movin' on."
And so I packed up me things and headed into the moun-

tains — "whence cometh my strength." *(Beat.)* Psalm 121? "I lift up mine eyes unto these hills, whence cometh my strength." Are you familiar with the scriptures, sir? *(Tod remains silent, his gun pointed at Rowen.)*

TOD.   I know, "An eye for an eye."

MICHAEL.   Ahh, an Old Testament man, are ya? A fellow after me own heart. The New Testament, it's ... it's a little watery now isn't it?

TOD.   You didn't finish your story. What happened to you?

MICHAEL.   Couple o' days ago, I ran into a catamount. Scared me horse so, he bolted off into a ravine carryin' everythin' I owned, includin' me rifle.

TOD.   Bad luck.

MICHAEL.   The devil's own! 'Course, I can't say I blame me horse, poor creature. When I seen that cat, I was off and runnin' meself, with about as much direction. I took a fall, knocked meself silly, ass over teacup, and turned this ankle in the bargain! Been wanderin' ever since. Real glad to see your fire.

TOD.   Then why didn't ye just step up, 'stead of sneakin' in?

MICHAEL.   Well, after Zion, I wasn't sure but ye might be Indians. *(Beat.)* Listen, Mr. ... uh...? *(No response.)* It's been very nice to chat with ya, but do ya suppose I could finish this conversation with me arms down and me belly full?

TOD.   Warm yourself. *(Michael drops his hands and limps to the fire. Tod turns quickly and strikes Michael a blow with the stock of his gun. Michael drops. Tod stands over him and searches his body for weapons. He finds a small knife in one boot and drops it in disgust. Michael moans. Tod crosses over to the other side of the fire. He tosses a canteen and a small leather pouch into the dirt in front of Michael.)*

MICHAEL.   *(Gasping, as he catches his breath.)* Son of a bitch!

TOD.   There's water, and pemmican in the bag.

MICHAEL.   Son of a bitch.

TOD.   Can't take no chances. Not with Cherokee and Shawnee runnin' about. Renegades runnin' wi' 'em. *(Michael struggles to sit up.)*

MICHAEL.   You seen Indians?

TOD.   Party o' bucks all painted up. Headin' North-West seven days ago.

MICHAEL.   *(Swallowing some water and digging into the pemmican.)* Shawnee?

TOD.   Cherokee.

MICHAEL.   Probably part of the same group what attacked Zion.

TOD.   What happened to Zion?

MICHAEL.   Ya don't know? Terrible thing. Tragic.

TOD.   You're the first man I've run into since I left Boonesboro two months ago.

MICHAEL.   White man.

TOD.   What?

MICHAEL.   First *white* man you've seen. You saw those Cherokee bucks a week ago. *(Beat.)* What're ya doin' out here? You a trapper?

TOD.   You didn't answer my question.

MICHAEL.   Oh, Zion. Terrible. About a hundred Cherokee savages attacked the settlement a week ago. Wiped it out. Man, woman, and child.

TOD.   *(Pointedly.)* 'Cept you.

MICHAEL.   I wasn't there. On me way back from Boonesboro, me horse threw a shoe, bless his soul, slowed me down and saved me life. I was in time to watch the massacre. Not "take part."

TOD.   You're a very lucky man.

MICHAEL.   With a very unlucky wife. And two children even more unlucky. *(Beat.)*

TOD.   That's hard. *(Michael shrugs.)*

MICHAEL.   May their souls rest comfortably in the arms of the Lord.

TOD.   Amen.

MICHAEL.   I've no way to repay your hospitality but this ... *(He reaches into his back pocket. Tod starts, and lowers his gun, cocked. Michael freezes.)* I've nothin' more dangerous in me back pocket than a small flask of poteen. With your permission? *(Tod nods. Michael pulls the flask out.)* You're a nervous man,

21

Mr....?

TOD. *(Ignoring the implied question.)* These are nervous times.

MICHAEL. That they be. When no man dare be sure of his neighbor and a white man'd ride with the murderin' red savages 'gainst his own kind. Nervous times. *(Beat.)* I'd toast the health of my host and savior, if I knew his name. *(Beat.)*

TOD. Tod. Earl Tod.

MICHAEL. Mr. Tod, sir, your health. Like the good Samaritan, ya have restored life to this poor wayfarer. *(He drinks, and then hands the flask to Tod.)*

TOD. Ye saw renegades at Zion?

MICHAEL. Well, I wasn't close enough to be sure, ya understand, but ... when did ya ever hear of Indians carryin' rifles?

TOD. Christ!

MICHAEL. I counted near a dozen rifles. Mebbe more. *(Beat.)* They looked new. *(Tod drinks.)* Ah well, way of the world, eh, Mr. Tod? I mean, we been sellin' 'em everythin' else. It was bound to happen sooner or later. And one man's profit ... is just another man's dead wife. *(Tod throws the flask back to Michael.)*

TOD. When there's light enough, I'll show ye where ye are. Give ye some water and jerky. Even with your ankle bad, should make Boonesboro in a week. Little less.

MICHAEL. You in trade, Mr. Tod?

TOD. What I do is none of your damn business.

MICHAEL. I meant no offense, to be sure, Mr. Tod. It's just that I find meself in your debt, sir, and I always pay me debts. I've friends in Boonesboro might be useful to a man like yourself, if he's in trade.

TOD. That's kind of ye. But what little tradin' I do, just keeps me in what I needs. Nothin' more.

MICHAEL. Aye, but that's the real question now, innit, Mr. Tod? What is it a man needs?

TOD. Meanin'?

MICHAEL. One man's needs are another man's luxuries. Take yourself now. What brings you to Kentucky, Mr. Tod?

TOD. Room. And quiet. And it don't look like I'm goin' to

get much of either this mornin'.

MICHAEL. *(Grinning.)* It's a beautiful country, now innit? *Look* at the size of them trees. Sure, but that's the King of Oaks there. And the water in that creek is so sweet, and so *clear,* b'God but you could read the date off a shilling on the bottom of it.

TOD. If you had one to throw in.

MICHAEL. Oh, no trouble there! It's a grand land of opportunity, it is, with plenty of scratch to be made for those with an itch! All that, and enough room for a man to stretch out and lose himself entirely. Become somethin' new. Somethin' different. A new *man.* That's what we're makin' here in Kentucky, Mr. Tod. New Men. *(Beat.)* Meself, I came by way of Georgia. Brought over indentured, don't ya know. Only, me and my Master disagreed over the length of me service.

TOD. And?

MICHAEL. And then there was this terrible accident, and the poor man up and died. Very sudden like. *(Tod laughs, in short, sharp barks.)*

TOD. Sad!

MICHAEL. *(Laughing.)* Yes! It was all very sad! Tell me, Mr. Tod, don't you worry 'bout sharin' all this lovely space of yours with them savages?

TOD. They don't bother me.

MICHAEL. They don't?

TOD. I leave them alone, they leave me alone.

MICHAEL. Is that a fact? You have an understandin' then, do ya, you and them?

TOD. I wouldna call it that.

MICHAEL. What would you call it? A deal, maybe? Ah, but I forgot, you're not a tradin' man, are ya? "Ha dlv digalowe?" [Where are the rifles?]

TOD. What ... what is that?

MICHAEL. Cherokee. As you well know. "Ha dlv digalowe?" Where are the rifles?

TOD. I don't know what you're talkin' about.

MICHAEL. That was a Cherokee greetin' you called out

when I first stumbled onto your campfire. Where *are* the rifles, Mr. Tod? *(Tod stands up nervously, pointing his gun at Michael.)*

TOD.   I don't know what you're talkin' about.

MICHAEL.   The rifles them Cherokee had at Zion. They come from you, didn't they? *(Beat.)* Where's the rest? *(Tod cocks his rifle.)* Don't be stupid as well as greedy, Mr. Tod. Ya don't think I walked in here unarmed, *alone? (A noise off-stage. Tod whirls and fires. As he does so, Michael leaps up and screams.)* DON'T KILL HIM! *(A single shot rips out of the darkness. Tod falls. Beat. Sam, a thin, nervous young man emerges from the woods holding a rifle.)*

SAM.   That him?

MICHAEL.   Yes, you little shit — that *was* him. *(Sam walks over to the body. He drops his rifle, kneels down, and begins to pummel the corpse with both his hands with increasing ferocity.)*

SAM.   You bastard! You bastard! YOU BASTARD! *(Michael strides over and hauls Sam roughly to his feet.)* He killed my family! He kilt'em! *(Michael slaps him across the face several times and then drops him to his knees with a blow to the stomach.)*

MICHAEL.   And mine! And everyone else's! And now he's *dead,* you little shit! I told you not to kill'im! *(Beat. With great disgust.)* Now wipe your face and shut up.

SAM.   *(Crying.)* He killed my Sarah.

MICHAEL.   Piss on your Sarah! *(He grabs Sam and throws him to the ground.)* You little turd! Them shots will have every Indian in two miles down on us.

SAM.   *(Blanching in terror.)* Cherokee?

MICHAEL.   Well, who do you think dear Mr. Tod was waitin' for? The Blessed St. Christopher? So unless you want to join your precious Sarah in the hereafter, you shut your mouth and do as I say. Now bring our packs in. *(Sam staggers off into the woods. Michael searches Tod's body closely, removing and keeping a knife. He discovers a gold pocket watch on a chain, which when opened plays a bright tune. He pockets it. He then searches through Tod's belongings, with increasing urgency and finally frustration.)* Damn! Damn it! *(Sam returns with two heavy leather packs, which he drops by the fire.)*

SAM.   What's wrong?

24

MICHAEL. I can't find anything! Not flints, powder, bullets or muskets. I don't know — mebbe he buried it somewhere. Worried, were you, Mr. Tod, 'bout the good word of our red brothers? *(Michael starts rummaging through one of the packs. He pulls out a worn, red blanket. He looks at it oddly for a moment, and then tosses it to Sam.)* Cover'im up.

SAM. Why?

MICHAEL. You're developin' an annoyin' habit, Samuel, of questionin' me. Just do as I say and we'll both live longer. Now cover him up! *(Sam obeys.)* How much powder and shot have you got, Sam?

SAM. I don't know. Mebbe two horns and a quarter pound of shot.

MICHAEL. Get it out.

SAM. You think we'll have to make a fight of it?

MICHAEL. I'm hopin' we can work out a trade.

SAM. What?

MICHAEL. Get out what you've got! *(Sam starts to comply but before he can move, four figures emerge from the woods, surrounding them. They are Cherokee Warriors, dressed simply in buckskin, but beautifully painted. They all carry rifles. One of the men steps forward. Unnerved, Sam tries to reach for his gun.)* Be still, for the love of Christ! *(Sam freezes, as every rifle is lowered at him. Two of the Indians — Taskwan and Dragging Canoe — openly contemptuous of the white men before them, converse in Cherokee.)*

DRAGGING CANOE. "Gago yunsti na anisgaya?" [Who are these men?] *(Taskwan shrugs.)*

TASKWAN. *(To Michael.)* "Tod di nah?" [Where is Tod?]

MICHAEL. Greetings to my Cherokee brothers.

TASKWAN. Who are you?

MICHAEL. *(Surprised.)* You speak English?

TASKWAN. It is easier than hearing you butcher Cherokee. I am Taskwan. Who are you?

MICHAEL. Friends.

TASKWAN. Whose friends?

MICHAEL. We could be yours.

TASKWAN. *(Indicating Tod's body.)* Was he a "friend?" *(Michael says nothing.)* Your friendship is very hard.

DRAGGING CANOE. "Tod is unihlv?" [Have they killed Tod?]

TASKWAN. "Hu tle gi." [Uncover the body.] *(One of the Warriors pulls the blanket off Tod. Taskwan steps over and looks into his face.)* "Vs kidv." [It is him.] *(Beat.)*

DRAGGING CANOE. "Didi luga." [Kill them.] *(The Warriors raise their rifles. Michael and Sam tense.)*

MICHAEL. We can still do business! *(Dragging Canoe gestures for the Warriors to hold.)*

DRAGGING CANOE. "Gado adi?" [What does he say?]

MICHAEL. You need us! *(Beat. Dragging Canoe gestures to his Warriors and they lower their guns.)*

DRAGGING CANOE. "Wiga wo ni hi." [Let him speak.]

MICHAEL. Ya had a deal, right, with Tod? Guns for pelts. Right? But how much powder and lead did the bastard give ya? Huh? Not enough, I bet. Not nearly enough.

SAM. What are ya doin', Michael?

MICHAEL. Shut up, boy! So, we'll step in for Mr. Tod, see. Here. Here's a good faith gesture ... *(He starts to move towards Sam's pack. The Warriors shift uneasily.)* Easy lads! Call'em off, Taskwan. *(Taskwan gestures.)* That's it. Here. Here now. *(Pawing through Sam's pack, he pulls out two powder horns and a small deerskin bag, which he lays out grandly on the red blanket.)* See here. Two horns of black powder and a half pound of the King's own finest lead! And I'll throw them blankets in too. Fine wool, both of 'em!

TASKWAN. And?

MICHAEL. And? And when the moon is full again, we meet you here, by that oak, with ten times that, twenty times ... whatever ye want.

TASKWAN. How much?

MICHAEL. Twenty pelts per horn. Ten for a quarter pound of shot. And none of your junk, mind ya! Good skins! Clean cuts!

DRAGGING CANOE. "Gado adi?" [What is he saying?]

TASKWAN. *(Smiling.)* "Adaweligisgi ale gani. Utloyi Todi jatuisdisgv. Gayoheigeski ussale." [Powder and shot. Just as Tod promised us. Only they are less greedy.]

MICHAEL. You need us, Taskwan! Without us, those muskets are just expensive firewood!

DRAGGING CANOE. "Gayolige jiliskododi na, Tod digesv aniskahv inisvgagwo. Nanu ina yigati gagogi." [I trust them less than Tod. They stink of fear and the tall one lies.]

TASKWAN. "Handadis sayani, Jiygasini? Galogwe gesvyusdi igadahlosvi. Sagwo gaduhv yugwony shla gohusdi yigunela. Kuni yididalewisdodani dunikaligi ale dodunadigaleyi digajeli yvwi. Uhloyi anishani jidedikehedolvi. Vskyusdi galogwe digiyadi. Galogwe adaweliski gideski. Na adaweligiski unaliskasdi." [Remember Zion, Dragging Canoe? The guns brought us a great victory. But one town burned is nothing to them. Unless we stop them now, they will cover this land and scatter our people as we drove off the Shawnee. For this we need guns. Guns need powder. Powder needs them.]

DRAGGING CANOE. "Hawa. Tadi na?" [So be it. What of Tod, though?]

TASKWAN. "Hawa." [Yes.] *(He turns to Michael.)* We accept your offer.

MICHAEL. Now you're talkin', me friend!

TASKWAN. Old debts before new business, my "friend." He is dead who was a brother to my people, and his blood debt is unpaid. *(Pause.)*

MICHAEL. As you will. *(Magically, his knife is out, and in one, swift, brutal motion he slams the blade into Sam's stomach. Sam drops to his knees, a look of incredulity laced with pain spreading across his face.)*

SAM. Michael? *(He collapses on the ground. Michael turns and ceremoniously drops the knife on the blanket with the other trading goods.)*

MICHAEL. He killed Tod. He's dead. We're even.

DRAGGING CANOE. "Gadousti inage ehnai ni hi?" [What kind of animal is this?]

MICHAEL. What'd he say?

TASKWAN. He says, "What kind of animal are you?"

MICHAEL. A necessary animal. Tell him. "A necessary animal!"

TASKWAN. He understands. We will meet you here in one

month. Twelve more rifles. Powder and shot for all.

MICHAEL. Two hundred pelts per gun.

TASKWAN. That is more than Tod wanted.

MICHAEL. You can still trade with Tod.

TASKWAN. I could still kill you.

MICHAEL. You could. *(Beat. He extends his hand.)* Deal? *(Taskwan looks at it with distaste but takes it. When he tries to turn away, Michael holds him.)* Just one more thing. I want me some land. Much as a man can walk around in one day, and your word that me and mine is safe on it.

DRAGGING CANOE. "Gado adi?" [What does he say?]

TASKWAN. "Gado uduli." [He wants land.] *(All the Warriors laugh.)* No one "owns" this land. It cannot be "given."

MICHAEL. Is that what you said when you drove the Shawnees off it?

TASKWAN. This land is cursed. We hunt on it, but no tribe lives here.

MICHAEL. I'll take me chances.

DRAGGING CANOE. "Ganegedi ale gigaha gadohi. Tla yegehadehvga." [It is a dark and bloody land. You cannot live here.]

MICHAEL. What'd he say?

TASKWAN. He says, you will find this a dark and bloody land.

MICHAEL. *(To Dragging Canoe.)* I'll take me chances. *(He turns back to Taskwan.)* Your word.

TASKWAN. You live here, it is not the Cherokee you need fear. *(He gestures to the powder, shot and blankets.)* "Ijutagesvhna. Idahnigia." [Take them. We go.] *(The Warriors gather up the blankets and exit. Dragging Canoe doesn't move. He remains staring at Michael.)* "Idahnigia!" [We go!] *(They exit. Michael stands for a moment, breathing hard, a look of triumph on his face. Sam moans.)*

MICHAEL. Ah, Samuel, you were more use to me than I could ever imagine. How can I ever repay you?

SAM. *(Faint.)* Water.

MICHAEL. Water? By all means, Samuel. *(He lifts Sam up*

tenderly, crouching behind, half-supporting him and helping him to sip at the canteen.)

SAM. Am I goin' to die?

MICHAEL. Oh, I should think so, Samuel. Otherwise, I should have to order you off my land. *(Laughs.)* "My land." Oh, there's a grand sound to that, isn't there? Course, if you and Mr. Tod want to stay here, permanent-like, make yourselves useful — fertilize me corn, mebbe — that'd be all right too! *(He laughs.)*

SAM. They'll kill you ...

MICHAEL. Who? The Cherokee? Oh no, Sam. Quite unlike their white brothers, they keep their word, they do. *(Beat.)* And even if they didn't, this lot will. I've seen to that.

SAM. What?

MICHAEL. Them blankets, Sam — they're *poxed*. Salvaged them from that Cutter family in Zion — them whose baby girl died of the pox three weeks ago. Remember? Sweet child. Hair like corn silk. *(Beat.)* Indians has thin blood. Pox'll cut through them like a hot knife through butter. *(Beat.)* So you see, Sam, you can rest easy now. Zion's been revenged after all. *(Beat.)* Sam? *(Beat.)* Sun's comin' up, lad. *(Beat.)* New day for a new land. *(Beat. Fade to black. Forest sounds hold for five beats and then fade.)*

END OF PLAY

PROPERTY LIST

Hat
Rifles
Blankets
Large leather pack
3 wooden "fire" logs
Small knife (MICHAEL)
Canteen (TOD)
Small leather pouch (TOD)
Small flask (MICHAEL)
Knife (TOD)
Gold pocket watch with chain (TOD)
2 heavy leather packs (SAM)
Worn, red blanket (in leather pack)
2 powder horns (in leather pack)
Small deerskin bag (in leather pack)

SOUND EFFECTS

Forest sounds
Wolf howling (distance)

THE COURTSHIP OF
MORNING STAR

❧

Cherokee Translations by
Wes Studi, and Levi and Virginia Carey

The Conqueror's threats weave a whole universe of resistances; holding out against him means keeping up an atmosphere of an armed truce.

... In his presence, the Occupied learns to dissemble, to resort to trickery ... for every contact between them is a falsehood.

— **Frantz Fanon**

War even to the knife.

— **Palofox**

CHARACTERS

MICHAEL ROWEN, age thirty-five

MORNING STAR, age sixteen, a Cherokee

DOUBLE FOR MORNING STAR (non-speaking role)

NARRATOR

The Courtship of Morning Star.

One year later. 1776.

A rude cabin in Southeastern Kentucky.

The Courtship of Morning Star.

THE COURTSHIP OF MORNING STAR

1776. Summer. The interior of a rude cabin in southeastern Kentucky. Michael Rowen's house is a simple, one room, pole structure chinked with mud and moss. There is a rough stone firepit, and a simple bed. The interior, like the rich woodland which surrounds it, is suggested rather than recreated.

Scene 1

Late Afternoon. Sound of birds and insects; then, in the distance, something else: the sounds of a struggle. Finally appearing downstage left is Michael Rowen. He is bearded, his hair is long, and he is dressed in a combination of buckskin and homespun. His hands and face are scratched and bleeding.

He is struggling with a young woman, Morning Star, whose dark complexion is lightly pockmarked and whose hands are tied. She never ceases to try to kick or claw at him, and she curses him non-stop in Cherokee, pausing only to catch a ragged breath.

STAR.   "Jegskini Eskiwhena!" [Go to hell, you devil!] "Yona wi gejkoja jaksheni!" [May the bears fuck you in the ass!] "Skini ikshi jahlstaydi!" [Make meals of devil shit!] *(Finally, Michael succeeds in dragging her into the room, where he unceremoniously dumps her onto the center of the floor. Both pause, breathing hard. They look at each other.)*
MICHAEL.   Welcome home.

Blackout

Scene 2

The next morning, early. Michael and Star are lying in bed. Both asleep. Michael has one arm thrown over her.

Star wakes up. Momentarily disoriented, she surveys the room. Then she remembers. Slowly, she tries to slip out from under the dead weight of his arm. He stirs. She freezes. Then, still asleep, he shifts his position and moves his arm, freeing her.

She bites her lip to keep her joy quiet. Then she begins to slide out of bed — only to discover that her left hand is tied to his right hand with a rawhide thong. She stops. She considers the knot ... gives up.

Frustrated, she looks around the room for some kind of weapon. There is a pile of cut logs and kindling near the fireplace. She reaches out for one of the logs. Michael stirs. She catches herself.

She reaches down slowly, grasps the log, and in one swift motion brings it up, over, and down onto Michael's head.

Or what would have been his head; in a move surprizing for a man of his size, Michael rolls and catches the log with his left hand. He twists it brutally out of her grasp and rolls over onto the floor.

Both come up in a slight crouch, facing each other, still linked by the rawhide thong. Beat.

Michael laughs.

Blackout

Scene 3

That evening. Star is seated at the table. She is no longer tied to Michael. He walks over from the fire with two crude wooden bowls, one of which he sets down on the table in front of her.

She doesn't react. He sits down and begins to eat; stops. He smiles at her, encouraging her to eat. She ignores him. He returns to eating.

MICHAEL.   Sure now, I'm not much of a cook, but it can't be all that bad. *(No response.)* My name is Michael. *(He indicates himself.)* Michael. You? *(He indicates her. No response.)* I didn't bring ya home to starve ya, ya know. Coulda left ya out there for that — eatin' roots with what's left of your poxy tribe. *(No response.)* Well, starve then, if you've a mind to. *(He starts to take her bowl away. She grabs it back. They stare at each another. He smiles. She turns away and attacks the contents of the bowl ravenously. She wipes the bowl clean and then throws it on the floor. She sucks and licks her fingers clean. Michael pushes his bowl across the table to her. She looks at it for a moment.)* Go on. Only I'd eat it a little more slowly if I was you. That is, if ya want to keep any of it down. *(She grabs the bowl and begins wolfing it down like the first one.)* I said slowly! *(Startled by the violence in his voice, she stops and stares at him. He gestures.)* Eat slowly. *(She obeys, cautiously. Michael smiles.)* My name is Michael. You? *(She stares at him. He repeats.)* Michael. You? *(She stares at him. Then.)*
STAR.   Michael you? *(Michael stares at her, then laughs. She laughs. He roars. She laughs harder. Then, abruptly, he slams both his hands down on the table. He points to himself.)*
MICHAEL.   Michael. *(He points to her. She looks at him warily.)*
STAR.   Knox Sanale.
MICHAEL.   Knox Sanale? *(She nods.)* That means ... Morning Star. *(He points to her.)* Morning Star. *(She shakes her head.)*
STAR.   Knox Sanale. *(He laughs.)*

MICHAEL. "And I saw Satan fall like lightning from Heaven." *(He laughs.)* Was that you, Morning Star? Tempter of our Lord? Lucifer's handmaiden here in the wilderness! Sure, but you've got some devil in ya. Like all women. *(Beat.)* Come here. *(She doesn't move.)* I said, come here! *(He gestures. She rises, uncertain, bowl in hand. She crosses to stand beside him. He takes the bowl from her hand and puts it on the table. He pulls her into his lap and kisses her. She remains passive. Gradually, she begins to embrace him. She kisses him harder and harder. He moans, kisses her throat, her breasts. With one hand, she reaches behind her and picks up the wooden bowl. He senses something and turns, but before he can move, she smashes the bowl into his face. Simultaneously, she slips off his lap and grabs him by his hair and pulls him to his knees on the floor. He struggles to rise, but she picks up the chair and brings it down on his head. She runs off. He shakes his head, now covered with blood and gruel, and bellows with rage.)* Goddamn it! Goddamn you!! Damn you! *(He staggers out after her.)*

Blackout

Scene 4

Lights up. Michael sits in a chair at the table. Perhaps he whittles. Star stands by the firepit and periodically stirs a large iron pot. Beat.

MICHAEL. I been killin' as long as I can remember. Ireland. Georgia. Here. Never for the pleasure innit, ya understand — though I'm good at it, and a man should take pride in what he does well. But if you go simple with blood you can lose your way. And I meant never to do that. I was always headed somewheres better. I killed my first man when I was seven. A bloody lobsterback. One o' them that was runnin' our piece of Ireland like his own bloody vegetable patch.

They'd have "hunts" on the land, see. Our land. Racin'
through our fields on their fine horses in their blacks and
scarlets. A beautiful sight! If you could just forget it was your
crops out there bein' trampled underfoot for their sport.
(Beat.)
Did you ever notice how like the distant bayin' of a fine pack
of hounds is the sound of a hungry child cryin' hisself to sleep?
(Beat.)
One of the silly bastards had too much to drink and lagged
behind the rest. He failed to clear a wall and took a bad fall.
His horse rolled over him. Must've broke him all up inside,
'cause he couldn't move none. I got to him first. I stood
there, over him, and I remember him lookin' up at me with
the queerest look on his face. What a sight I must've been:
little snot-nosed, barefoot boy, more dirt than clothes. I won-
dered what he thought now; him and his kind always bein' so
high and mighty. And then I stepped on his neck and broke
it. Like St. Patrick crushin' a snake.
(Beat.)
But there was no sport innit. See, I learned early, blood's
just the coin of the realm, and it's important to keep strict
accounts and pay your debts. That's all. And now here, at last,
I'm a man of property meself, on the kind of land ya only
dream about. Dirt so rich I could eat it with a spoon. I've but
to piss on the ground and somethin' grows. I've corn for
whiskey and white oaks for barrels to put it in and a river to
float it down and sell it. I've everythin' I've ever wanted: the
land, and to be left alone on it. I'm richer than that snot-
nosed boy ever dreamed he'd be. But somethin' isn't right.
(Beat.)
I'm gettin' in and layin' by more food than one man could
eat in a year. And instead of feelin' full, I feel empty. I feel
hungry. What's the point, after so much blood and so much
sweat, if ten years after I'm gone, the damn forest covers my
fields again? Or worse, some *stranger* does? Will I have built all
of this for nothin'? For no *one*? Michael, me boy, what you
want is a family. And for that, you need a *wife*.

(Star limps over slowly to the table and ladles out stew into a bowl for Michael. For the first time, we notice a clumsy, bloodstained bandage wrapped tightly around her right ankle and calf. Finished serving, Star starts to cross back. Michael stops her with a touch. She freezes instantly. He looks at her leg.)

Still swollen some, but gettin' better. It'll heal. I cut the tendon cleanly. You'll always limp, but you'll walk soon enough just fine. No pain. But you'll never be able to run. Not fast enough. Not far enough.

(He releases her. She crosses back and stands by the fireplace. She stares at him as he talks. He raises his glass.)

Here's to our first born. A *son!*

(Beat.)

Gimme a daughter, and I'll leave it on the mountain for the crows.

Blackout

Scene 5

"Star's Vision"

Three pools of light. Michael stands upstage left. Upstage right is a body double for Star. She squats, her back to the audience, and grips the posts of the bed.

She is in labor, and her groans and cries counterpoint, accent, and build with Star's speech. The rest of the ensemble breathes with her. Downstage center facing the audience, is Star.

STAR.   This child will kill me! Like the leaves in the time of changing colors, I am torn and scattered.

(The Double screams.)

Where are you, Grandmother?! You have turned your back on your people and we are no more. Cloudy Boy and even your Dog have abandoned us. The Four Witnesses hide their eyes and are mute. The Four Winds are still. All is death.

(The Double screams.)

It is the time of the Fall Bread Dance, and we gather to give thanks, Grandmother, for your bounty. The Great Game is close this year, but we women win and the men must gather the wood for the twelve days of feasting and dancing! Aaiiiieee! Laughing Eagle smiles at me, and my sisters whisper that his Mother will soon be talking to mine and bringing the gift of skins. Father frowns, but secretly I think he is pleased. Brother is chosen as one of the Twelve who will provide for the feast, and my heart swells so with pride it will burst! At dawn on the third morning, we gather to greet them at the Council House. See how he steps forward with the Grandfather of Deer — horns like the branches of an oak tree!

(The Double screams.)

That night, my brother grows ill. Hot, like a fire, his skin burns to the touch. No amount of water can touch his thirst. He drinks streams and lakes. The Shaman dances, but he, too, is ill. We burn now, all of us. Two days later, the blisters appear, stinging like red ants, like bees. I claw at my skin, my nails black with my own blood.

(The Double screams.)

The first to die are dressed and painted by their friends, as the great Grandmother taught us. Each is given proper burial in the earth, but as more and more are dying, there is no one with the strength to carry his brother to the burial ground. My father dresses in his finest skins and feathers. He paints his face and sings his death song. He takes his shield and his lance and dares the Red Death to fight him in the Council House. The Red Death smiles at him and he dies.

(The Double screams.)

Everywhere is death. And I am the Noon-Day Sun who dreamed once, that she was a woman named Morning Star.

(The Double screams.)

Where are my sisters?! Who will build my birthing hut? Where is my mother? Who will guide me through my time? Where are you, Grandmother! Why have you turned your face from your people?! THIS CHILD WILL KILL ME!

(The Double screams.)

How I hated you, little one. When my blood stopped and my belly grew, how I hated you! You were a part of *him,* my enemy, only now he was inside me. No longer could I shut him out, for there you were, always! How I hated you!

(The Double screams.)

But when I felt you move, child, when you whispered to me that you were *mine* — aaahhh, how then I laughed at my fears! *Mine!* You are *my* blood, and *my* flesh! We are *one* breath, and *one* heartbeat, and *one* thought, and that is DEATH TO HIM!

(The Double screams.)

Hurry, child — how I long to hold you!

(The Double screams.)

Hurry, child — my breasts ache for your touch!

(The Double screams.)

Hurry, child, and grow strong!

(The Double screams one last time and collapses. Silence. Star raises an imaginary infant up to the audience.)

Michael Rowen, you have a son.

(Michael turns. She looks at the baby and smiles.)

He is born with teeth.

Blackout

Scene 6

Night. The cabin. Star sits at the table. Michael stands by the fire, watching her. Star rocks the baby and sings to him.*

STAR. "Jaslinigohi adage tahlihi," [Grow strong, young warrior,]

* See music at back of text.

"Jaslanigohi hatvhi iniyigati." [Grow strong, grow tall.]

"Agado alteluhe hatohisgvi," [The land shakes with your war cry.]

"Uganowi kosti ale uhisodi ojigotisgo jalosohnvhi." [Warm ashes and grief, mark your passing.]

MICHAEL.   What are ya singin' to him?

STAR.   Just words I make up to quiet the child.

MICHAEL.   You ought to sing him a proper lullabye.

STAR.   Then teach me one. *(Beat.)*

MICHAEL.   I don't know any.

STAR.   There you are then.

MICHAEL.   Don't be smart with me, girl. I don't want you talkin' Cherokee to him, you understand? He's not to grow up like some savage. He's a Rowen! *(She coos to the baby.)*

STAR.   Sssshhhh. What a baby. What a baby.

MICHAEL.   Is he hungry?

STAR.   He just ate.

MICHAEL.   Did he piss himself?

STAR.   No.

MICHAEL.   Then why does he cry? *(Star shrugs, laughs derisively.)*

STAR.   Who knows? He's a baby. Babies cry. *(She coos to the child.)* What a baby. What a baby.

MICHAEL.   Do your breasts still bleed?

STAR.   A little.

MICHAEL.   *(Matter-of-factly.)* It's not natural.

STAR.   What do you know of babies 'cept how to get them?

MICHAEL   *(With distaste.)* Milk and blood.

STAR.   He's a Rowen. *(Beat.)* Sure you won't like to hold him? *(Beat.)* Here. *(She rises up and offers the child. He backs up and waves her away.)*

MICHAEL.   No.

STAR.   Go on.

MICHAEL.   I said *no! (Beat.)*

STAR.   You afraid of him? Your own son?

MICHAEL.   I've no gift for babies, that's all! *(Michael walks outside. Star watches him go, then returns to her chair. Michael*

45

watches them from outside, disturbed by forces he has set in motion but doesn't understand, can't articulate. Star croons to her baby; maybe she dangles the gold watch over him.)

STAR.   Afraid of his own son. Hmmmmm? *(Beat.)* What a baby. What a baby. *(She laughs softly. Michael watches. Slow fade to black.)*

END OF PLAY

PROPERTY LIST

2 crude wooden bowls (MICHAEL)
Large iron pot
Soup ladle
Bowl (STAR)
Rowen watch

SOUND EFFECTS

Birds
Insects

THE HOMECOMING

❧

Cherokee Translations by Wes Studi

*"This thing shall be done with speed.
The hand gropes now, and the other
hand follows in turn."*

— Aeschylus

CHARACTERS

PATRICK ROWEN, age sixteen, Michael's son

REBECCA TALBERT, age sixteen, a neighbor

STAR ROWEN, age thirty-two

MICHAEL ROWEN, age fifty-one

JOE TALBERT, age forty-seven, Rebecca's father

SALLIE, age twenty-two, a slave

NARRATOR

The Homecoming.

Sixteen years later. 1792.

A ridge in eastern Kentucky. Later, the Rowen homestead.

The Homecoming.

THE HOMECOMING

Scene 1

1792. Late morning. A ridge overlooking a vast expanse of mountains and valleys in eastern Kentucky.

As the lights come up, we see a young man, Patrick Rowen, staring out past the audience. He rests easily on his haunches and seems as much at home, as much a part of the wilderness that surrounds him, as any tree or bush.

He thoughtfully chews on a grass stalk and he cradles a long rifle lightly in his large hands. He shifts slightly and smiles. He picks up a handful of dirt and sifts it through his fingers.

From behind him, a sixteen-year-old girl, Rebecca Talbert, steps quietly out of the woods. She is slender and attractive in a blunt and unaffected manner. The emerging woman in her is plainly visible. She carries a wicker basket. She stands and considers Patrick.

REBECCA.   If I was an injun, you'd be dead six ways from Sunday by now.
PATRICK.   *(Unperturbed.)* Ain't been no injuns 'round here for five years.
REBECCA.   Well, if there was, I'da had your scalp for sure.
PATRICK.   *(Laughs.)* I heard you comin' days ago.
REBECCA.   Oh yeah? How'd you know it was me?
PATRICK.   'Cause as much noise as you were makin', it had to be you or some pack of razor-back hogs. I'm sittin' down wind of you and decided early on it couldn't be them hogs.

REBECCA. Well. That's a nice thing to say.

PATRICK. Coulda been a lot worse. I coulda said I was still guessing till I saw you! *(She swings at him. He ducks and laughs.)* I take it back!

REBECCA. You better. *(Beat.)* Pretty up here. Maybe we oughta have us a house up here when we get married. What'ya think?

PATRICK. Don't stand there. *(She ignores him. He pulls her down beside him.)* I said, don't stand.

REBECCA. Why not?

PATRICK. 'Cause we're on a ridge, facin' the sun, and you stand there you stick out like a sore thumb. Might just as well fire off a cannon for folks.

REBECCA. What's to worry, "Ain't been no injuns 'round here for five years." Not countin' you or your ma.

PATRICK. There's worse things than injuns.

REBECCA. I been missin' you somethin' fierce. You miss me?

PATRICK. Yeah. I reckon.

REBECCA. "You reckon?" Well, whyn't you gimme some sugar and we'll find out for sure. Come on. *(He kisses her.)* Well, what you think?

PATRICK. Yeah. I missed you. *(Beat.)*

REBECCA. I knew you'd be up here. Know how I knew? When you weren't in the fields I asked Star ...

PATRICK. *(Concerned.)* I told you, you shouldn't oughta bother my ma like that ...

REBECCA. All right by me! Didn't so much as give me back a how-do-you-do. Just grunted and pointed off towards the woods. She don't like me much.

PATRICK. She likes you fine.

REBECCA. Shoot! She'd just as soon put that gimpy leg of hers up against my backside as look at me.

PATRICK. Don't make fun of her!

REBECCA. I wasn't ... makin' fun of her.

PATRICK. Just don't talk about my ma like that.

REBECCA. Well, how come she don't like me? I ain't never done nothin', ain't never looked crossways at her but whenever she come visitin', you'd think I was a chair or somethin' for all the notice she give me. *(Beat.)*

PATRICK. *(Surprised.)* My ma's been visitin' over to your place?

REBECCA. Sure. Coupla times.

PATRICK. She don't visit nobody. Ain't never been acrost to the other side of the Shilling as far as I ever knew.

REBECCA. Well, it warn't no social call you understand. My daddy, he had a cut on him that went bad and everythin' and I thought maybe he was gonna lose that arm or die, maybe. Well, it ain't no secret round here that your ma got healin' hands. I guess Jeremiah gone and fetched her, 'cause she just shows up — bled my daddy and cooked him up a poultice o' herbs and his arm healed up just fine, nice as you please. *(Beat.)* Since then, she been back, oh, I don't know, a buncha times — to look in on him, I guess. Sure wasn't to say howdy to this girl.

PATRICK. She ain't never said nothin' 'bout that to me.

REBECCA. So?

PATRICK. So nothin'. It's just ... nothin'. *(Beat.)*

REBECCA. Anyways. So, you know how I found you? I knew you was out here somewheres but I didn't know exactly where. And like I said, your ma wasn't goin' to be any help. So, I did that thing you talked about. I tried to think like you — like you was some kind of animal or something? I thought, "Now, where would I go if I was you?" And then, I just had the strangest feelin', like a goose stepped on my grave or somethin', and ...

PATRICK. Don't have nothin' to do with thinkin'.

REBECCA. What don't?

PATRICK. When I hunt, I don't "pretend" I'm a deer or nothin'. I just *am.* I'm out here in the woods and things just get real ... still ... or somethin' ...

REBECCA. You talk like that, you sound like your ma when she conjures over them herbs of hers ...

PATRICK. It ain't magic or nothin'. It's just ... *(Then shyly.)* When I reach that place, when I just am, there, with the forest, then it's like I can call the deer or somethin'. I call'em and they come. Like I was still waters and green pastures, 'stead of hunger and lead. *(She strokes his face.)*

REBECCA. Nobody hunts as good as you, that's a fact, not in these hills.

PATRICK. My pa can hunt.

REBECCA. Shoot! He can't hold no candle to you.

PATRICK. Yeah?

REBECCA. Oh yeah. *(He kisses her. She pulls him on top of her.)* I want lots of kids, don't you? *(He moans assent.)* Bunches and bunches. *(He kisses her throat.)* What'd your pa say when you talked to him? *(He freezes.)* You talked to him, right? *(He rolls off her onto his back.)* You didn't, did you! You promised you would and you didn't! I swear, sometimes I think you're just scared of him!

PATRICK. I ain't scared!

REBECCA. Well, fine, then. Talk to him about it!

PATRICK. It ain't all that easy.

REBECCA. What's so hard about it? You just tell him — "Pa, me and Rebecca Talbert's wantin' to get married."

PATRICK. You don't know him. You can't just say nothin' like that to him.

REBECCA. Well, don't say nothin' then! Let's just run off! Get outta here! We don't need'im.

PATRICK. I AIN'T LEAVIN' THIS LAND! It's MINE! I don't want anywhere's else! *(Beat.)*

REBECCA. Then talk to him.

PATRICK. I will.

REBECCA. When?

PATRICK. Soon.

REBECCA. When?

PATRICK. As soon as he gets back from Louisville!

REBECCA. When'll that be?

PATRICK. Any day now. He's late. We spected him back last week. *(Beat.)*

REBECCA. You think mebbe he got kilt or somethin'?

PATRICK. Not unless a mountain fell on him.

REBECCA. What's that supposed to mean?

PATRICK. It's just ... he ain't dead, that's all. I'd know it if he was.

REBECCA. Well, how come your pa's so late gettin' back, you suppose?

PATRICK. I don't know. Cain't never figure him. Maybe.... Ever year, on each of these trips to Louisville, he makes a big show outta buyin' somethin' for Ma. Maybe that's what's takin' so long.

REBECCA. Well, that's nice.

PATRICK. No it ain't. There's always some meanness in his givin'. First time, it was a hand mirror.

REBECCA. So?

PATRICK. Well, Ma ain't never seen a glass before, and it scared her half to death. She thought it was bad magic or somethin'. He said not to worry — any old devil she saw in there, he'd been lookin' at for years and it ain't never kilt him yet! Well, she threw that mirror at him, busted it into a thousand pieces. This is a *two dollar* mirror, mind you!

REBECCA. No!

PATRICK. Next trip, he brung her that big tin tub that sits up in the yard there so's she could soak her leg whenever it stiffin' up on her.

REBECCA. What's so mean about that? *(He hesitates, then looks away.)*

PATRICK. Nothin'. *(Beat.)* He got somethin' special in mind, this time — been thinkin' hard on it all winter. I watch him. He's figurin' somethin' out.

REBECCA. How come you talk about him like that?

PATRICK. Like what?

REBECCA. Callin' him "him" and "he" instead of "my pa" or "my daddy." You never call him nothin' like that. It's like you ain't really kin or something. *(Beat.)*

PATRICK. I had me a sister, onct. 'Bout tore my Ma inside out, havin' her. Tore her up fierce. I never saw so much blood.

REBECCA. And the baby? *(Beat.)*

PATRICK. He took her away, somewheres.

REBECCA. Your pa?

PATRICK. He said he was doin' her a mercy. Said she was

sick and wasn't goin' to last. But she looked fine to me. Star had beaded this piece of buckskin for her so fine, it looked liked she pinned all the stars in the sky to it. He wrapped the baby up innit and took her away and we never saw her agin. Only time in my life I ever seen Ma beg him. Usually she just quiet as the grave no matter what he do or say, but she cried and begged him for that baby. Didn't seem to make him no never mind. *(Beat.)* He ain't never even told Ma where she's buried. I usta look for her grave all the time but I ain't never found nothing. *(Beat.)* Waste of time.

REBECCA.   Gimme goosebumps just thinkin' about it. You reckon mebbe she ain't at rest, bein' buried like that?

PATRICK.   You mean, is she a haint, or somethin'? *(She nods.)* Nah. I seen a whole lotta death, and I ain't never seen nothin' dead get up and walk agin. I don't worry none about the dead. *(Beat.)* What're you supposed to be doin' over this way, anyhow? *(She indicates the basket.)*

REBECCA.   Huckleberries. My daddy's real partial to 'em. Well, leave a few! I gotta look like I been doin' somethin' when I get back or he'll tan my hide.

PATRICK.   *(Re: berries.)* Good.

REBECCA.   'Course, gettin' round my daddy's not all that hard. But Jeremiah? Now, he's a nosey one. Always wantin' to know where I'm goin', when I'll back.

PATRICK.   He's just lookin' out for you.

REBECCA.   That's what he says! But he's just lookin' out for himself. Have a fit if he thought I was gettin' away with somethin' that he wasn't.

PATRICK.   I'm sure he ain't that bad. Probably real nice to have a brother.

REBECCA.   Well, you can have Jeremiah if your heart's so set on it! *(Beat.)*

PATRICK.   Hold on! *(Beat.)* See that?

REBECCA.   What?

PATRICK.   In gap there.

REBECCA.   I don't see nothin'.

PATRICK.   There's a glint there. Like metal. There it is agin! Somebody's comin' thru there. In a hurry.

REBECCA.   Is it your pa?
PATRICK.   More'n likely. I'm gonna go finish up, then git back to home. *(He rises, starts to exit.)*
REBECCA.   You gonna talk to him about us?
PATRICK.   I said so, didn't I?
REBECCA.   When?! *(He stops and thinks.)*
PATRICK.   I'll do it tonight. He's always feelin' good when he gets back from one of these trips. Gets good and likkered up, anyway. You bring your pa over after dark'n they can make a deal.
REBECCA.   What's your pa gonna want, you think?
PATRICK.   *(Smiling.)* What's your pa got? *(He kisses her.)* I love you. *(She bends down to get her basket and as she does so he disappears into the woods.)*
REBECCA.   It's gonna be fine, I know it. I just gotta feelin'. I ... *(She looks up but he is gone. Then to the trees and the darkness around her.)* I love you.

Fade Out

Scene 2

Dusk. The front yard of the Rowen house. The original single room has been expanded. Among other additions is a simple front porch and steps. The house and the yard are bare and unadorned, strictly functional.

There is a pile of logs on the porch and an old axe. In the yard is a tin tub, partially filled with water.

Patrick enters, cradling his rifle and a leather bag containing a pair of dead rabbits.

Star limps in, carrying two wooden buckets full of water. She stops and looks at Patrick.

STAR. "Ostas hindhalid?" [Good hunting?]

PATRICK. Couple of rabbits. Here, gimme those, Ma. (*He throws his bag on the porch, lays his rifle down and takes the buckets from her. He pours them into the tub.*)

STAR. "To hi ju?" [How are you?]

PATRICK. I'm fine.

STAR. It embarrasses you now to speak the language of your grandfathers'?

PATRICK. No. It don't embarrass me. I just don't see the point.

STAR. Not to forget who you are, that is the point.

PATRICK. Not much danger of that around here, is there? (*Beat.*)

STAR. I'll bring your supper out. Cooler on the porch. (*He sits. She goes in, returns with a bowl of food. She picks up the rabbits while he eats.*)

PATRICK. Good.

STAR. Took you all day to get these? Losin' your touch.

PATRICK. Didn't take me all ... (*Before he can finish protesting, Star goes inside with the rabbits. She returns.*) Most of the mornin' I sat up on the ridge.

STAR. Oh. Corn gonna plant itself this year?

PATRICK. I finished that piece on the Shilling.

STAR. Uh-huh. What's on the ridge worth a visit?

PATRICK. Nothin'. Just did me some thinkin'.

STAR. Alone? (*Beat.*)

PATRICK. Mostly.

STAR. I knew when that Talbert girl come sniffin' 'round here this mornin' you wasn't gonna get a lick of work done.

PATRICK. I planted the damn field!

STAR. Don't curse in front of your ma.

PATRICK. Don't see what you got against the Talberts. From what I hear you're a regular visitor over there. (*Beat.*)

STAR. What is it you hear?

PATRICK. You doctored her Pa.

STAR. His name is Joseph.

PATRICK. Joseph? Michael know about it?

STAR. What do you think?

PATRICK. I think he hears about it, he'll skin you alive.

STAR. Are you gonna tell him? *(Beat.)* Folks think I have the Gift for healin' and readin' dreams. Because I'm different. Because I'm Cherokee. Michael laughs, but as long as they pay, he laughs to himself. I think, why should he have all this money? Why not my son? And so, when I can, I see people secretly. Like Joseph.

PATRICK. For me?

STAR. Someday you'll want land of your own. A woman of your own.

PATRICK. Why hide it from me?

STAR. So if Michael finds out, he'll be angry only with me. *(Beat. He crosses over and hugs her knees, puts his head in her lap.)*

PATRICK. "Do yu jiskanoqi. Skidoliga?" [I am sorry. Forgive me?] *(She kisses him on the top of his head, strokes his hair roughly.)*

STAR. "I gvkewidina." [It is forgotten.] You want this Ruth Talbert?

PATRICK. Rebecca.

STAR. Whatever. What she wants, you can give her easy enough. You don't have to marry her for that.

PATRICK. She ain't like that.

STAR. I see. Maybe she's smarter than I thought.

PATRICK. I love her.

STAR. You love her. Now. Today, you love her. But tomorrow? Next year? Chuji. Why so much hurry? Why marry her? *(Beat.)*

PATRICK. If I marry her, maybe her pa'd gimme that piece of bottom land next to ours. *(She cuffs him.)*

STAR. You are your father's son. Truly.

PATRICK. Not so's he'd notice.

STAR. I never understand this. What you two have is never enough. You work from sunrise to sunset and you can't plow all what you have now, but you want *more*. More *land!* Why?

PATRICK. It's the only thing that lasts. *(Beat.)*

STAR. You live like that, Chuji, you live a lonely life.

PATRICK. Somethin' diferent.

STAR. Everybody gotta right to some happiness, osta Chuji.

You gotta right.

PATRICK. She makes me happy. Rebecca. *(Beat.)* You help me?

STAR. How?

PATRICK. Talk to him for me. 'Bout us. *(She walks to the tub, runs her hand through the water.)*

STAR. Michael don't listen to me.

PATRICK. He's comin' back. *(She hesitates.)*

STAR. You seen him?

PATRICK. This mornin'.

STAR. You sure?

PATRICK. Somebody was movin' thru the gap in a hurry.

STAR. Coulda been anybody.

PATRICK. Who?

STAR. When'll he get here?

PATRICK. Tonight mebbe. Tomorrow for sure. But tonight I think. *(Beat.)* You could tell him ... tell him that Talbert bottom land'd give us a third agin as much.

STAR. It give your *pa* a third agin as much. *(She takes his bowl and starts into the house.)*

PATRICK. Same thing. It's all gonna come down to me, innit?

STAR. Is it? *(She sits on the porch. Patrick stares at her in confusion.)*

PATRICK. What're you talkin' 'bout?

STAR. I'm not sayin' nothin'. Said too much already. *(Preoccupied, she absent-mindedly strokes her injured leg.)*

PATRICK. Your leg botherin' you a lot? *(She shrugs. Looks off into the woods where Michael is.)* Here. Lemme rub it for you. *(He sits next to her. She hikes up her skirt and swings her leg into his lap. He begins to knead her scarred calf. She leans back against a post, her eyes closed.)* What'd you mean about ... about the land not comin' to me. I'm his only son.

STAR. Are you?

PATRICK. What d'you mean, "Are you?" — "Is it?" You know somethin' why don't you just say it, 'stead of dancin' around!

STAR. Lower.

PATRICK. What?

STAR. Rub lower. *(He does so.)* What does Michael do in Louisville?

PATRICK. I don't know.

STAR. How come?

PATRICK. 'Cause I ain't never been.

STAR. How come?

PATRICK. 'Cause I gotta stay here and take care of things! *(Beat.)*

STAR. He got a woman down there.

PATRICK. How do you know?

STAR. I seen her in a dream.

PATRICK. You seen her?

STAR. Blue eyes, corn-silk hair. She always be crossin' a muddy river in my dreams.

PATRICK. Muddy water? That's death. *(She nods.)* Mebbe she's dead already.

STAR. Mebbe.

PATRICK. What I care if he got some woman down there? Specially if she's dead now.

STAR. Mebbe she had him a baby.

PATRICK. He ... he got him another family down there?

STAR. Why else he always got to go alone? You a growned man, Chuji. With your help, he could pack in twice as much on these trips. You ever knowed Michael to turn his back on a dollar? How come he don't take you?

PATRICK. You seen the baby in your dream?

STAR. Clear as the bottom of the Shillin'.

PATRICK. Boy or girl?

STAR. She give him a *son.*

PATRICK. A son!

STAR. Where does that leave you?

PATRICK. I'd still be the oldest! It'd all still come to me! That's the law!

STAR. Law? *(She laughs.)* Michael ever pay a whole lotta mind to the *law?*

PATRICK. Why wouldn't he let me have my share?

STAR. You know why.

63

PATRICK. Why!

STAR. 'Cause he hates you.

PATRICK. That's a lie!

STAR. Look me in the face and tell me it is! *(He can't.)*

PATRICK. Why? Why's he hate me? Nothin' I ever do is right. Never has been. He looks at me like I was some kinda mad dog, gonna tear somethin' precious away from him.

STAR. He's afraid of you.

PATRICK. Afraid?! Hell, Michael Rowen ain't afraid of nothin'!

STAR. Look at yourself, Chuji, *look!* See yourself as you really *are* — not like that hungry dog he turns you into, the one who whines and licks the hand that beats him. You are bigger than him now. And stronger. He sees you and he feels old. He feels tired. He sees his *death* in you. That's how you scare him, Chuji, and that's why he hates you. Because there is no forgiving that. And that's why he will never give you your rightful share of this land. *Your* land. Not till you bury him innit! *(Beat.)* Ask him. You don't believe me? Ask him for your share and see what he says.

MICHAEL. *(Off-stage.)* Halllooooo the house!

PATRICK. You help me? *(She nods. Michael walks on carrying an enormous pack. He stands and considers them.)*

MICHAEL. There's a sight to warm your heart. Lovin' wife and lovin' son, anxiously waitin' up for the master of the house. You're like one of them fancy paintin's, the two of you! "The Homecomin'! *(He drops the pack.)* Take it inside, boy, and bring me a jug. *(Patrick goes inside.)*

STAR. You hungry?

MICHAEL. Only for the sight of you, beloved.

STAR. What'd you bring me this time?

MICHAEL. "What'd you bring me?" Well, that's nice. No warm embrace first? No kisses on my old grey head? Just, "What'd I bring you?" *(Patrick returns with the jug.)* You've grown.

PATRICK. Yeah?

MICHAEL. A head taller at least. Still ugly as sin, but bigger. *(He drinks.)* Was that you standin' up on the ridge this mornin' in front of God and everybody?

PATRICK.   I was up on the ridge.

MICHAEL.   Gonna get your ass shot off like that, boy. 'Course in your case that'd probably be fatal, seein' as how that's where all your brains are. *(He drinks and then wanders over to the tub.)* Has your leg been botherin' you?

STAR.   I was gonna soak it, but maybe you'd rather wash up first?

MICHAEL.   I might at that.

STAR.   There's hot water on the fire.

MICHAEL.   I can't tell you how it warms my heart to see you so glad of the little gifts I bring you. It's like when we were young and courtin' all over again.

STAR.   What have you brought?

MICHAEL.   Greedy, greedy, greedy. Gimme, gimme, gimme. In time, love. But first, I bring news!

PATRICK.   What?

MICHAEL.   We're a *state!* A full member of the United States!

PATRICK.   Yeah.

MICHAEL.   *(Drily.)* Your enthusiasm is overwhelming, boy. Yes! As of June 1st, born in a tavern in Lexington! Whiskey and politicians, boy, a terrible combination!

PATRICK.   What do we care?

MICHAEL.   Don't make the mistake of your ignorant neighbors and think these mountains is some kinda magic, gonna protect ya! Mark my words, boy, the day'll come when those flatlanders in the city sneeze, it's us in the hills'll catch cold! *(He drinks again.)* Enough of that! I said I'd bring you back somethin' special and by God, somethin' special I have. I've insured the future of the Rowen family in a single blow! *(He whistles. Beat. Out of the shadows steps a young Black woman, Sallie, carrying a large pack. Her face is bruised and her hands are manacled.)* Step in, step in! Let'm get a good look at ya! *(Patrick stares at her and then starts to laugh at Star.)*

PATRICK.   Blue-eyed?! "Cornsilk hair?!"

MICHAEL.   What's that? What're you laughin' about?

PATRICK.   Nothin! Foooolishness! *Dreams.* I'd like a drink.

(Michael looks at his son curiously and then hands him the jug. Patrick drinks deeply, coughs, and then hands it back.)

MICHAEL.   A Guinea princess! *Full*-blooded. How do you like that, eh? My father never owned a pot to piss in, but his son owns the daughters of kings! What a country! Go on. Take a look at her, she won't bite — not anymore, anyway, believe me! *(He laughs.)* Thirty silver dollars, that's what I paid for her. Every penny I had saved for years and a bargain at twice the price. I stole the man blind!

STAR.   What'll you use her for?

MICHAEL.   Field work, of course.

STAR.   Field work! Look at her — she wouldn't last a week, a *day!*

MICHAEL.   Oh, *she* won't be workin' in the fields. Or maybe only a little bit at first. And then ...

STAR.   Then what? *(Beat.)*

MICHAEL.   Take a lesson from your old pa here, boy, on how to get ahead in the world. You got to think further than your own nose; further than your neighbor's nose. You don't get ahead just thinkin' about tomorrow or the day after. You got to think years down the road. *(He drinks.)* With a slave, we can work half again as much land. More land, more corn. More corn, more whiskey. More whiskey, more slaves. More slaves — more *LAND!* I'll own these damn mountains before I'm through. *(They both laugh.)*

STAR.   You won't get much work outta one slave and certainly not out of that one. You were robbed, old man — you've grown soft in the head.

MICHAEL.   Have I? Here's your choice, boy, you can have one strong buck or one little woman. What do you choose?

PATRICK.   I ... I don't ... know ...

MICHAEL.   One man in the fields is just one man, you're right. But a woman? She's a half-dozen men in the fields. A half dozen *sons.*

STAR.   You'll breed her. To who? *(Michael just grins at the two of them.)*

MICHAEL.   Let's just hope this new litter is an improvement over the old! *(He laughs, drinks. Star looks at Patrick. He avoids her eyes. When she speaks, she is careful to control any hint of the triumph she is feeling.)*

STAR.   Go get that hot water for your pa, Patrick. Don't stand there. Your pa's water for his bath! *(Patrick goes off into the house.)* It's a good plan, Michael, you're right.

MICHAEL.   *(Suspicious.)* You think so?

STAR.   Did you think I'd be angry? A long time ago, mebbe. But all that's past. In the past. The *future* — you're right, that's what bears watchin'. *(Patrick enters and pours the water into the tub.)* Get the soap. *(Patrick goes inside. Star gestures to the tub.)* Who will wash Master Rowen, now that he's home again: Slave? or Wife? *(Michael grins at her. He drains the jug and drops it to the ground.)*

MICHAEL.   Wife! *(As Patrick returns with a bucket of soap, Michael pulls out the pistol which hangs on a lanyard around his neck and puts it on the ground. He quickly drops his buckskin shirt and pants, and then, in his tattered and nearly black with dirt longjohns, climbs triumphantly and a little drunkenly, into the tub. Star pours water over his head. Michael hoots and hollers. Star rubs his shoulders and his chest and then begins to wash his hair, working the soap into a thick lather. Patrick watches, his eyes unnaturally bright.)*

STAR.   Your son is thinkin' of gettin' married, Michael.

MICHAEL.   Married?! The boy's not out of his diapers yet!

STAR.   Has his eye on that Talbert girl.

MICHAEL.   That titless creature?

STAR.   She's a pretty thing.

MICHAEL.   She's no Rowen. You wait, boy. Wait and some-day you can pick and choose any woman in these hills.

PATRICK.   I don't wanta wait. We're ready now.

MICHAEL.   Then pack up and go. I won't stop you. *(Beat.)*

PATRICK.   We need us some land.

MICHAEL.   Then talk to her pa.

STAR.   He ain't got a third of what you got and he got a boy of his own.

MICHAEL.   Then go find your own! Country's full of land West of here ...

PATRICK.   Full of Injuns ...

MICHAEL. Well, it didn't stop me, now, did it! And I didn't have your great advantage, bein' half-brother to them savages and all.

PATRICK. I want a share of this. It's *mine*. I want a piece of what's comin' to me.

MICHAEL. Are you slow, boy? Did you hear what I said to you? I've got plans for this land. For these *mountains!* I'm not goin' to start cuttin' it up like some half-wit, Irish bog trotter. They've more stone walls than fields over there because they've more sons than vision! You tuck your pecker back in your pants and don't talk to me about marryin'!

PATRICK. It's all for m ... m ... me, innit?! It's all comin' to m ... m ... me anyhow! There's no one else!

MICHAEL. Your concern for my health is touchin', lad, but it's a little early to be worrying about your inheritance.

PATRICK. Then what's the d ... d ... diference! What's the difference between me out there workin' the land for you, and s ... s ... some *slave!*

MICHAEL. I can "*s ... s ... sell*" the slave! It's *worth* somethin'!

PATRICK. Tell me! I got a right to know!

MICHAEL. Don't push it, boy!

PATRICK. DOES IT COME TO ME OR DON'T IT!

MICHAEL. I'd sooner give it to my slaves, first! I'd sooner the forest covered my fields than turn them over to some half-blooded, half-witted, droolin' excuse for a man! You were never *my* son. She saw to that! Never a *Rowen!* Not from the first! I SHOULD HAVE LEFT YOU ON THE MOUNTAIN WITH YOUR SISTER! WATCH WHAT YOU'RE DOIN', NOW! GODDAMMIT, WOMAN, MY *EYES!* AAAAHHHH! *(Star has deliberately pushed the lye soap into Michael's eyes. He frantically splashes water in his face, in his burning eyes, then staggers upright in the tub, tears streaming down his face.)* GODDAMMIT! GET ME SOMETHIN' FOR MY EYES! DAMN YOU! *(Star backs slowly away from the tub.)*

STAR. Help your father, Patrick. *(Patrick pulls his knife out and stabs Michael once in the back. Michael staggers. He looks up, virtually sightless, at Patrick.)*

MICHAEL.   Is that your best, boy? WELL, COME ON THEN! COME ON! *(Patrick steps in and stabs him repeatedly. Michael grapples with him, his arms around his neck. Patrick pulls away and stabs him one last time, then backs away. Michael lies half in and half out of the tub, bleeding profusely. His eyes close. There is silence.)*
STAR.   Chuji? *(Patrick staggers off to the side of the house and throws up. She hurries to him and kneels beside him, stroking his head.)* Chuji. Sshh. Sshh.
PATRICK.   I kilt him.
STAR.   Sshh.
PATRICK.   I kilt him!
STAR.   All right now. Hush.
PATRICK.   What ... what'll we do now?
STAR.   We'll bury him somewheres. Where nobody'll ever find him. And nobody'll ever know. Just us.
PATRICK.   She saw it. *(Star looks to Sallie.)*
STAR.   She didn't see nothin'. Ain't that right?
SALLIE.   Yes'm.
PATRICK.   I didn't wanta kill him. I didn't.
STAR.   Sshh. What you bein' so scared for? It's over now. Listen to me. He woulda kilt you one of these days. You didn't hardly have no say innit. We free now, Patrick. You freed us! Ain't nothin' we can't do now! *(Patrick continues to sob. Star walks over to Michael.)* I dreamed you dead so much, I'm 'fraid if I touch you I'll wake up. *(Star reaches out and strokes his face.)* Ain't nothin' like what I thought'd be. *(She lifts his head.)* Who was there, old man, in the darkness? Who raised their hands to you? My father? My brothers? Our daughter?
PATRICK.   Leave him alone.
STAR.   You hear your son, old man? His hands are still wet with your blood but he won't have you mocked. Aaahhh, a son's love is a wonderful thing.
PATRICK.   I SAID, LEAVE HIM ALONE! *(Star releases Michael. She stops, then calls out into the darkness.)*
STAR.   Who's out there?! *(Rebecca steps out of the shadows. Behind her and carrying a rifle, is her father, Joe Talbert.)*

REBECCA. Patrick?

PATRICK. What ... what're you doin'...?

REBECCA. I was supposed to ... you told me to ... *(Beat.)*

STAR. We free now, Joe. We free.

JOE. It's all right now. *(Patrick stands.)*

PATRICK. You Joe Talbert?

JOE. That's right. *(He gestures towards the body.)* You kill him? Kill your own pa?

PATRICK. Yessir.

JOE. Lord have mercy on your soul. *(Patrick starts to cross into the house. Joe raises his rifle.)* I'd feel a whole lot better iffen you'd just stay where you are, son. *(Patrick freezes.)* 'Becca? Go git your daddy that gun offen that porch.

REBECCA. Pa?

JOE. Just do as I say, Rebecca.

PATRICK. Rebecca?

JOE. Git it, Rebecca! *(She gets the gun and brings it to Joe.)*

STAR. Joe?

JOE. We didn't talk about nothin' like this, Star. You was just to walk away. That's all. There warn't 'sposed to be no killin'.

PATRICK. Talk about what?

STAR. I told you what he was like. He'da *killed* me. He'da killed *you*. He wouldn't've just let us walk away!

JOE. That don't mean.... Who's that?

STAR. A slave! Michael bought him a slave in Louisville, gonna breed her to *himself!*

JOE. Sweet Jesus.

STAR. That's the kind of man he wuz! Ain't no curse in his death! Ain't nothin' but a judgement and a blessin'!

JOE. Ain't no question but what he was a wicked man but I cain't turn my back on this. Murder's murder.

STAR. What do you mean?

JOE. I'll take Patrick on down to Morgan. Get him a fair trial, in front of a real judge.

STAR. A fair trial? He's half-Cherokee, done kilt a white man — what kinda trial he gonna get, 'cept a quick one?

JOE. What we done talk about all this time, Star, but how

you gotta be trustin' in God?

STAR.   I ain't got no problem with God, I gotta problem with some white man in Morgan gonna hang my boy!

JOE.   I know he's your only child, Star, but we ain't a bunch a savages no more, up some holler, squattin' round a camp-fire. The law be full-time and you cain't be pickin' and choosin' with it.

STAR.   Nobody's hangin' my son! If you love me, Joe, you stop this. You stop it right now.

JOE.   You know how I feel about you, Star, but the boy done tied my hands.

PATRICK.   You love him? Ma?

STAR.   Chuji ...

REBECCA.   Pa?

PATRICK.   Do you *love him*?! (*Beat.*)

STAR.   Everybody gotta right to some happiness. I gotta right.

PATRICK.   He's just after the *land!* Can't you see that?!

JOE.   Land don't mean nothin' to me; not when you by yourself. I love her, boy. I mean to marry her.

PATRICK.   This is what you meant to happen all along, innit? Innit?!

STAR.   No.

REBECCA.   What if Patrick and I just went away? Went off somewhere's? We wouldn't bother anybody — nobody'd have to know!

JOE.   You ain't goin' nowhere, Rebecca.

STAR.   But what about Patrick?

JOE.   What about him?

STAR.   What if *he* went away? Give him a *day*, that's all. Just one day.

PATRICK.   Ma?

STAR.   You'll be safe, Chuji! You move fast enough, the way you know these mountains, ain't no man alive gonna catch you.

JOE.   I cain't do that — Just let him run off.

STAR.   You take my boy down to Morgan, you gotta take me.

JOE. Star...!

STAR. No! I was right there, I'm as guilty as he is. They gonna hang him they gotta hang me.

JOE. Star, you cain't ...

STAR. You ready to live with that? That'll be *my* blood on your hands! Don't your God say nothin' 'bout forgiveness? *(Beat.)*

JOE. What you want me to do?

STAR. He leaves right now! Tomorrow, you go into Morgan. Tell'em what he done. Tell'em whatever you want. Tell'em how you tracked him up the Shilling and clear over to the Buckhorn and then you lost him.

JOE. You askin' me to lie for you, too.

STAR. I give you your life back there, Joe, and I didn't ask fur nothin'. Now I'm askin' you to give me back mine. Give me my son? *(Beat.)*

JOE. It won't work.

PATRICK. You hear him? He wants me dead!

STAR. Why not? Why won't it work?

JOE. 'Cause I don't trust him, that's why! 'Cause I don't aim to spend the rest of my life lookin' over my shoulder.

STAR. He's no threat to you! Tell him, Chuji.

JOE. The hell he ain't!

STAR. He'll give you his word — to go away and never come back. You will be safe, Joe, you and yours. On my life, I swear it. Tell him, Chuji. *Tell him! (Beat.)*

PATRICK. Yes.

STAR. Yes, what?

PATRICK. Yes. He's safe.

STAR. Your word?

PATRICK. My word.

STAR. You hear him? His word. And mine. Joseph? *(Beat.)*

JOE. All right. *(Star hugs Joe.)*

STAR. Thank you.

PATRICK. I'll need my gun.

JOE. Your rifle stays here.

REBECCA. You cain't do that to him, Pa!

JOE. Be quiet!

PATRICK.   What kinda chance I got without a rifle?

JOE.   The only chance you get. *No,* Star! No *gun.* That's the deal. He leaves like he is, right now, or he don't leave at all.

PATRICK.   Ma? *(Beat. She looks to Joe, and then to Patrick.)*

STAR.   "Do yu jiskanoqi. Skidoliga." [I am sorry. Forgive me.] *(Patrick stands and looks at her. He crosses to the tub and looks at Michael's body.)*

PATRICK.   All my life, you two been pullin' and tearin' at me. Not so much 'cause you wanted me, but 'cause you didn't want the other one to have me. I been a blade that you both ground down so much that I ain't nothin' left but edge. *(Beat.)* You mind if I bury my Pa 'fore I go? Or you figure I'm gonna be too dangerous with a shovel in my hands? *(Joe is about to object but Star cuts him off.)*

STAR.   That'd be all right. *(Patrick moves to the pile of clothes by the tub.)*

PATRICK.   I ain't buryin' him naked. Man's gotta right to that much at least. *(Joe nods and then looks away. Patrick kneels down and then pulls out his father's pistol.)*

STAR.   JOOOEEEE! *(Too late. Patrick fires and Joe drops.)*

REBECCA.   Pa?! *(Star crouches over Joe's body keening. Patrick crosses quickly and grabs Joe's rifle and his own. He retreats to the porch.)*

STAR.   You were free, Chuji! You heard him! All you had to do was walk away.

PATRICK.   This is *my* land! *Rowen* land! I ain't leavin'!

STAR.   They'll hang you for this. I'll see to that.

PATRICK.   Who's gonna witness against me, a black slave and a Cherokee squaw? Ain't no man gonna hang in Kentucky on their say-so, not even no half-breed.

STAR.   Rebecca.

PATRICK.   A man's wife cain't witness against him.

REBECCA.   Wife?

STAR.   Don't listen to him!

REBECCA.   No.

PATRICK.   Get inside the house, Rebecca!

REBECCA.   NO!

PATRICK.   GET INSIDE THE HOUSE! *(Patrick grabs Rebecca*

by the arm and pushes her into the house. Patrick turns to Star.) Get outta here! I'll give you till mornin' and then I'll come lookin' for you. If I find you anywhere on my land, I'll kill you. *(Beat.)*

STAR.   *(Quietly.)* I wish you and your wife long life together. And many sons to comfort you in your old age.

PATRICK.   I had a dream last night, Ma. I saw a woman who looked like you crossin' a muddy river. *(She exits. He watches her go and then crosses to Sallie.)* What's your name?

SALLIE.   Sallie, suh. *(She shivers.)*

PATRICK.   You sick?

SALLIE.   No suh.

PATRICK.   You scared?

SALLIE.   Yes suh.

PATRICK.   Me, too. *(Beat.)* He must have him a key, somewhere's.

SALLIE.   Suh?

PATRICK.   For them irons.

SALLIE.   Yes suh. *(Beat.)* 'Round his neck. *(Patrick crosses to his Father and finds a piece of twine around his neck with a small key attached. He tears the key off, returns to Sallie, and slowly unlocks her manacles.)*

PATRICK.   You sleep in the barn, for now. There's a shovel in there. You take it, follow that creek down there about a mile. Stay on the path and you come to a big oak tree. We'll bury my pa there. *(Beat.)* I'll carry him down — be after you directly. *(Sallie points to Joe.)*

SALLIE.   What about him? *(Beat.)*

PATRICK.   He's not for buryin'. *(Sallie exits slowly off. Patrick crosses again to Michael and goes through his clothes. He finds the gold watch. He crosses up to the porch and sits. He opens the watch and listens to the music it plays. He closes the watch.)* I'm gettin' married tonight, Pa. Give me your blessin'. *(He starts to cry. Slow fade to black.)*

END OF PLAY

PROPERTY LIST

Grass stalk (PATRICK)
3 long rifles (PATRICK, MICHAEL, JOE)
Basket (REBECCA)
Old axe
Tin tub with water
Leather bag with a pair of dead rabbits (PATRICK)
2 buckets of water (STAR)
Bowl (STAR)
Manacles (SALLIE)
Large pack (MICHAEL, SALLIE)
Jug (PATRICK)
Pistol on lanyard (MICHAEL)
Knife (PATRICK)
Key on twine (MICHAEL)
Rowen watch (MICHAEL)

TIES THAT BIND

❧

*"Blest be the tie that binds
Our hearts in Christian love;"*

— Traditional Hymn

CHARACTERS

PATRICK ROWEN, age forty-three

EZEKIEL (ZEKE) ROWEN, age nineteen, his son

ZACHARIAH (ZACH) ROWEN, age seventeen, his son

SALLIE BIGGS, age forty-nine, a slave

JESSIE BIGGS, age twenty-six, Sallie's son, also a slave

JUDGE JIM GODDARD, circuit court judge

DEPUTY GREY, court deputy

DEPUTY O'SULLIVAN, court deputy (nonspeaking role)

JEREMIAH, age forty-five

STAR, age fifty-nine

NARRATOR

Ties That Bind.

The year is 1819.

The Rowen Homestead.

Ties That Bind.

TIES THAT BIND

Summer, 1819. Darkness. Then the sound of labored breath-
ing. Finally, a tight spot comes up slowly to reveal two
Young Men, one African-American and one white, standing
head to head, their arms wrapped around each other's shoul-
ders. They move in slow motion against each other, muscles
straining, each one struggling for leverage and position
against his opponent. A long beat. Suddenly, the lights come
up full and the two wrestlers move against each other at full
speed. It's a friendly match, but neither man is sparing
much. The winner, however, is never in doubt. The African-
American, Jessie, is considerably bigger and stronger and he
consistently drops and pins his opponent, Zachariah. In the
full light we can now recognize where we are: the front
"yard" of the Rowen homestead. From the physical additions
to the house itself, the new iron pump in the yard, and the
tools and hardware stacked neatly on the porch, the Rowens
appear to be doing well.

A third young man, Ezekiel, sits on the porch reading a
bible and trying to ignore his younger brother Zach's pleas
for help.

ZACH. Three outta four!
JESSIE. Ain't gonna make no difference.
ZACH. Come on — three oughta four! Or ain't you got the
stomach fur it?!
JESSIE. Don't you be talking that way.
ZACH. Or what? Come on!
JESSIE. Shoot, you ain't won one yet.
ZACH. Hell ...
ZEKE. Don't you curse, Zach.
ZACH. Mind your own business, Zeke.

JESSIE.   Your daddy come back, find us wrestlin', he ain't gonna be too happy 'bout that.

ZEKE.   Daddy's little darlin' ...

ZACH.   Come on, Jessie! I ain't hardly been tryin' yet. Just been lettin' you win.

JESSIE.   Oh, you been *lettin'* me win!

ZACH.   Sure! I just been playin' with you so's you'd get to feelin' confident. Get you all swole up like a lizard on a hot rock, and then let your guard down! *(He launches himself at Jessie. Jessie ducks and trips Zach, who hits the ground hard.)*

JESSIE.   Only thing I see down around here regular-like is you, Zach.

ZACH.   Hold on, I don't feel so good. Let me catch my breath a minute, will ya? *(He tries to get up and can't.)*

JESSIE.   You want me to getcha some water?

ZACH.   Nah. Jist got the wind knocked outta me.

ZEKE.   Don't know what you expect, wrestlin' on the Lord's Day.

ZACH.   Now, what's the Lord got against wrestlin'? Weren't you just bendin' my ear the other day about a Jacob or somebody? Didn't he wrestle him an angel or somethin'?

ZEKE.   He didn't wrestle him no field hand, and he sure didn't wrestle him on the Sabbath!

ZACH.   Ezekiel, that preacher may have saved your soul, but he sure turned your brains to spoonbread.

JESSIE.   Praise the Lord!

ZACH.   Amen!

ZEKE.   You boys laugh all you want now. Ain't gonna be no singin' where you headed —

ZACH.   Oh no!

JESSIE.   Save me, Jesus!

ZEKE.   — and you both gonna be a whole lot thirstier!

ZACH.   Hold on there, I think mebbe I broke somethin'.

JESSIE.   What?

ZACH.   I don't know what! Somethin' inside. Oh shit, Jessie, I'm spittin' blood.

ZEKE.   You see!

ZACH.   Shut up, Zeke.

JESSIE. I'll get your daddy.

ZACH. No! Pa hears I hurt myself 'fore we get that second plantin' done, he'll nail my hide to the door. Gimme a hand — get me in the house and wrap this side of mine up. *(Jessie bends down to lift Zach up. Zach grabs him and flips him over, pinning him to the ground.)* I told you! I told you I'd git ya!

JESSIE. You sneaky piece of shit.

ZACH. I got you now, boy!

JESSIE. You got me, huh?

ZACH. Yessir!

JESSIE. You sure of that?

ZACH. Sure as my redeemer liveth!

JESSIE. All right then. *(Jessie flips Zach over and pins him.)*

ZACH. Ahhh! You're chokin' me!

JESSIE. What?

ZACH. You're chokin' me!

JESSIE. Cain't hear you, Zach, you sound all choked up.

ZACH. Chkkkngmmmeee ...

JESSIE. Did you say, "uncle?"

ZACH. Uggghhhh ...

JESSIE. Sound like "uncle" to you, Zeke?

ZEKE. Sound like "more" to me.

JESSIE. You think so?

ZEKE. Well, give him a squeeze, let's find out.

ZACH. UNCLE! *(Jessie releases him.)* Damn, Zeke! You just gonna sit there while somebody chokes the life outta your little brother? What the hell kinda family feelin' is that?!

ZEKE. I told you, Zach, you supposed to remember the Sabbath and keep it holy. Hurt me somethin' fierce to watch you suffer like that but I figure if it brings you closer to God, well, that's just the price I gotta pay.

ZACH. Shoot! You listen to that, Jessie? Man's just a natural-born coward, hidin' behind the scriptures.

JESSIE. No sir, I think Mr. Zeke done got him the Spirit, all right. But it ain't Jesus got him by the short hairs.

ZACH. You ain't talkin' 'bout that mousy little thing live up on the Buckhorn, are ya?

JESSIE. Miss Joleen Johnston?

ZACH.   That's the one!

ZEKE.   That's enough of that.

ZACH.   You pullin' my leg?

JESSIE.   No sir! I hear that woman got your brother on a short rope.

ZACH.   Well, I'll be! You mean all this prayin' and studyin' ...

JESSIE.   Them clean hands and shiny boots ...

ZACH.   That six mile walk over and back to meetin's ever Sunday ...

JESSIE.   Yes sir.

ZACH.   That all for some *woman*? That true, Ezekiel? Ol' Joleen got you towin' the line here and that's why you become this overnight holier-than-thou, pain in the butt!

ZEKE.   You keep your smart mouth offa Joleen!

JESSIE.   Look out, kettle's boilin'!

ZACH.   Well, I reckon I can keep my mouth offa her but can anybody else?

ZEKE.   You gonna eat them words!

JESSIE.   Boilin' over!

ZACH.   Way I heard it, 'fore she found Jesus, Joleen get down on her knees for just about anybody!

ZEKE.   YOU SON OF A BITCH! *(Zeke throws himself off the porch and onto Zach , who is laughing so hard he can hardly defend himself. They roll over and over on the ground, Zeke flailing away at his brother. Patrick Rowen enters.)*

PATRICK.   What're you boys doin'! *(Jessie snaps to immediately but the brothers are too involved to hear anything.)* You break it up now, you hear me! *(He wades into the middle of them, picking them up and apart in his big hands like puppies.)* THAT'S ENOUGH! *(He pushes Zach away and grabs Zeke with both hands.)* What I tell you 'bout scrappin' with your brother?!

ZACH.   I started it, Pa. It was my fault.

PATRICK.   Shut up, Zach ! What you got to say for yourself, boy?! Huh? You the oldest, Zeke. You s'pose to look after things. But no, I cain't turn my back for a second, can I, without you gettin' everbody into trouble! *(He cuffs Zeke and pushes him towards the house.)* Now git in there and get changed! We got people comin'! Jessie!

JESSIE.   Yessir!

PATRICK.   You go clean up and then git back here. Tell your ma I want her up here at the house right now.

JESSIE.   Yessir! *(Patrick hangs his gun on the porch.)*

PATRICK.   Look like he done bust up your lip good.

ZACH.   I tole you, it were my fault.

PATRICK.   Get over here, let's get you cleaned up. *(He leads Zach over to the pump and wets an old handkerchief in the water. With a tenderness and a delicacy surprizing for a man of his size, he cleans Zach's face.)* Now. What was all that about?

ZACH.   I was teasin' Zeke. It were my fault, Pa. Honest.

PATRICK.   That's good, you stick up for your brother but he knows better'n that. *(Patrick stops and stares at Zach.)*

ZACH.   What's wrong?

PATRICK.   Nothin'. Just ... sometimes I see your mama real strong in you. That's all. Now get inside and get changed. Hurry up! *(Zach starts inside as Zeke comes out.)* Zeke! You beg your brother's forgiveness, you hear? *(Zach looks miserable, embarrassed.)*

ZEKE.   *(Coldly.)* I'm sorry.

ZACH.   That's all right. *(Zach escapes inside. Beat.)*

ZEKE.   He started it.

PATRICK.   Ain't no excuse! That boy ain't half your size — ain't got his health. You oughta be ashamed. *(Beat.)* Gotta 'nough on our hands without you two scrappin'.

ZEKE.   Didn't know we were 'spectin' company.

PATRICK.   This ain't social.

ZEKE.   Circuit Court? *(Patrick nods.)* How bad you think this gonna get? *(Patrick shrugs.)* We ain't gonna lose any of it, are we?

PATRICK.   Not if I can help it. You and your brother, you load your rifles but keep'em just inside the door. We give'em a handshake first, 'fore we show'em a club. Let's go! Shake a leg! *(Zeke goes inside. Jessie runs back on.)*

JESSIE.   My mama's comin', Mr. Rowen, it's just her hip be actin' up on her today. She be along directly.

PATRICK.   Go to the springhouse, Jessie, bring me a jug.

JESSIE.   Yessir.

PATRICK. Jessie!

JESSIE. Yes sir.

PATRICK. When these folks git up here, I'm gonna send you down to look after their mules. Just like I always do. But if you hear any shootin', you make sure them mules ain't too easy to come by.

JESSIE. Shootin', Mr. Rowen? How'm I sposed to ...

PATRICK. Whatever that takes. You follow me?

JESSIE. Yes sir.

PATRICK. Go on and get that jug now. Make it a bigun! *(Jessie exits the yard. Zeke and Zach re-enter from the house.)* You boys just smile and don't say nothin'. If I send you in the house for some reason, you look and see if I scratch my head first. See me do that, you come out with them rifles.

JUDGE. *(Off-stage.)* Halllooo the house!

ZACH. What's goin' on, Pa?

PATRICK. Just be patient, son, we all gonna find out soon enough. *(They hold while a Fat Man in a black coat, tie and hat makes his way slowly onstage. One leg is wooden below the knee and he leans heavily for support on the arm of one of his Deputies for support. A second Deputy follows closely behind. Both Deputies carry rifles and pistols. The Fat Man stops and tips his hat grandly.)*

JUDGE. Good day to you sirs, one and all. Mr. Patrick Rowen, I presume?

PATRICK. That's me.

JUDGE. I'm Judge Jim Goddard — "Razor Jim" to my friends, among whom I hope to count you, Sir! I wish I could tell you that I earned that nickname on the bench, for the sharpness of my decisions, or the cut of my clothes — hah! hah! *(He coughs loudly, his face growing crimson.)* But the sad truth is — and it's truth, sir, and only truth we jurists care about — the sad truth is I earned both that name and this leg ... *(He thumps his wooden leg impressively.)* ... during an unfortunate hunting accident! Hah! Hah! *(Patrick and the boys stand dumbfounded in the face of this rotund, off-kilter whirlwind.)* Allow me to introduce my staff, Deputies Grey and O'Sullivan. The rest of our party will be joining us momentarily.

PATRICK. My sons, Zachariah and Ezekiel.

JUDGE.   Zachariah and Ezekiel! Great men, learned men, men of judgement and of the law! An auspicious beginning. I always find that a house in which there is respect for God's laws, also respects the laws of this great country of ours. They follow one another as night does follow the day. Would you not agree, sir?

PATRICK.   Their mama named'em. Iffen God helps them as much as He helped her, they ain't got much to look forward to. My oldest there, Zeke, he been baptised. But Zach and me, we ain't heard no call. (A tall, slender, expensively dressed man, Jeremiah, walks up quietly and joins the Judge. He carries a small strongbox under his arm.)

JUDGE.   So, you're a Christian, are you, young man? Read your bible do ya?

ZEKE.   Yessir.

JUDGE.   Well, that's fine.

ZACH.   Hell, he can't read any more'n I can!

ZEKE.   Shut up!

PATRICK.   Both of you be quiet. (Jessie and Sallie enter with a jug of whiskey.)

JUDGE.   Is that a jug, your nigger has there?

PATRICK.   Thought you might be a bit dry after all your traveling.

JUDGE.   Well, sir, you were surely right about that. Justice is a thirsty business.

PATRICK.   Give'em the jug, Jessie. Jessie here'd be happy to go on down and look after your mules for you.

JUDGE.   Well, that's kind of you sir, but we have found it prudent to care for our own livestock, seein' as how our business is frequently subject to ... what shall we call it, ... uh, "disagreements," sometimes of a rather violent nature. Hah! Hah! As you can see, I'm not a man much built for walkin'. I'd rather ride, both comin' and goin'. My thanks, sir, for your hospitality. (He drinks.) "Let schoolmasters puzzle their brain,/With grammar, and nonsense and learning;/Good liquor, I stoutly maintain,/Gives genius a better discerning!" Hah! Hah! (Jeremiah touches the Judge's sleeve.) Ahh! And now our party is complete and we can get down to the business at hand, perhaps?

PATRICK.   Get the judge a chair, Jessie.

JESSIE.   Yessir. *(Jessie exits into the house, and returns with a chair.)*

PATRICK.   I didn't catch your name.

JUDGE.   My fault! This is, ... uh ... Mr....?

JEREMIAH.   Jeremiah. You there, boy. Mr. Preacher Man ...

ZEKE.   Ezekiel.

JEREMIAH.   Ezekiel. *(He smiles.)* Do you know who Jeremiah was in the bible, boy?

ZEKE.   A prophet?

JEREMIAH.   A great prophet. He sent the whole Hebrew nation into Exile. Tore'em from their homes and sent them wanderin' in the desert for seventy years! *(Beat.)*

JUDGE.   Shall we get started, gentlemen?

JEREMIAH.   Of course.

JUDGE.   Then by the power vested in me by the great state of Kentucky, I hearby declare this session of the Sixth Circuit Court on July seventeenth, eighteen hundred and nineteen open! Mr. Grey, will you please do the honors as our bailiff?

GREY.   You want me to say that thing?

JUDGE.   That's right.

GREY.   The ... uh ...

JUDGE.   Honorable ...

GREY.   Honorable ...

JUDGE.   Judge Jim Goddard ...

GREY.   Judge Jim Goddard ... pre ... pro ... somethin'.

JUDGE.   Presiding.

GREY.   That's it.

JUDGE.   Mr. Grey only recently joined us — one of those unfortunate disagreements I mentioned having suddenly left his position vacant.

GREY.   Nobody said nothin' to me about talkin'. All they wanted to know was if I could shoot good, and by God I can do that!

JUDGE.   Indeed sir, if you can't, you're liable to lose more than your job! Hah! Hah!

GREY.   I could shoot good enough for Andrew "By God"

Jackson, I reckon I could shoot good enough for anybody!

JUDGE.   I'm sure your War Record is very impressive, Mr. Grey ...

PATRICK.   You fought with old Hickory at New Orleans?

GREY.   I'm proud to say I did ...

JUDGE.   Gentlemen ...

GREY.   And you...?

PATRICK.   Under Col. Henderson till he got his ass shot off in them Cypress Swamps. Then me and some of them Tennessee boys decided we'd cut our own orders and do us a little huntin!

GREY.   I heard you did! *(Singing.)* "We fed them lead fer breakfast,/And we fed them lead for dinner," ...

PATRICK.   "And the ones that didn't say their prayers,/went straight to hell a sinner" ...

GREY/PATRICK.   "We shot them in their big round eyes,/ We shot their chins and noses,/We shot all the buttons off./ Their coats as red AS ROSES!"

PATRICK.   Damn!

GREY.   By God, that was somethin', wasn't it? We stacked them redcoats up like cordwood! You boys there?

ZEKE/ZACH.   No sir.

JUDGE.   Gentlemen ...

GREY.   Well, you missed yourself somethin' there, that's for damn sure!

PATRICK.   Naw, my boys stayed here, looked after things. But Jessie over there, his daddy come with me. Died of a fever in them swamps.

GREY.   I'm sure sorry to hear that.

JESSIE.   Thank you, sir.

JUDGE.   GENTLEMEN! *(He pulls a pistol from his coat pocket and fires it into the air. Everyone stops.)* I'm sure as comrades-in-arms you must have a hundred old stories to share, but this is not a social call, gentlemen, it is a COURT OF LAW! Mr. Grey, try to keep that in mind, will you?

GREY.   Yessir.

JUDGE.   Mr. Rowen, we are here to proceed with the issue of your bankruptcy. Do you have a lawyer, sir?

PATRICK. You can see I don't.

JUDGE. No need to be embarrassed, Mr. Rowen, it's potentially a blessing. I have found in matters of this sort that a defense attorney only prolongs the issue and that the result is always the same. Could I have the documents in question, please? *(Jeremiah unlocks the strongbox and hands a number of papers to the Judge.)* What the court finds before hisself are three personal loans to one Patrick Rowen near Shilling Creek from the Bank of Kentucky in Morgan. All notes secured by what appears to be extensive and growing land titles here in Howsen county.

PATRICK. I own three hundred acres of land — good bottom land along the Shilling and most of what's between there and the Buckhorn North Fork. Along with the original thirty-nine acres my pa bought from the Injuns, that give me three hundred and thirty-nine acres.

JUDGE. No sir, you just own the *paper* on that land. And a veritable mountain of delinquent debt.

PATRICK. I pay my debts!

JUDGE. Mr. Rowen, really. If you paid your debts I wouldn't be here.

PATRICK. I tried! But them bastards changed the rules on me! Look here, I bought that land with *paper* money, *Bank of Kentucky* money — good as gold, they told me. Then two years later they won't take their own money! Told me to chink the logs in my house with it, light ceegars, or wipe my ass — all they wanted now was *hard* coin.

JUDGE. You signed a contract, Mr. Rowen. You agreed to pay a certain amount of interest on these loans.

PATRICK. When I signed them loans corn was sellin' for a dollar five a bushel in *paper* money. Bank switch to *silver* and suddenly that same bushel of corn is only worth twenty cents. That ain't my fault.

JUDGE. It's nobody's fault, Mr. Rowen. It was the War.

PATRICK. When we was fightin' I was doin' fine — it's *peace* that's killin' me! Hell, I thought we won the war! Look to me like I'd a been better off if we'da lost the damn thing!

JUDGE. Better off under the British? They burned Washington and drove your fellow countrymen out of their homes!

PATRICK. Well, ain't that what you aimin' to do to me and my family! *(Beat.)*

JUDGE. The government is not without understanding and ... and a great deal of sympathy for you and the *hundreds* of citizens who find themselves in your predicament. Even as we speak, replevy laws are being introduced in the legislature.

PATRICK. So you ain't gonna throw me outta here? *(Beat.)*

JUDGE. Unfortunately, until such time as those measures are enacted, this court must continue to enforce the existing statutes. Your total debt, Mr. Rowen, principal and interest, now runs to, ... uh, to ... *(The Judge searches for a moment among his papers.)*

JEREMIAH. Nine hundred and eighty-seven dollars and thirty-five cents.

JUDGE. Yes! Exactly. Are you prepared to repay that sum in full?

ZEKE. Mister, I thought that bank in Morgan folded?

JUDGE. Yes, it did.

ZEKE. Well, if the bank's gone, how can we still owe it anything?

JUDGE. Good question. The answer, my young friend, is that your father's debts were purchased in total by Mr. Jeremiah, here, just prior to the Bank's collapse. A stroke of fortune, sir, having just the one creditor. I have presided over cases with multiple creditors, each one howling for *Par Conditio Creditorium* like so many alleycats over a rotting fishhead.

PATRICK. I don't know how I got so lucky.

JUDGE. Hmmm? Oh yes. Hah! Hah! I meant, sir, that it will simplify matters greatly. Now, the question remains, are you prepared to repay your debt?

PATRICK. I got fourteen dollars and eighty cents in cash.

JEREMIAH. Silver?

PATRICK. Silver.

JUDGE. Well, that's a start.

PATRICK. I can't give you none of that. That's my seed money. How'm I gonna get a crop in next year without seed?

JUDGE.   *(Gently.)* I don't think under the present circumstances, Mr. Rowen, that you're gonna need to worry about
next year. Now, what else have you got? *(Beat.)*

PATRICK.   I got the land. The land I bought with that
money. I'll give it back. All of it. Every damn acre. That's fair,
ain't it mister?

JEREMIAH.   How much is that land worth?

PATRICK.   It cost me nine hundred and forty dollars.

JEREMIAH.   I didn't ask you what you paid for it, I said,
"What's it worth?"

PATRICK.   *(Confused.)* Nine hundred and forty dollars!

JUDGE.   Mr. Rowen, land at one time in these parts was
worth nearly two and a quarter dollars an acre ...

PATRICK.   I paid *two dollars and forty-two cents an acre* in '15
for that section near the Buckhorn!

JUDGE.   Your memory does you credit, sir. But today, that
same piece of land — indeed all the land in this area — is
worth only half that much.

JEREMIAH.   A dollar sixty-five, to be exact.

PATRICK.   HOW CAN THAT BE?! It's the same piece of
land, innit? Same trees, same rocks, same dirt. Only I been
workin' it — made it better.

JUDGE.   Land is just dirt, Mr. Rowen. It's worth only what
the market is willing to pay for it. No more, no less.

PATRICK.   IT AIN'T JUST DIRT! It's *land.* It's a *live* thing.
It's got moods and tricks and secrets like me or you or any
other living thing. Man who farms and don't know that, he
gonna bust out quick, 'cause the land, it don't tolerate no
fools. I know that don't mean nothin' to no bank man
pushin' his little pieces of paper, but just 'cause he don't
know it, that don't mean it ain't so.

JUDGE.   We are not here, Mr. Rowen, to argue Philosophy.
It is *facts* that we are concerned with and the *facts* of this
matter are that you are in *default.* Less your cash assets, your
debt to Mr. Jeremiah is now ...

JEREMIAH.   Nine hundred and seventy-two dollars and fifty-
five cents.

JUDGE.   Thank you. Turning over the land you purchased,

some ...

JEREMIAH.   Three hundred acres ...

JUDGE.   At the current value of ...

JEREMIAH.   A dollar sixty-five an acre ...

JUDGE.   For a total worth of ... *(He looks to Jeremiah, who does not disappoint him.)*

JEREMIAH.   Four hundred and ninety-five dollars.

JUDGE.   Exactly. The balance on your debt is now ...

JEREMIAH.   Four hundred and seventy-seven dollars and fifty-five cents. *(Beat.)*

PATRICK.   That's it, then. I'm busted flat. You can't get blood outta no rock.

JEREMIAH.   I think we're a long ways from bedrock, yet.

JUDGE.   What Mr. Jeremiah is suggesting is that you still possess some valuable assets: the original homestead, this house, your tools, etc....

PATRICK.   I ain't sellin' this land! I got family buried here — my pa, my wife, a baby sister and my first two children. Ain't no stranger gonna walk over them bones. No sir. You want this land, you gonna have to kill me and my boys first. *(Beat.)*

JUDGE.   While it would grieve the Court to see things come to such a state, there is always that possibility, of course. *(Beat. The Deputies shift their guns slightly.)*

JEREMIAH.   *(Quickly.)* Gentlemen, please. Please! I'm sure we can work something out. Mr. Rowen, surely there is something? What else have you got? *(Beat.)*

PATRICK.   I got two mules, traces and harnesses for both ...

JEREMIAH.   Sixty dollars.

ZEKE.   We paid forty dollars for Tucker alone, and that was just a year ago...!

JEREMIAH.   Fifty-five dollars ...

ZEKE.   They're worth a lot more'n that...!

JEREMIAH.   Fifty dollars.

ZEKE.   IT AIN'T FAIR!

PATRICK.   Be quiet, Zeke. Go in and lay down 'fore you have yourself one of those fits.

ZEKE.   I'm fine, Pa.

PATRICK. Go ahead and do what I tell you. *(Patrick scratches his head. Zeke starts in but the Judge stands up, alerting the Deputies.)*

JUDGE. I think your boy looks fine to me, Mr. Rowen. Fresh air, that's all he needs. You need something from inside, why, one of my men here, he be glad to fetch it for you. *(Beat. Then Patrick waves Zeke back.)*

PATRICK. *(To Jeremiah.)* What exactly you want from us here, mister?

JUDGE. It's nothin' personal, Mr. Rowen. Mr. Jeremiah here, he's just looking for justice.

JEREMIAH. No offense, Judge, but a man who goes to a Court of Law looking for " Justice," he gonna be pretty disappointed. I think Mr. Rowen there'd be the first one to agree with me on that point. No sir, you go to Court to get the law enforced. We'll leave "justice" up to God, eh, preacher man? All I want here's my money. *(Beat.)* And even at fifty dollars for them mules, I figure I'm still some four hundred and twenty-seven odd dollars shy.

PATRICK. You a farmer, Mr. Jeremiah? You don't look much like a farmer to me.

JEREMIAH. Oh, I been a lot of things in my time. I guess what I am now, you could call me a ... a speculator.

PATRICK. Spec...?

JEREMIAH. Spec-u-late-er.

PATRICK. What's that exactly?

JEREMIAH. That's a man who buys things people need, before they know they need'em.

PATRICK. Man can make a livin' doin' that?

JEREMIAH. *(Smiling.)* Oh, I do all right. Like you, I did a whole lot better when we was at war. In my line of work, peace is a mixed blessin' but I take comfort in the fact that, human nature bein' what it is, it ain't likely to last long. *(Beat.)* Four hundred and twenty-seven dollars and fifty-five cents.

PATRICK. You just bought yourself a whole lot of land, and I know you ain't aimin' to work that land with your bare hands. You gonna need you some tools.

JEREMIAH. Yessir, I guess I am. What you got?

PATRICK. I got smithy and shoeing equipment, two plows, a scythe, axes, ...

JEREMIAH. Guns?

PATRICK. The guns ain't for sale.

JEREMIAH. Too bad. I'm like to pay handsome for them rifles of your'n.

PATRICK. Not for sale.

JEREMIAH. Suit yourself. Eighty dollars for the tools — lock, stock and barrel. Ever piece of iron, ever scrap of leather.

PATRICK. Except the rifles.

JEREMIAH. Three hundred and forty-seven dollars and fifty-five cents. *(Beat.)*

PATRICK. I got these slaves here.

ZACH. Pa?!

PATRICK. The woman is full-blooded Guinea ...

ZACH. You can't sell Sallie ...

PATRICK. His daddy was Bantu ...

ZACH. Tell him, Zeke ...

PATRICK. Be quiet, boy ...

ZACH. Zeke!

PATRICK. Jessie's in good health ...

ZEKE. Bible don't say nothin' agin it. Joseph hisself was sold into slavery ...

ZACH. BY HIS FAMILY!

PATRICK. SHUT UP! I'm tryin' to *save* somethin' here — save somethin' for you and your brother!

ZACH. Ain't nothin' worth this! Jessie...?

JESSIE. Hush up, now, Zach. When it rains you take cover — yellin' at them clouds ain't gonna get you nothin' but wet.

PATRICK. He's a hard worker. He don't talk back and he got him some sense in him. You can see that.

JEREMIAH. Woman's too old for breeding.

PATRICK. She's healthy, though. And she carries her weight around here. She can outwork any of my boys in the field any day, long as you ain't makin' her lift heavy ...

JEREMIAH. I can see the boy's strong but I got no use for

the woman.

SALLIE.   Mr. Rowen ...

PATRICK.   I ain't breakin' 'em up. That Jessie, he was raised right alongside my boys ...

SALLIE.   Mr. Rowen, sir ...

PATRICK.   I just wouldn't feel right about it.

JEREMIAH.   Can't sell a man what he don't want.

PATRICK.   Take 'em together, or leave it alone. It don't make me no never mind. *(Beat.)*

JUDGE.   Mr. Jeremiah?

JEREMIAH.   Two hundred and twenty dollars for the both of 'em. You take it quick 'fore I change my mind.

PATRICK.   That's a deal.

SALLIE.   Mr. Rowen ...

PATRICK.   It's all right, Sallie, you and your boy gonna be together.

SALLIE.   That ain't what I'm askin' you about, sir. You gonna sell me, well, I can't do nothin' about that but I'm beggin' you, sir, don't you be sellin' my boy. It ain't right.

PATRICK.   Sallie, you gonna be together, I promise you ...

SALLIE.   For twenty-seven years, you ain't never had to raise a hand to me or my son. And when Miss Rebecca died birthin' your Zach, I nurse him, and raised him and his brother both, just like they was my own children.

JUDGE.   Mr. Rowen ...

SALLIE.   I ain't never asked you for nothin', sir, but I'm askin' you now, don't you be sellin' Jessie.

JEREMIAH.   The boy's all I'm interested in, Rowen.

SALLIE.   I ain't askin' this for me, sir, I'm askin' for you.

JESSIE.   It's all right, Mama.

PATRICK.   I ain't got no choice here, Sallie.

SALLIE.   No sir, man always got a choice! And you sell Jessie, you buyin' yourself a world of pain, in this world and the next. I'm beggin' you, sir. Don't you sell him.

JEREMIAH.   I ain't buyin' no crazy woman.

PATRICK.   Two hundred and twenty leaves me owing what?

SALLIE.   YOU BE SELLIN' YOUR OWN BROTHER! *(Beat. Everyone stares at her.)* John Biggs was a good man and I always felt bad 'cause I couldn't give him no children his own but our blood was bad and them babies always die.

JESSIE. Who's my pa?

SALLIE. You ask Mr. Rowen there. He see how things be now, don't you? John Biggs, he come over with Miss Rebecca, but I already be carryin' Jessie by then. I tell him what's what and ask him what he want to do about it and John Biggs he tell me, "You see how things is. Man kill his own daddy ain't gonna spare no baby no sword. We just gots to keep quiet and pray that baby take after his mama." And the Lord, He heard them prayers 'cause my Jessie was born black as night and I knew he was gonna live. *(Beat.)* You see how it be now, dontcha?

ZACH. Pa?

SALLIE. Your daddy use me 'fore we got here. By the time we buried him, I was already carryin' his son. *(Beat.)*

PATRICK. My brother.

SALLIE. He gonna do right by you now, Jessie. Now he knows.

ZACH. We ain't got no deal here, right, Pa? No deal, Mister. *(Patrick is silent.)* Tell him, Pa! *(Long beat.)*

PATRICK. Two hundred and twenty. What's that leave on what I owe?

ZACH. You can't do that!

JEREMIAH. One hundred and twenty-seven dollars and fifty-five cents.

ZACH. You can't sell your *brother!*

PATRICK. I ain't sellin' no brother, I'm just sellin' a *slave.*

ZACH. He's your flesh and blood, god dammit — HE'S YOUR FAMILY!

PATRICK. On my land, don't nobody tell me what I CAN AND CANNOT DO! YOU HEAR ME! NOBODY! *(Patrick knocks him to the ground. Zeke moves between his brother and his father.)*

ZEKE. Pa! *(Patrick steps back, breathing hard. He turns to Jeremiah.)*

PATRICK. One hundred and twenty-seven dollars and fifty-five cents.

JEREMIAH. What else you got?

PATRICK. I got ... I got ... (Beat.)

JEREMIAH. This house and the original thirty-nine acres. (Beat.)

PATRICK. (Barely audible.) How much?

JEREMIAH. Thirty-nine acres at a dollar sixty-five an acre is sixty-four dollars and thirty-five cents.

PATRICK. The house?

JEREMIAH. Don't need a house.

PATRICK. It's gotta be worth something! (Beat.)

JEREMIAH. Thirty dollars for the house.

PATRICK. That leaves me ... I got ... uh ... I got this here watch. My daddy's. Been in this family I don't know how long. It's real gold, see there? And it ... it plays this little music when you open it. Real sweet.

JEREMIAH. Twenty dollars.

PATRICK. This here watch is real special ... my pa give it me ...

JEREMIAH. I buy gold 'cause I can sell it at a profit. Ain't no market for sentiment. Twenty dollars. (Beat.)

PATRICK. Twenty dollars. That leaves ... uh ... I'm still short.

JEREMIAH. Thirteen dollars and twenty cents.

ZEKE. Let it go, Pa. Let'em have it.

PATRICK. I ain't finished yet! (Beat.) You got family, Mr. Jeremiah?

JEREMIAH. Not anymore. My pa was kilt, and my sister ... she died in childbirth.

PATRICK. I'm sure sorry to hear about your trouble. My ... my pa ... he's dead and my wife, 'Becca, she died birthin' my youngest, Zachariah. So I know what ... it's like ... we got somethin' ... we share somethin' here. This here ... this land ... it's all I ever knowed. All I ever wanted. I know ... know ever foot of this place. I bet if you was to blind me and take me somewheres on it, anywheres, I could tell you where we wuz just by the smell and the taste of the dirt. I could do that. I did a wrong thing, here. I see that. And the law don't smile on no poor man when he do wrong. But my boys ...

they didn't do nothin'. You gonna toss me off this land, well you gotta right to do that, but I'm askin' you to think of your own family, think of your pa and that sister of yours, and let my boys stay on. I'm beggin' you ... *(Beat.)*

JEREMIAH. Do it.

PATRICK. Do...?

JEREMIAH. Beg me.

JUDGE. Mr. Jeremiah — really sir...!

JEREMIAH. Shut up! *(Beat.)* Beg me. *(Patrick sinks slowly to his knees.)*

PATRICK. I'm begging you ...

JEREMIAH. Mr. Jeremiah.

PATRICK. Mr. Jeremiah ...

JEREMIAH. Sir.

PATRICK. Sir ...

JEREMIAH. Don't throw me off my land.

PATRICK. Don't throw me off my land. *(Beat.)*

JEREMIAH. Tell you what I'll do. You're right, what you said about me not bein' no farmer. Not for a long time now, anyways. I'm gonna need help to work this land. I'll let your boys, I'll even let you, I'll let you stay here on my land, in my house here, and sharecrop for me.

PATRICK. What's "sharecrop?"

JEREMIAH. You work this land, and I take half of whatever you grow here. Corn, tobaccee, whatever.

PATRICK. We ain't got no tools.

JEREMIAH. No sir, you don't. No tools, no mules and no seed. And you gonna need all of that. So I'll give seed and tools ... for another quarter of what you grow.

PATRICK. That don't leave me and my boys but a quarter of that to live on.

JEREMIAH. Guess you better work hard then. *(Beat.)* Take it or leave it, it don't make me no never mind. *(Patrick rises slowly.)*

PATRICK. We'll take it.

JEREMIAH. 'Course you still owe me twelve dollars and sixty-five cents but you catch me in a generous mood, today. So, what do you say, we just let it ride?

PATRICK. That'd be mighty generous of you.

JEREMIAH. Cost you, say, ten percent a year to carry it. *(Beat.)*

PATRICK. All right.

JEREMIAH. Cash, of course.

PATRICK. Of course.

JEREMIAH. Since you asked me in my pa's name, I'll go you even one step further. Just to show you that my heart's in the right place, I won't put no time on that loan. You pay me the balance whenever. Won't cost you one penny more.

PATRICK. I appreciate that.

JEREMIAH. But each year, what you can't pay on the interest? That gets added to the rest of it. *(Beat.)*

PATRICK. All right. *(Beat.)*

JUDGE. Well, gentlemen, if both parties are satisfied, this court approves the settlement and is adjourned. Mr. Jeremiah, if you will be so kind as to have the necessary documents drawn up and filed with this court in Lousiville.

JEREMIAH. If you could hold on just a minute, Judge, there is one more piece of business I'd like to introduce. *(The Judge looks at him in confusion. Jeremiah whistles loudly. Then, a figure wearing a hooded cape, limps on. The figure looks at Jeremiah.)* It's over. *(The figure pulls off her hood and a cascade of long, grey hair tumbles down. It is Star Rowen. She stares at her son.)*

STAR. "To hi ju?" Chuji. [How are you?] *(Beat.)*

PATRICK. I thought you were dead.

STAR. Maybe I am. Maybe you dream me. Crossin' a muddy river ...

PATRICK. Dead ...

STAR. They's lots of times I wisht I were. But the thought of you always kept me goin'.

ZACH. Who is she, Pa?

STAR. Ain't you gonna make me known to my own kin? I'm Star Rowen. Your grandma. Who you boys?

ZEKE. I'm Ezekiel.

ZACH. Zachariah. *(Beat.)*

PATRICK. Why'd you come back?

STAR.   I don't know.   See you humbled. Curse you to your face. Something like that. But I think hating you so long just done burned me out inside 'cause I stand here and I don't feel nothin' for you one way or t'other. *(Beat.)* Maybe I come home to die. I think maybe that's it. *(To Jeremiah.)* I seen all I need to. *(She exits slowly. Patrick looks over to Jeremiah.)*

JEREMIAH.   I'm Jeremiah Talbert.

PATRICK.   Talbert.

JEREMIAH.   Star come get me the night you run her off. The night you killed my pa and took my sister, Rebecca. For the longest time, I was gonna kill you. But somehow that didn't seem enough — just killin' you. So I decided to let you live, but take away everything in your life that meant anything to you, just like you done to me. And now I own you, Rowen — own all of you Rowens. *(Beat.)* You know, I never thought I'd hear myself say this, but I hope you live a long time, Patrick. I hope you live a long, long time. *(Beat.)* Two weeks from today, I 'spect to see all you Rowens over at what used to be the Talbert homestead. Your daddy knows the way, boys. You're gonna build your Uncle Talbert a new house. With a *big* porch. And ever mornin' I get up I'm gonna sit on my big porch and drink a big cup of coffee and watch you Rowens workin' my land. *(Beat.)* I'm done, Judge. Court's adjourned. *(Jeremiah exits. The Judge rises.)*

JUDGE.   Mr. Rowen.... Good day to you Sir. *(The Judge tips his hat and then he and the two Deputies start to exit. Grey stops.)*

GREY.   I'm ... I'm sure sorry for all your trouble, Mr. Rowen. I wisht I could help you but ... *(He gestures helplessly, then exits.)*

JEREMIAH.   *(Off-stage.)* Sallie! Jessie!

SALLIE.   I can't curse you, Mr. Rowen — you done that yourself when you sold the best part of you. You take care of yourself, Mr. Zach. *(She and Jessie exit. Patrick stands and then goes over to where the Judge sat. He picks up the jug, hefts it, and then turns it upside down.)*

PATRICK.   Man didn't even leave me a drink. Ain't that just like the law. *(Zachariah goes into the house. He returns with his rifle and starts to exit the opposite direction of the Judge.)* Where you think you're goin'?

ZACH.   I don't know. Anywheres.

PATRICK.   Don't you look down your nose at me, boy. What I did, I did here for you and your brother. All of it!

ZACH.   I know that, Pa — that's the worst part of it.

PATRICK.   What kinda man turns his back on his own family?!

ZACH.   You and Zeke know more about that'n I do. *(He starts off again.)*

PATRICK.   YOU LEAVE HERE, DON'T YOU EVER COME BACK! YOU HEAR! YOU LEAVE, YOU AIN'T PART OF THIS FAMILY NO MORE! I CUT YOU OUTTA ME LIKE A BOIL! *(He turns on Ezekiel.)* How about you, boy! You gonna turn tail and run off, too!

ZEKE.   I ain't goin' nowhere, Pa.

PATRICK.   I don't need you, you know! Don't need any of you! AAAAHHHH!! *(Patrick falls to his knees sobbing.)* My b ... b ... boy, gone. He gone. All gone. All gone. *(Zeke holds his Father.)*

ZEKE.   It's all right, Pa, I'm here. You still got me. Ezekiel's here.

PATRICK.   All gone. Everything. All g ... g ... gone ...

ZEKE.   Listen to me, Pa. Listen to me. Stop it! Cryin' ain't gonna bring nothin' and nobody back, you hear!? Listen to me. You get angry. You hear? Get angry! You hear me! YOU GET ANGRY! *(Ezekiel slaps and shakes his father until Patrick pushes him away.)* You angry now? You listenin' to me?

PATRICK.   I'm listenin'.

ZEKE.   We gonna get it back, you hear? All of it! We gonna get it all back and more! You hear me? Don't matter how long it take, how many years, we gonna get ours agin!

PATRICK.   I'm listening.

ZEKE.   We ain't lost no war, here. War's just startin'. We got to be patient. Got to hide our hearts and put on our stone faces and smile these people to death.

PATRICK.   Smile?

ZEKE.   That's right. We gonna "yessir" Mr. Talbert, and smile on him and his, and we gonna wait. *(Patrick begins cry-*

ing again. Zeke cradles him in his arms.)

PATRICK.   Ain't never gonna see my b ... b ... boy, no more. My Zach!

ZEKE.   It's all right, Pa.

PATRICK.   My b ... b ... boy's gone and I ain't never gonna see him again.

ZEKE.   Hush now. Got to be strong. Got to be stone. The Lord, he ain't gonna forget us. No way. No sir. He just be testin' us.

PATRICK.   My boy ...

ZEKE.   We got to wander in this desert here, like them Hebrews, but then he gonna bring us home.

PATRICK.   My boy ...

ZEKE.   And then ... *(Beat.)* Then we gonna settle up. *(Slow fade to black.)*

END OF PLAY

PROPERTY LIST

Tools
Bible (ZEKE)
Gun (PATRICK)
Old handkerchief (PATRICK)
Rifles (DEPUTIES, ZACH)
Pistols (JUDGE, DEPUTIES)
Small strongbox with papers (JEREMIAH)
Jug (JESSIE)
Chair (JESSIE)
Rowen watch

GOD'S GREAT SUPPER

In the desert
I saw a creature, naked, bestial,
Who, squatting upon the ground,
Held his heart in his hands,
And ate of it.
I said, "Is it good, friend?"
"It is bitter — bitter," he answered;
"But I like it
Because it is bitter,
And because it is my heart."

— Stephen Crane

CHARACTERS

JED ROWEN, age twenty-eight

EZEKIEL ROWEN, age sixty-one, Jed's father

PATRICK ROWEN, age eighty-five, Jed's grandfather

JOLEEN ROWEN, age fifty-five, Jed's mother

RICHARD TALBERT, age thirty-nine, landowner,
    son of Jeremiah Talbert

RANDALL TALBERT (BOY), age ten, Richard's only son

ROSE ANNE TALBERT, Richard's daughter

JULIA ANNE TALBERT, Richard's daughter

FIRST SHARECROPPER

SECOND SHARECROPPER

UNION COLONEL

FIRST REBEL

SECOND REBEL

BOATMAN

TOMMY NOLAN

CARL DAWKINS

GUS SLOCUM

WILLIAM CLARKE QUANTRILL

FIRST UNION SOLDIER

SECOND UNION SOLDIER

CHURCH CHOIR

MOURNERS AT GRAVESIDE

NARRATOR

God's Great Supper.

42 years later. The year is 1861. The Rowen Homestead.

God's Great Supper.

GOD'S GREAT SUPPER

Darkness. We hear a sound which is vaguely familiar but unrecognizable. Perhaps it has been slightly altered electronically. The sound grows louder and more insistent — threatening. Then the backdrop explodes with a collage of giant images, and we recognize the sound: angry scavenger birds, crows mostly, fighting over a meal. The sound of their feeding grows to a crescendo and then stops.

A single spot comes up center on Jed Rowen. He speaks directly to the audience.

JED.   When I hear the crows, I know I'm dreamin'. My dream always begins with me in church. *(In the darkness behind him, can dimly be seen a large group of Men and Women quietly singing "Blessed Be the Tie That Binds.")* My pa, Ezekiel, preaches from the dark chapter of the bible, the one that always scared me as a kid: the Book of Revelations. *(A second spot comes up on Ezekiel. The power of the Word fills him like a bonfire. His face is flushed and wet with sweat as he guides his congregation through the glory of John's vision of Armageddon.)*
EZEKIEL.   "Then I saw an angel standing in the sun, and he cried aloud to all the birds flying in mid-heaven, 'Come and gather for God's great supper, to eat the flesh of horses and their riders, the flesh of all men, slaves and free, great and small!'" *(Spot fades out on Ezekiel.)*
JED.   I sneak out of church and into an apple orchard where the trees are so full of crows the branches crack under their weight. The fruit rots on the ground. The trees are all beaks and eyes and appetite. There's a cold church picnic laid out on tables underneath the trees, and I sit down and a

ragged woman puts a plate of food in front of me. She goes and kneels next to her sister. I'm hungry and I eat. I eat alone 'cept for this one man who sits acrost from me, his hat pulled low so I can't see his face. I can see his hands, though, and his nails are torn and bleeding. When I finish my plate the woman brings another one. And when I finish that, another one. And then another. I eat till I am full to burstin', but I'm afraid to stop. Afraid what might happen to me if I stop eatin'. I make myself sick, and when I look up again the man removes his hat and I know him now — he's Quantrill. William Clarke Quantrill. "Have some more, Jed," Quantrill says, and he laughs. And then the women begin to speak. *(Two spots come up to reveal two women — Rose Anne and Julia Anne — kneeling on either side of the stage. Both women are so gaunt and haggard it is impossible to determine their real ages. Their faces are raw and sunburnt. They are dirty, barefoot, and their clothes are in tatters. They speak directly to the audience without apparent notice of each other.)*

ROSE ANNE. These are the names:

JULIA ANNE. These are the names:

ROSE ANNE. Tom Nolan ...

JULIA ANNE. Tom Nolan ...

ROSE ANNE. Carl Dawkins ...

JULIA ANNE. Carl Dawkins ...

ROSE ANNE. Sam Jackson ...

JULIA ANNE. Sam Jackson ...

ROSE ANNE. Isaac Gatlin ...

JULIA ANNE. Isaac Gatlin ...

ROSE ANNE. Josh Gatlin ...

JULIA ANNE. Josh Gatlin ...

ROSE ANNE. Edward Hayes ...

JULIA ANNE. Edward Hayes ...

ROSE ANNE. Jed Rowen ...

JULIA ANNE. Jed Rowen ...

ROSE ANNE. Jed Rowen ...

JULIA ANNE. Jed Rowen ...

ROSE ANNE. Jed Rowen ... *(Beat.)*

JED. And then I wake up. *(The light on the two women fades out and then Jed's spot goes out. Darkness. The lights come up and we recognize the front of the Rowen cabin. The structure shows signs of disrepair and neglect. It is early summer, 1861. Patrick Rowen, now 85, sits on an old chair on the porch, his lap covered with a threadbare blanket despite the heat. He is blind. His son Ezekiel, sits leaning against a porch post, apparently asleep. A small boy, ten-years-old, darts across the stage. He is well dressed, perhaps even a little over-dressed for the country. Tucked under one arm, he carries a bundle wrapped in cloth. The boy considers Ezekiel and Patrick nervously and then whispers loudly into the cabin.)*

RANDALL.   Jed? *(No response. He tries to sneak past both men and into the house. With surprizing agility, Patrick grabs him by the scruff of his neck, emitting a weird, high-pitched laugh as he does so. Immediately, Ezekiel is awake. He grabs the terrified boy from Patrick and drags him kicking and screaming into the yard.)*

EZEKIEL.   What do you think you're doin' here, boy?

RANDALL.   Lemme go! Lemme go!

EZEKIEL.   Didn't I tell you not to come snoopin' 'round here, you damn devil's whelp!

RANDALL.   I wasn't doin' nothin'!

EZEKIEL.   The hell you say! What were you doin' on my porch?

RANDALL.   I just wanted to talk to Jed!

EZEKIEL.   Liar! You was sneakin' and spyin', weren't ya?!

RANDALL.   No I wasn't! *(Joleen Rowen, Ezekiel's wife, comes out onto the porch.)*

JOLEEN.   Ezekiel, what is it? I'm tryin' to get me some rest in here.

EZEKIEL.   God damns all liars, boy! He gives'em to the devil and Satan rolls'em in cornmeal and frys'em up like catfish! Terrible is the fire that burns'em and terrible is the sound of their screams! *(The boy is sobbing now.)*

RANDALL.   I wasn't doin'nothin'!

JOLEEN.   What you got there, Ezekiel?

EZEKIEL.   Got me that Talbert boy, Randall! Put the big pot on, Joleen, we gonna eat tonight!

JOLEEN.   Shoot, not enough on that boy to make two mouthfuls. *(She moves to Patrick and wipes his chin and strokes his head.)* Calm down, Pappaw, it ain't nothin'. Ain't nothin' to worry about.

RANDALL.   Lemme go, *please,* lemme go!

JED.   Let 'em go, Pa. *(Jed stands SR with a hoe in one hand.)*

RANDALL.   Jed! *(The boy tears himself out of Ezekiel's hands and throws himself at Jed.)*

JED.   All right now, Randall, what's goin' on here?

RANDALL.   I just ... I wanted to ... I just wanted to see you and ... and ... Preacher said ... said he was gonna damn me to hell and ... and then they was ... they was gonna eat me and ... and...!

JED.   Ma?

JOLEEN.   Boy's a natural-born liar, say anythin' come into his head.

RANDALL.   I am not!

JOLEEN.   Hush now, Pappaw, it's all right. Sshhh.

JED.   Pa, what's your side o' this?

EZEKIEL.   All them Talberts gonna burn, don't need no special curse from me!

RANDALL.   See!

JED.   *(Amused.)* Didn't Jesus say somethin' about "suffer the little children to come unto me?"

EZEKIEL.   Oh, he gonna suffer'em all right!

JED.   He's just a kid, Pa.

EZEKIEL.   Little snakes grow into big ones!

JOLEEN.   Amen.

JED.   Pappaw all right?

JOLEEN.   He just fine. Little excited that's all. Aren't you Pappaw?

PATRICK.   Zchkk ghckkkk ...

JOLEEN.   Huh? I think he wants some tobaccee, Zeke. *(Ezekiel crosses over and puts a twist of tobacco into his father's mouth.)*

JED.   What'd you want to see me about that's so all fired important, Randall? My pa here may damn your soul but everybody knows his bark's a whole lot worse'n his bite ...

EZEKIEL.   Say's who?!

JED.   ... But *Mr. Talbert* catch you here and he gonna whip your butt up one side and down the other.

RANDALL.   I know.

JED.   So, what is it? Hurricane? Tornado? What?

RANDALL.   I wanna come live with you! *(Beat.)*

JED.   Well, and we'd love to have you, right Pa?

EZEKIEL.   Lord have mercy!

JOLEEN.   Amen.

JED.   But I don't think your daddy he gonna be too happy about that.

RANDALL.   I don't care, I hate him!

JED.   Don't talk that way about your pa, boy — it ain't right.

RANDALL.   He's goin' away anyhow. He don't have to know anything about it. *(Jed and Ezekiel share a quick look.)*

EZEKIEL.   Told ya.

JED.   That a fact, now? Where's he goin'?

RANDALL.   He's goin' off to fight them Yankees! And I wanted to go off with him but he said I was too young and that's when I decided I was gonna run off and live with you! I reckon I can kill Yankees as good as anybody.

EZEKIEL.   Bloodthirsty little savage. *(Jed waves him quiet. Randall unties his bundle.)*

JED.   When's your daddy takin' off?

RANDALL.   He rode off this mornin' collectin' folks. They all gonna leave tomorrow. See here, I took his pistol!

JED.   Well now, that's really somethin', innit? That's one of them new Colts, I bet! Look at that, Pa.

EZEKIEL.   Lemme see.

JED.   Now I know you're angry, Randall, but I sure don't think you shoulda gone and borrowed that gun off'n your daddy without askin' him.

EZEKIEL.   Gotta mighty sweet action on it.

RANDALL.   If I'd asked him he'd a just said no.

EZEKIEL.   Boy's gotta point.

JED.   Whatever. Ain't none of our business, nohow. But as to your stayin' here, Randall, well that dog just don't hunt. Your daddy have a fit he even know you *visitin'* us. You know that.

RANDALL.   I know.

JED.   So, what I'm gonna do, I'm gonna suggest you just

sneak on back to home and put that gun away afore your daddy sees it's missin'.

RANDALL. Don't see why I can't stay. I like you a lot more'n my daddy. He isn't gonna miss me.

JED. Sure he would — he'd miss you somethin' fierce. Your daddy, he's just a busy man, that's all.

EZEKIEL. Yeah, bleedin' folks dry is a full-time job.

JED. Now my mamma's gonna fix you somethin' to eat and then you gotta get on to home, you hear? *(Randall drops despairingly to the ground and rolls his bundle back together.)*

JOLEEN. Feed him? I'm so hungry I can't sleep and I'm sposed to feed him?! Feed him what?

JED. Give'im a little piece of cornbread, Maw.

JOLEEN. Hit's comin' outta your supper it is. Ain't comin' outta mine.

RICHARD. Randall! What are you doing here, son? *(Randall freezes as his father, Richard Talbert, strides on. Richard is 41. He's a tall, thin, impatient man with a condescending attitude. He wears a new and rather garish Confederate Lieutenant's uniform topped by a wide-brimmed hat with an enormous plume.)* I said, what are you doing here!

RANDALL. Nothing, I just ...

RICHARD. Did I tell you not to come down here?

RANDALL. Yes sir.

RICHARD. Did you disobey my order?

JED. Boy didn't mean any harm, Mr. Talbert ...

RICHARD. I reckon I know how to raise my own son without your help.

RANDALL. It wasn't his fault, he ...

RICHARD. You speak when you're spoken to! Now come here! *(Randall trudges over reluctantly.)* You disobeyed my orders, didn't you?

RANDALL. Yes sir.

RICHARD. What do you think I ought to do with you?

RANDALL. Punish me.

RICHARD. How do you think I ought to do that?

RANDALL. *(Hopefully.)* Send me to bed without any supper? *(Richard just stares at him.)* Whip me.

114

RICHARD. You sure?

RANDALL. Yes sir.

RICHARD. Put your hand out. *(He does so. Richard strikes his hand several times with his riding crop.)* Are you crying?

RANDALL. No sir.

RICHARD. Don't you shame me in front of these people. You're a Talbert! These people work for your daddy and some day they are gonna work for you. Now how're these people gonna look up to you if you cry? Put your hand back out there. *(He does so. Richard hits him again.)* Now say you're sorry.

RANDALL. I'm sorry.

RICHARD. Now go home. Go on! *(Randall grabs his bundle and runs off behind the house. Richard turns to the Rowens.)* They grow up fast, don't they? *(Silence.)*

JED. You ride in on the grey mare?

RICHARD. On the roan. Mare's doin' all right, though. You did a good job — look like she's gonna be fine.

JED. I'm sure glad to hear that, 'cause that's a mighty fine horse.

RICHARD. Oughta be, what I paid for her.

JED. I was fixin' to come up to the big house tonight after I got cleaned up and take another look at her.

RICHARD. I appreciate that, Jed, but that wasn't what I came by for.

JED. Yes sir. *(Beat.)*

RICHARD. I'd like a drink of water, if you don't mind. *(Beat. Nobody moves.)*

JOLEEN. Help yourself.

JED. Here, let me get that for you, Mr. Talbert.

EZEKIEL. Man can get his own water, Jed.

JED. It's no trouble, Pa. *(Jed pumps a cup of water and hands it to Richard. Richard drinks and then swaggers over to the porch. He addresses Patrick.)*

RICHARD. Afternoon. *(No response.)* Can he hear me?

JED. Hard to tell when he can and when he won't.

RICHARD. How old is your Pappaw?

JED. Eighty-five this spring.

JOLEEN. We think.

EZEKIEL.   Nobody's too sure.

RICHARD.   Eighty-five. Isn't that something? I tell you, you gotta cherish'em when they're alive. Isn't a day goes by I don't miss my daddy. *(Patrick spits a stream of tobacco juice amazingly close to Richard, who beats a hasty retreat.)*

JOLEEN.   Pappaw! Look at the mess you gone and made! *(She wipes Patrick's chin. Ezekiel grins.)*

JED.   Mighty fancy uniform you wearin' there, Mr. Talbert.

RICHARD.   You like it?

EZEKIEL.   Puuuurty.

JED.   *(Quickly.)* Very impressive.

RICHARD.   My girls made it for me.

JED.   That a fact? Miss Rose Anne and Miss Julia Anne did that themselves, did they?

RICHARD.   Well, their momma helped, of course. But they designed it and did all the work. Hey, what do you think of this plume, huh? You wouldn't believe what that feather cost.

JED.   Well, I was just gonna ask you about that, sir. That a real feather, off a real bird?

RICHARD.   Oh yeah.

JED.   I'll be darned. Sure wouldn't want to run up against that critter.

RICHARD.   Must be big as mule!

JED.   Big as a horse!

RICHARD.   Horse feathers! *(They laugh. Richard tosses what's left of his water on the ground.)* Sweet water.

JED.   Any sweeter 'n' you could boil it down for molasses.

RICHARD.   *(Laughing.)* I reckon.

EZEKIEL.   Somethin' on your mind, Mr. Talbert, or you just come by to whip kids 'n' waste water.

RICHARD.   Spare the rod, Preacher, spoil the child. As to wasting water, I reckon I can do whatever I like with it, seein' as how it's mine. It and everything else around here. *(Beat.)* The fact of the matter is, I come down here to talk to you, Jed.

EZEKIEL.   I'm head of this family, and anything you got to say you can say it to me!

JED.   Easy, Pa.

116

RICHARD. Whoa — easy there, Preacher. Nobody's gonna run off with your flock. He always this touchy?

JED. Only when he ain't had his nap. You know.

RICHARD. Oh, I see. They do get that way, don't they?

EZEKIEL. Well, I reckon I don't need to stand around here and be insulted to my face! Joleen, get inside that house! Come on, Jed! *(Ezekiel moves up to the porch and turns back to Jed.)* You comin'?

JED. You go on inside if you've a mind to, Pa — I'm gonna hear what Mr. Talbert come all this way to say.

EZEKIEL. I can tell you what he come over here for, he come over to make trouble.

JED. Let the man speak, Pa, 'fore you go damning him to hell.

RICHARD. See now, you always been a level headed fellow, Jed — unlike some of your kin. And I admire that about you. I know there's been bad blood between us, beween my daddy and your pappaw, but it doesn't always have to be that way don't you think?

JED. No, I reckon it ain't written in stone.

RICHARD. Of course not. Times change, people change. We got a lot in common, you know? We're like two people sharing the same well — doesn't matter how much we might disagree, it doesn't make any sense for either one of us to piss in the water.

EZEKIEL. Make a lot more sense just to shoot the other fellow.

JED. Pa.

RICHARD. What I'm trying to get at here, Jed, is maybe it's time to bury our common differences and to join forces against a common foe. Those cowards down in Louisville may have voted Kentucky neutral, but when this war heats up there won't be any such thing.

JED. Long as we mind our own business, don't see why anybody ought to bother us out here.

RICHARD. Lot easier said than done. You sure gonna feel different after old Abe Lincoln come in here and take your slaves away.

EZEKIEL. We ain't got any slaves here.

RICHARD. It isn't just slaves. They take our niggers away they aren't gonna stop there. They gonna come take our cows and our horses and everything else we got.

JOLEEN. We ain't got any cows or horses either.

RICHARD. I know that Joleen, I'm trying to get to a bigger principle here!

EZEKIEL. Oh, a *principle*.

JOLEEN. What's a principle, Zeke?

EZEKIEL. That's one of those sweet nothin's the big boys whisper in your ear while they pull your pants down.

RICHARD. Now, look here ...

JED. Pa's got a point, Mr. Talbert. It sure look like a rich man's war to me. Don't see why poor folks oughta be inna hurry to go die innit.

RICHARD. It isn't about property! It's about somebody livin' miles and miles away tellin' you and me how we got to live. That isn't why your granddaddy and my granddaddy came out here and whipped the indians off this land. Now, there's a Confederate army getting organized down in Bowling Green. I'm looking to raise a company of men to go down there and show those boys how to make war! I reckon you can shoot about as good as anybody in these mountains, and I know there isn't anybody here or in the bluegrass can touch you for your way with horses. I want you to ride with me. *(Beat.)*

JED. Well, that'd be a real honor, sir, but I just don't know. Who's gonna look after things here? We just set out the corn, who's gonna bring it in? We owe you seed and tools and I don't know what all, how we gonna make enough to pay you anything on what we owe with me gone?

RICHARD. My field niggers'll get in your crops. Isn't white man's work anyway, is it? And for every week you ride with me I'll knock a nickel off what you owe. Now that's fair, isn't?

EZEKIEL. He just tryin' to buy you, Jed. Tell him you ain't for sale, you or any other Rowen!

RICHARD. Hell, Jed, everybody says the war's gonna be over in six weeks. What have you got around here that's so much more exciting?

EZEKIEL.   That's the devil talkin' in him, son, sure as I'm standin' here!

RICHARD.   Don't you ever want to get out of these mountains, Jed, and have a look see? You want to spend the rest of your days looking at the south end of a northbound mule?

EZEKIEL.   He ain't goin' and that's that!

RICHARD.   Well, if your daddy won't let you ...

JED.   I can make up my own mind.

EZEKIEL.   You ain't goin'!

JED.   And why the hell not!

EZEKIEL.   'Cause I'm tellin' you not to!

JED.   Save your preachin' for Sundays, Pa.

JOLEEN.   Jed!

EZEKIEL.   Don't you dare talk to me like that, boy!

JED.   I'm the one does the work around here, I reckon I'm the one should make up my own mind. You gettin' old and ...

EZEKIEL.   Old!? You hear him, Jesus, spittin' in your face and violatin' your most sacred commandments! Exodus! Chapter Twenty! Verse Twelve! Honor thy father and thy mother!

JOLEEN.   Amen!

EZEKIEL.   Fall to your knees, sinner, and beg for forgiveness! *Old!* If Jesus could roll that stone away and rise up outta his cold tomb, I can surely come down offa this porch, *old as I am,* and still whip your butt!

JED.   When do you ride out?

RICHARD.   First thing tomorrow morning.

EZEKIEL.   You ride with that thing there, don't you bother to come back!

JED.   Count me in.

EZEKIEL.   You hear me! You go and I'll put the curse of God on you boy! He'll rot you the from the inside out and send your unrepentent soul straight to Hell!

JOLEEN.   Ezekiel!

EZEKIEL.   "A place of unquenchable fire!" Matthew, chapter 3, verse 12! "A place of memory and remorse!" Luke, chapter 16, verse 19! "A place of misery and pain!" Revelatioι chapter 14, verse 10!

JED.   Pa. I'm tired of Jesus, and I'm sure tired of these

mountains, but most of all ... I'm tired of you. I'm goin'.

EZEKIEL.   Come on, Joleen. *(They go inside the cabin, slamming the door.)*

RICHARD.   Didn't mean to ...

JED.   You didn't light the fire, you just stirred the pot. That's been comin' for a long time, and I'm obliged to you for makin' it sooner rather'n later. *(Beat.)* Sunup?

RICHARD.   Want to make an early start. Get to Bowling Green by week's end.

JED.   I'll be there. *(Jed gives Richard an awkward salute. Richard starts off.)* Mr. Talbert?

RICHARD.   Yeah?

JED.   All I got to wear's what I got on ... I ... uh ...

RICHARD.   Need some kind of uniform?

JED.   Now, I don't need any kind of big, fancy feather or nothin' but ...

RICHARD.   I'll see what we can do when we get to Bowling Green. *(Richard exits. Jed watches him go. Beat. Ezekiel and Joleen step cautiously outside.)*

EZEKIEL.   He buy it?

JED.   Hook, line and sinker.

EZEKIEL.   Hell, he swallowed the damn pole! *(Everybody bursts into laughter.)*

JOLEEN.   How you kept a straight face talkin' about that uniform I will never know!

JED.   Had to pinch myself! Got the blood on my palms to prove it.

EZEKIEL.   Oh lord! I thought I'd bust a gut.

JOLEEN.   Amen.

JED.   "Horse feathers!"

EZEKIEL.   For a horses ass!

JED.   Damned if he didn't look like some kind of giant, grey chicken! Brwwwkkkk! Brwwwwkkk! *(Both men collapse on the porch. Joleen hugs Patrick.)*

JOLEEN.   What you think of your family now, Pappaw? Huh?

PATRICK.   Chkkzz bddgghh.

JOLEEN.   He says you're bad boys, you are.

EZEKIEL.   Now, I know you gonna want to get to it quickly

son, but you just take your time, you hear? We waited a long time for this ...

JOLEEN.   Long's I can remember ...

EZEKIEL.   ... and we can wait a few more weeks.

JED.   What's good, you think?

EZEKIEL.   You gonna have to feel your way about that ...

JED.   Late at night? Maybe when everybody's asleep ...

EZEKIEL.   Too risky. I was thinkin' more like sometime in the middle of some battle, somewheres. When everything's crazy and nobody'll pay you no mind. Even if somebody should ask questions, well, these things happen, don't they?

JED.   Then what?

JOLEEN.   Lay low and try to work your way back here.

EZEKIEL.   No! No! Don't desert. You gotta get *permission* to come home.

JOLEEN.   Yeah, mebbe you gotta get back and let his poor widow know the terrible news.

EZEKIEL.   Somethin' like that. Then ...

PATRICK.   Chkkzz arggg ...

EZEKIEL.   Look to him will you, Joleen? Then I think ... *(Ezekiel stops suddenly. He gestures to Jed to keep on talking while he sneaks over to the edge of the porch.)*

JED.   What about the fellows I'll be ridin' with? Do I just lose 'em, you think? Or do I need to make 'em part of this or what? *(Ezekiel suddenly reaches over the edge of the porch and hauls in a very frightened Randall.)*

EZEKIEL.   GODDAMMITT! How long you been hidin' under there!? Huh! Answer me dammit or I'll tear your guts out and feed 'em to the damn hogs!

RANDALL.   NOOOO! *(Ezekiel slaps him several times.)*

EZEKIEL.   What'd you hear, huh? You little pissant! You tell me word for word! WHAT DID YOU HEAR!

RANDALL.   Nothin'! I didn't hear nothin'! PLEASEEEEE!

JED.   Let'im go, Pa!

RANDALL.   JEDDD!

EZEKIEL.   WHAT'D YOU HEAR!!

JED.   LET'IM GO! *(Jed tears Randall away from Ezekiel. Beat.)*

EZEKIEL.   Get inside Joleen. Get dinner ready. *(She exits.)*

121

We gonna have to kill'im now.

RANDALL.   JED?! *(Beat. Then Jed starts laughing.)*

EZEKIEL.   WHAT'S SO GODDAMN FUNNY!

JED.   The look on your face! Damn Pa, you sure had me goin'! How about you, Randall, you think he was angry?

RANDALL.   *(Still crying.)* Yeah.

JED.   What? Did he really scare you? You believe all that?

RANDALL.   Uh-huh.

JED.   We was just pullin' your leg, boy! Isn't that right, Pa? We knew you was there that whole time, didn't we? *(Beat. Ezekiel smiles.)*

EZEKIEL.   Yeah. *(Ezekiel starts to laugh with Jed. Randall looks from one to the other.)*

RANDALL.   It was just a joke?

JED.   What? You think my ol' pa here was really gonna feed you to them hogs? Shame on you for scarin' him like that, Pa! You apologize to him right now! You hear me!

EZEKIEL.   I'm ... sorry boy.

JED.   I'm *real* sorry, and I beg your pardon.

EZEKIEL.   What?! ... I'm real sorry ... and ... I beg your pardon.

JED.   That's better. We wuz just foolin' with you.

RANDALL.   Yeah?

JED.   Well, of course. You think I let anybody, *anybody,* touch a hair on your sweet head? Not on my life! 'Cause you and me, we's friends, right?

RANDALL.   Yeah.

JED.   'Course we are. *Best* friends!

RANDALL.   Best friends?

JED.   Sure! In fact, we can be *blood brothers* if you like. What do you think about that? Huh? You got a pen knife on you?

RANDALL.   Yeah.

JED.   Let's see it. *(Randall pulls a knife out of his pocket and shows it to Jed.)* Whooee. Look at that, Pa. Ain't that a beaut. With a real ivory handle and all. Now what you gotta do, you gotta knick my thumb ...

RANDALL.   Cut you?

JED.   Oh, just a little bit, nothin' to write home about. Right there. Go on. *(Randall cuts him.)* There. Now, I got to knick you ... *(Jed does so.)*

RANDALL. Ow ...

JED. Now, that didn't hurt none, did it?

RANDALL. Nooo.

JED. And we got to squish our thumbs together, see, like this. This is how the Indians did it.

RANDALL. Yeah?

JED. Sure! I'm part Cherokee, you know? Now you are too. Now we got the same blood runnin' in us. Now Pa here, is goin' to give us a blessin', make it proper.

EZEKIEL. A what?!

JED. A "blood brother" blessin'. You know.

EZEKIEL. Oh. Right. *(Beat.)* Jesus! Look down on these two sinners ... and bless'em to thy Holy Name. Let the blood they share ... purge ... and ... join them together even as your blessed blood did redeem us of our sins and bring us together with God, in whose Holy Name, we pray.

JED. Amen.

RANDALL. Amen.

EZEKIEL. *Amen.*

JED. How you feel?

RANDALL. I don't know.... Different.

JED. Well, I 'spect so. We both changed now, we blood brothers. Now, let's get your face washed up here. Pa, get me some water would you. *(Jed washes Randall's face.)* Now you can't go around tellin' everybody about this, you know? What we done here today is special. It's sacred. It's just between me and you. It's goin' to be our secret, right?

RANDALL. Sure.

JED. I mean, we can tell your daddy if you want ...

RANDALL. No! He'd be real mad about this!

JED. You think? Well, maybe you're right. I reckon you know best. We'll just pretend that you went on back to home when your daddy sent you and that you didn't sneak on back here and hear us or nothin'. All right?

RANDALL. All right.... Can I tell Julia Anne?

JED. Your sister? Nooo, you can't tell no women about this.

This is secret man stuff. You understand?

RANDALL.   Yes, sir.

JED.   All right now, you look halfways presentable. I think you better scoot on to home and get there 'fore your daddy does.

RANDALL.   All right. *(Randall starts off.)* Jed?

JED.   Yeah?

RANDALL.   Thank you. *(They watch carefully as Randall exits. Beat.)*

EZEKIEL.   You really think he gonna keep his mouth shut?

JED.   Oh, yeah. Nice prayer, Pa. Real ... movin'. *(Jed sucks his thumb thoughtfully as Ezekiel crosses up to the porch.)*

EZEKIEL.   Come on, Pappaw. *(He helps Patrick to stand and then crosses with him to the door. He turns to Jed.)* You really like his boy, don'tcha?

JED.   He's all right.

EZEKIEL.   Ain't no point gettin' too fond of Randall, Jed. Make your mind up to it — we gonna kill'em all. *(They exit into the house. The lights fade out to a single spot on Jed who again addresses the audience directly. As characters and scenes are invoked by Jed, they will appear and disappear in isolated pools of light. Jed will walk in and out of the scenes.)*

JED.   We rode out the next mornin': Lieutenant Richard Talbert, the house nigger who shaved and dressed him every mornin', and a handful of sharecroppers. Talbert's army! *(Talbert "inspects" his troops.)*

RICHARD.   Men of Kentucky! Today, we ride out of our ancestral homes safe in the natural fortress of these beloved mountains to do battle with a godless enemy who would strip us bare of our most cherished traditions. Well, even as we drove those red savages from these hills, so shall we send these bastard sons of John Brown back to the Babylon that sired them! Death or Dishonor! Glory above all! *(Talbert starts out.)*

JED.   Mr. Talbert! Lieutenant! Sir!

RICHARD.   Yes, Jed!

JED.   Bowlin' Green is that way, sir! *(Talbert hesitates only a fraction and then reverses his direction.)*

RICHARD.   Thank you, Jed! *(The "Army" marches out and almost immediately we hear loud thunder and the sounds of a torrential rain, with gunfire and cannons in the distance. The men enter and huddle miserably.)*

JED.   *(Aside.)* Down near the Cumberland river, we got baptized pretty quick. *(The First Sharecropper makes a mad dash across the stage and joins Jed's group.)*

SECOND SHARECROPPER.   How's it look?

FIRST SHARECROPPER.   Just up that hill and over that picket fence are more damn Yankees than you can shake a stick at. Must be twice our size.

RICHARD.   Well, that's all right, we've got the element of surprize. *(Loud cannon explodes nearby.)*

SECOND SHARECROPPER.   They don't sound too damn surprized to me.

RICHARD.   Hell, any Confederate worth his salt is worth five of them Blue Bellies!

FIRST SHARECROPPER.   S'pose them Yankees know that? *(In the distance, a Union Colonel stands up and yells contemptuously.)*

UNION COLONEL.   Why don't you rebels stand up and fight like men!

RICHARD.   Come on men, let's show 'em what we're made of!

JED.   Sit down, Lieutenant.

UNION COLONEL.   Well, what are you cowards waitin' for!

RICHARD.   You hear that?

JED.   How far is that son of a bitch?

FIRST SHARECROPPER.   Eighty, ninety yards. *(Jed sights his gun and fires.)*

UNION COLONEL.   Why don't you rebels stand up and ... *(The Union Colonel falls. Jed turns to Richard.)*

JED.   Why don't you sit down, Lieutenant, before you get your ass shot off. *(Richard sits. The cannons get louder. We hear the screams of an advancing Army in the distance.)*

FIRST SHARECROPPER.   Jesus Christ, they're comin'. Look at 'em.

RICHARD.   Steady, men. Steady.

SECOND SHARECROPPER.   There must be hundreds of 'em!

RICHARD.   Steady.

FIRST SHARECROPPER.   To hell with this. Let's get outta here!

SECOND SHARECROPPER.   Get to the river! *(The cannons are deafening. The men panic and begin to run. Jed grabs Talbert's arm.)*

JED.   Let's go, Lieutenant! LET'S GO! *(They stagger off. Talbert falls and grabs his ankle, dropping his pistol in the process.)*

RICHARD.   Oh, Christ! *(Jed leans over him.)*

JED.   What?!

RICHARD.   It's my ankle!

JED.   Come on, Mr. Talbert!

RICHARD.   I think it's broke!

JED.   Let's go!

RICHARD.   Oh Jesus, they gonna kill me!

JED.   Nobody's dead yet — come on!

RICHARD.   I can't make it! Don't leave me, Jed, please don't leave me! *(Jed picks up the pistol, and aims it at Talbert.)*

JED.   I ain't gonna leave you, Richard.

RICHARD.   PLEASE GOD — DON'T KILL ME, JED! *(Suddenly, a Union Soldier runs in behind Talbert. Jed shoots the Soldier and then holsters the pistol.)*

JED.   Shit, I ain't gonna kill you, Richard. Give me your arm — we gotta get out of here. *(Jed picks him up and half-carries Richard off. They join a large crowd of frantic men jostlin' and milling about.)*

FIRST SHARECROPPER.   Let me on!

SECOND SHARECROPPER.   You got room!

FIRST REBEL.   Quit pushin'!

SECOND REBEL.   Sweet Jesus! Quit pushin' back there!

SECOND SHARECROPPER.   Quit pushin' goddamnit!

JED.   What's the holdup?

FIRST SHARECROPPER.   Ain't no way cross the river 'cept that boat and he says he won't take no more!

JED *(Calling out.)* The Lieutenant here's hurt bad — he needs some help!

BOATMAN.   Ain't nobody gittin' on this boat lessen he got orders!

JED. That's us!

BOATMAN. Yeah, where's your papers?! *(Jed pulls his gun out.)*

JED. His order's been signed by *Colt,* by God — now get outta my damn way! *(The Boatman backs out of their way and they push onto the boat with the crowd and stand pressed against the rail. The boat casts off. The sound of battle fades.)*

RICHARD. Thank you, Jed. I ain't never gonna forget this.

JED. Yessir.

RICHARD. I think we're gonna make it, Jed, I really do.

JED. Yessir, I think so. *(Jed pushes him into the river.)*

RICHARD. Jed! Help me, Jed! FOR THE LOVE OF CHRIST! JEEEDDDDDD! *(Richard disappears. Beat. The other men move off the boat leaving Jed alone.)*

JED. *(Aside.)* I just gave him a smile colder'n the Cumberland River and watched him sink to the bottom. And I told myself, it's over now — it's all over. *(Beat.)* There wasn't any way back into Kentucky now with that Union army on the other side of the river and I wasn't all that much safer where I was. Missouri seemed as good a place as any and it looked like at least I'd have company on the way. *(Jed and a small group of men warily approach one another.)*

TOMMY. Hey.

JED. Hey.

TOMMY. You look lost.

JED. No, I know where I am. It's everybody else I marched out here with I can't seem to find.

CARL. Us too.

TOMMY. I'm Tommy Nolan. That's Carl Dawkins. Gus Slocum there.

JED. Jed Rowen.

GUS. Where you goin'?

JED. Nowheres in particular. How 'bout you?

CARL. We fixin' to join Quantrill — ride along if you like.

JED. Who's Quantrill? *(The men laugh and exchange looks.)*

GUS. Oh, nobody special — just the greatest guerilla fighter there ever was! Where you been, country boy? William Clarke Quantrill is God in these parts!

TOMMY. Wanta come? *(Beat.)*

JED. Sure. *(Quantrill steps forward. Jed turns front. Aside.)* First time I ever seen Quantrill, he tied two cats together by their tails and hung'em over a clothesline. Laughed himself silly while they clawed each other to death.

QUANTRILL. That's the war, boys — two critters joined at the tail and tearin' each other's asshole out! *(Beat.)* We take the war real personal round here. An eye for an eye. Ain't a man ridin' with me ain't lost some family to them Federals. My own little brother Charlie was butchered in his sleep by Captain Lane's Kansas Redlegs, and I won't rest till I killed every damn one of 'em!

JED. *(Aside.)* Quantrill fought the war full-time and by his own set of rules: ambush, bushwack, and the like. But I think his favorite trick was to dress up in a Yankee uniform and walk into a Union camp ... *(Two Union Soldiers sit around a campfire. One stands and challenges Quantrill as he walks up.)*

FIRST UNION SOLDIER. Who goes there!

QUANTRILL. Captain Clarke of the 4th Missouri! You got room for one more around that fire?

FIRST UNION SOLDIER. Yessir.

QUANTRILL. I don't know what you boys are eatin' but it sure smells good.

SECOND UNION SOLDIER. Just beans and what passes for bacon around here.

QUANTRILL. Mother's milk! I haven't eaten in so long my insides are knockin' together.

SECOND UNION SOLDIER. Help yourself.

FIRST UNION SOLDIER. Kinda far from your outfit aren't you, Cap'n?

QUANTRILL. Damn bushwackers cut us up t'other side of Big Sandy and scattered my command all to hell. I reckon it was that Quantrill fellow.

SECOND UNION SOLDIER. No shit!

FIRST UNION SOLDIER. Goddamn guerillas! Hangin's too good for'em!

QUANTRILL. Amen!

FIRST UNION SOLDIER. Buncha damn cowards! Always

shootin' at you from behind some damn tree. Boy, you give me five minutes with that bunch face to face, and I'd tear their balls off with my teeth!

QUANTRILL. Well, Christmas come early, son, looks like you gonna get your chance. He's standin' there right behind you. *(The First Union Soldier whips around. Quantrill stands up and pulls his gun.)* I said, "right behind you." *(He calmly shoots both Union Soldiers. Jed walks into the campsite and looks around at the bodies, appalled.)* Gotta problem, Jed?

JED. No sir. *(The sound of flames begins to build through the following. Aside.)* I'da left then if there'd been any way out, so I just told myself it was war and to keep my head down and my eyes open. But I couldn't do that after what we did in Lawrence. Killin' soldiers was one thing, and if we didn't take no prisoners, well, hell, neither did they. But Lawrence, Kansas was just murder, and there weren't two ways about it. *(General pandemonium breaks out: the sound of women crying, men cursing, glass breaking, horses screaming etc.)* We just rode into town, shootin' everythin' in pants, set the place on fire, took everything that we could carry that warn't nailed down and then rode out again. *(Quantrill pushes three civilian prisoners, hands tied behind their backs, DC. They kneel. While he does so, Jed, Carl, Tommy and other Quantrill soldiers cross the stage carrying armfuls of plunder. Jed notices Quantrill and yells to him.)* You want any of this stuff, Colonel? *(Quantrill ignores him and proceeds to execute each prisoner with a shot to the back of the head. As he kills each one he shouts.)*

QUANTRILL. THAT'S FOR MY BROTHER CHARLIE! *(He fires.)* THAT'S FOR MY BROTHER CHARLIE! *(He fires.)* THAT'S FOR MY BROTHER CHARLIE! *(He fires. Quantrill notices Jed watching him in horror. Quantrill gestures towards the loot in Jed's hands and shakes his head disapprovingly.)* Lord don't love a thief, boy. *(Quantrill walks off.)*

JED. *(Aside.)* After Lawrence, we headed east into Kentucky with a whole damn army after us. Maybe Quantrill was tired or maybe he just didn't give a damn anymore but he got careless one night and they killed four of our men and chased the rest of us barefoot into the woods without our horses. *(Quantrill's men, exhausted, collapse around a campfire. Carl is wounded and he moans deliriously. Quantrill drinks heavily from a bottle.)*

TOMMY.   Colonel?   Carl's hurt bad sir, I don't think he gonna make it 'less he get some help. *(Beat.)* Colonel?

QUANTRILL.   Do I look like a doctor to you? *(The Soldier backs quickly away. Jed edges cautiously over to Quantrill.)*

JED.   Sir? I wonder if I could ask you somethin'? *(Beat.)*

QUANTRILL.   What.

JED.   Your family ... you reckon they at rest now?

QUANTRILL.   My family?

JED.   Your brother ... Charlie. *(Beat.)*

QUANTRILL.   I ain't never had no brother.

JED.   But I thought ... *(Quantrill smiles.)*

QUANTRILL.   What difference it make, Jed? *(Jed backs away. Quantrill begins to laugh.)* What difference it make!

JED.   *(Aside.)* The next mornin' Tommy and me got Carl and with a couple of others, slipt outta camp. We stole some horses and headed East into the mountains. Towards home. *(Jed approachs a crowd gathered around an open grave singing "Amazing Grace." The hymn falters and then dies out as they see Jed. Ezekiel and Joleen come out of the group and face Jed.)* Pa? *(Beat.)* It's Jed, Pa.

EZEKIEL.   Jed? *(Joleen hugs Jed.)*

JOLEEN.   Zeke, it's Jed, honey.

EZEKIEL.   Pappaw died this mornin'. I'd give my right arm if he were alive to see this. *(He wipes the tears off his face.)*

JOLEEN.   Who your friends, Jed?

JED.   That's Tommie Nolan, and Carl Dawkins, and Sam Jackson, and that's Isaac and Josh Gatlin over there, and Edward Hayes.

JOLEEN.   You boys are welcome! Why don't you come down and get yourself somethin' to eat and somethin' to drink. There's a cold supper in the orchard. *(To one of the mourners.)* Show'em the way, Lallie.

TOMMY/CARL/etc.   Thank you, ma'am. God bless you, ma'am. Yes'm. *(They exit leaving Jed, Joleen and Ezekiel alone.)*

JED.   Richard's dead. *(Ezekiel embraces Jed.)*

EZEKIEL.   You rest tonight, son, then tomorrow we'll ride over to the Talbert place.

JED.   Ain't no need for that, Pa. They ain't got nothin' we need.

EZEKIEL.   I just this mornin' laid my daddy in the cold ground, his back bent and his heart broke by them people, and you stand there and you tell me "they ain't got nothin' we need!" They breathin' our air, ain't they! THEY WALKIN' ON OUR *LAND*, AIN'T THEY!

JOLEEN.   Easy, Zeke. The boy's just tired — he didn't mean that. That's his land too.

JED.   I don't see why there got to be any killin', Ma! We can just run'em off. Hell, they ain't probably nothin' now but a bunch of women and children, handful of slaves. Ain't a growed man on the place!

JOLEEN.   Your pappaw showed'em that kind of mercy once.

EZEKIEL.   And then they come back and made him grovel in the dirt. I was there, boy, I saw it! And then they took everything he had and worked him like a nigger in his own fields! WORKED *ALL* OF US! Bible says, "An eye for an eye" ...

JOLEEN.   "And a tooth for a tooth" ...

JED.   When's it ever gonna STOP! I'M SICK OF IT! *(Beat.)*

EZEKIEL.   It's gonna stop tomorrow.

JOLEEN.   Jed, honey, you want your *own* family, don'tcha? Babies of your own? Honey, they ain't gonna be safe with any of them people around. You always gonna be lookin' over your shoulder worryin' about your babies. *(She hugs him.)* You a good boy, Jed Rowen, don't you ever forget that. The Lord is askin' a terrible thing of you, I know, but you got to be strong, honey. You just keep His promise in your heart and you think about your *own* children.

EZEKIEL.   Jed? *(Beat.)*

JED.   One more day ...

EZEKIEL.   And then you can rest. Just like the Lord did when His work was done. *(Beat.)*

JED.   All right.

JOLEEN.   Let's get you somethin' to eat now, honey — you

must be starved to death. *(Joleen exits. Jed and Ezekiel stand on opposites sides of the stage. They face the audience directly.)*

JED. *(Aside.)* We rode out the next mornin'.

EZEKIEL. "O Lord God, to whom vengeance belongeth show theyself! For the day of their calamity *is* at hand, and the things that shall come upon them make haste."

JED. *(Aside.)* They saw us comin' a course, and took shelter in the big house Ezekiel and Pappaw had built for'em like slaves.

EZEKIEL. "You rich men, weep and wail over the miserable fate descending on you! You have lived on the earth in wanton luxury and the day for slaughter has come!"

JED. *(Aside.)* Those walls were thick but I hadn't studied under Quantrill for nothin'; I had Tommie Nolan fire the house and then all we had to do was wait.

EZEKIEL. Can you see the flame, sinner?! Can you feel it's heat?! God has not forgotten your crimes! No! He will pay you back in your own coin! Can you see the flame, sinner!

JED. *(Aside.)* I could hear Pa preachin' hellfire and Judgement on'em, but all I could think of was Quantrill laughin' about his brother Charlie, and I knew what we did had nothin' to do with God.

EZEKIEL. Come and gather for God's great supper to eat the flesh of all men, slave and free, great and small!

JED. *(Aside.)* We killed most of the men straight up, slave and free — 'cept for this nigger family name of Biggs; Pa let them go. Then he took Stephen Talbert, Richard's younger brother, hitched him up like a mule, and crackin' a whip over his back, plowed table salt into their fields.

EZEKIEL. "That the whole land thereof is brimstone and salt, that it is not sown nor beareth nor any grass groweth therein!"

JED. *(Aside.)* We buried him that way, with the traces still on'im and the bit in his mouth, and those fields are still barren to this day.

EZEKIEL. "The land thereof shall become burning pitch. It shall lie waste and the raven shall dwell in it."

JED. *(Aside.)* But that wasn't the worst of it. *(He pulls his gun out and enters the scene.)* Randall! *(A terrified Randall creeps in.)*

RANDALL. Jed? Please God don't kill me, Jed! *(Jed hugs him.)*

JED. Get to the barn. Work your way into the woods and don't stop for nothin'! *(Randall nods and turns to go. He runs right into Ezekiel who grabs him.)*

RANDALL. Jed!

JED. Let'im go, Pa!

EZEKIEL. We can't do that Jed.

JED. Let'im go!

RANDALL. Jed!

EZEKIEL. You agreed, Jed!

JED. Please, Pa!

EZEKIEL. What good does it do to crush the snake if you don't kill its young!

RANDALL. JEDDDDDDD!!! *(Ezekiel breaks Randall's neck and leaves him dead on the ground. Beat. Jed kneels down by Randall's body. He speaks directly to the audience.)*

JED. After that, the men poisoned the well and burned everythin' else that was still standin', and what animals they didn't kill, they took off with'em. Pa took nothin' 'cept for an ole gold pocket watch he said belonged to pappaw. *(Ezekiel stands in a spot.)*

EZEKIEL. Lord don't love a thief, boys. *(Ezekiel exits. As he does so the two women from Jed's dream come DR and DL and kneel as before. A spot comes up on each woman.)*

JED. After my men was finished with'em, I spared both the girls, Miss Rose Anne and Miss Julia Anne. Pa was all set to kill them too, but I'da shot him first and crazy as he was, I think he knew it. "War's over, Pa," I said, "War's over. And 'sides, they're just women. What can women do?" *(Beat.)* And then I went home. *(Beat. Rose Anne and Julia Anne speak exactly as they did in Jed's dream. As they speak, Jed will begin to bury Randall with his bare hands.)*

ROSE ANNE. Come here.

JULIA ANNE. Come here.

ROSE ANNE. Listen up.

JULIA ANNE. Listen up.

ROSE ANNE.	These are the names:
JULIA ANNE.	These are the names:
ROSE ANNE.	Tommie Nolan ...
JULIA ANNE.	Carl Dawkins ...
ROSE ANNE.	Sam Jackson ...
JULIA ANNE.	Isaac Gatlin ...
ROSE ANNE.	Josh Gatlin ...
JULIA ANNE.	Edward Hayes ...
ROSE ANNE.	Ezekiel Rowen ...
JULIA ANNE.	Jed Rowen ...
ROSE ANNE.	Jed Rowen ...
JULIA ANNE.	Jed Rowen ...
ROSE ANNE.	Jed Rowen ...

JULIA ANNE. Jed Rowen ... *(The lights close down around Jed as he finishes burying Randall. He rocks back on his haunches, exhausted, a fistful of dirt in one hand. We hear the crows again. The entire company stands just outside the light, surrounding Jed. He feels but does not see them.)*

JED. In my dreams, pa still preaches Revelations and the trees in the orchard bear crows instead of apples and ragged women feed me a meal I don't dare refuse. Even when I'm awake, planting my fields or rocking my daughter to sleep, I can feel the shadows movin' closer. But at night, in my dreams.... In my dreams, it's always spring and the first, dark shoots reach up through the soil towards me and mine. Whole fields of decay. Fields of appetite. Spring. *(Beat.)* And then the harvest. *(He pours the dirt onto Randall's grave and the lights fade out. Blackout.)*

END OF PLAY

END OF PART ONE

PROPERTY LIST

Wrapped bundle with pistol (RANDALL)
Hoe (JED)
Tobacco (EZEKIEL)
Riding crop (RICHARD)
Cup (JED)
Pen knife (RANDALL)
Rifle (JED)
Pistol (RICHARD, JED)

SOUND EFFECTS

Crows fighting over a meal — builds and out
Thunder
Torrential rains
Gunfire (distance) (1861)
Cannons (distance) (1861)
Cannons (close) (1861)
Battle sounds (close) (1861)
Fire
Pandemonium: women crying, men cursing, glass breaking,
   horses screaming

THE KENTUCKY CYCLE

Part Two

"Ill fares the land, to hastening ills at prey, when wealth accumulates and men decay."

— Oliver Goldsmith

PART TWO

— Intermission —

TALL TALES

"Some men rob you with a sixgun,
Some with a fountain pen."

— Woody Guthrie

CHARACTERS

MARY ANNE ROWEN, age fourteen

ADULT MARY ANNE ROWEN, age forty-nine

JT WELLS, a storyteller

TOMMY JACKSON, age fifteen, a neighbor

JED ROWEN, age fifty-two, Mary Anne's father

LALLIE ROWEN, age forty-seven, Mary Anne's mother

NARRATOR

Tall Tales.

The year is 1885. The Rowen farm in the hills of eastern Kentucky, in Howsen County, near the Shilling Creek.

Tall Tales.

TALL TALES

1890. Summer. The Prologue and Epilogue are approximately ten years later.

PROLOGUE

The hills of Eastern Kentucky, in Howsen County, near the Shilling Creek. A young girl, Mary Anne Rowan, kneels by a creek and arranges her hair. Standing off to one side is the woman she will become in thirty-five years. The Adult Woman watches her younger self and speaks directly to the audience.

ADULT MARY ANNE.   Spring usta explode in these mountains like a two-pound charge of black powder hand-tamped down a rathole. After months of grey skies and that damp mountain cold what bores into your bones like termites in a truckload of wood, it's your dogwood trees that finally announce what everythin's been waitin' for.

First thing some mornin', you might see a single blossom hangin' there, light pink, the color of a lover's promise ... if lies had a color. And then later that afternoon, damned if that bud ain't been joined by a hunnert of his brothers and sisters all sittin' 'round, chattin' each other up, Sunday-go-to-meetin' style. 'Course, dogwood's just the beginnin'.

The spark what lights the fuse for spring, that's the azaleas. When they get to goin', you'd swear somebody'd scattered a whole handful of lit matches across those hills. Bible story is how old man Moses talked to a burnin' bush. But for my money, he was just conversin' with a scarlet azalea in full bloom. Story just got a little expanded in the retellin' ... the way stories do.

143

Fella once told me a story, said these ain't no real mountains here at all — that if you stood high enough, you could see it was all just one big mound that had been crisscrossed and cut up into so many hills and valleys by the spring runoff, that it just looked like mountains. Leastways, that was his story.

Only, I don't put no truck in stories no more.

Scene 1

The lights fades out on the Adult Mary Anne and come up on the younger. A man, JT Wells, enters and stands quietly behind her. Smiling, he watches for a moment, and then picks up a pebble and tosses it over her shoulder and into the water. She turns, startled.

JT.   Friend. I'm a friend.

MARY ANNE.   Shouldn't sneak up on a body like that!

JT.   No, you're quite right, young lady, I shouldn't have. And under any other circumstances, my rudeness would merit your harshest disapprobation.

MARY ANNE.   Huh?

JT.   You'd a right to be pissed off. But the fact of the matter is, if you hadn't been in mortal danger just now, I probably would've walked right on by, 'stead of savin' your life.

MARY ANNE.   My life?

JT.   Well, you're immortal soul at least.

MARY ANNE.   How you figure that?

JT.   Why, starin' into that stream like that. I've heard it said from them that knows, that the devil himself hides his bleak heart in the muddy bottom of slow-movin' pools, just like this.

MARY ANNE.   *(A little uncertain.)* You're just foolin'.

JT.   Would that I were, ma'am. But 'tis a widely known fact that the Father of Lies often assumes the shape of an Ictalurus Punctatus and ...

MARY ANNE.   A what?

JT.   Channel catfish.

MARY ANNE.   You use more twenty-five cent words when a nickel word would do than any man I ever met. *(JT grimaces, mimes being shot by an arrow, pulls it out and hands it to Mary Anne.)*

JT.   I think this is yours. *(Laughs.)* Where was I? Oh yeah, and thus disguised, he lies in wait for an innocent virgin to come along.

MARY ANNE.   Devil hafta wait a might long time for one of those in these parts.

JT.   Well, he's a mighty patient fella, the devil is. *(They both laugh.)*

MARY ANNE.   There is an old catfish in this crick.

JT.   Oh yeah? *(He moves down beside her. Both of them roll over onto their bellies and look into the stream. He is close to her, with just the slightest suggestion of sexuality.)*

MARY ANNE.   I ain't never seen him, but my daddy has. Almost caught him onct. So's Tommy, but I think he wuz lyin'.

JT.   That your brother?

MARY ANNE.   Nah, he's my boyfriend. *(JT moves away slightly.)* Leastways, *he* thinks he is. *(JT moves back.)*

JT.   Mighty pretty here.

MARY ANNE.   Yeah. *(Both are quiet for a moment.)* I jist love them old trees. 'Specially that oak there? That's my favorite.

JT.   That's a beaut all right.

MARY ANNE.   Folks 'round here call that the "Treaty Oak" 'cause my great-great-grand-daddy, Michael Rowen, that's where he bought this land from the Injuns.

JT.   That a fact?

MARY ANNE.   That's what my daddy says. I don't think there's a tree in these hills comes close to touchin' it for size. Leastways, I ain't never seen one. When I was a kid, I used to think that tree was all that kept the sky off my head. And if that tree ever fell down, the whole thing, moon and stars and all, would just come crashin' down. I think sometimes how that tree was here way before I was born and how it'll be here way after I'm gone and that always makes me feel safe. I think this is just about my favoritest spot in the whole world. Not that I seen a lot of the world, but my daddy took me to Lousiville onct when I was six. You ever been there?

JT. ` Well, it just so happens, I was in Louisville three weeks ago.

MARY ANNE. Yeah? I bet you been a whole heap of places, way you talk 'n' all.

JT. Oh, I been here and there.

MARY ANNE. Where?

JT. Well, places like ... Atlanta.

MARY ANNE. You been to Atlanta, GEORGIA!?

JT. Hell, that ain't nothin'. I been to *New York City!*

MARY ANNE. *(Almost inarticulate with wonder and envy.)* NOOOO.

JT. Yes ma'am, I have. And lived to tell the tale.

MARY ANNE. What's it like?

JT. Well, I tell you, it's ... it's pert near indescribable. It's hundreds of buildings, each and every one taller'n that ole granddad oak of yours. "Skyscrapers." That's what they call'em. Sky*scrapers.* Clawin' up at the very fabric of heaven, threatening to push old Jesus Christ himself off his golden throne! And not more'n two months ago, I's standin' in the top a one of them golden towers and John D. Rockefeller himself shook me by this hand.

MARY ANNE. No.

JT. Yes ma'am, he did. And me, just a poor boy outta Breathitt County. Said to me, he said, "JT, you've got a future here!" Imagine that — the richest man in the country — The "Standard Oil King" himself — standin' no further from me than you are now. *(Beat.)*

MARY ANNE. *(Shyly.)* Is that your name?

JT. *(Still lost in reverie.)* Huh?

MARY ANNE. JT. I was wonderin' what your name was.

JT. Oh Lord, isn't that just like me? Here I get to jawin' so much I clean forgot to introduce myself. JT Wells at your service. The JT stands for Just Terrific. And who do I have the honor of speaking to?

MARY ANNE. *(Mumbling, embarrassed.)* Mary Anne Rowen.

JT. Say what?

MARY ANNE.   Mary Anne Rowen. *(Quickly.)* Most folks just call me Mare, though.

JT.   "Mare?" Well, I don't know. That's not a proper name for a pretty thing like you. Let me see here. You know what your name is in Spanish?

MARY ANNE.   No.

JT.   *(Savoring it.)* Marianna.

MARY ANNE.   *(Delighted.)* Yeah?

JT.   Now that sounds about right, don't it? Got all the right colors in it and everything. Marianna.

MARY ANNE.   Marianna. *(Giggles. Beat.)*

JT.   Marianna. *(He moves closer to her. Begins to kiss her. A stick snaps underfoot. Both turn, startled, as a Teenage Boy steps out of the underbrush, cradling a shotgun loosely under one arm.)*

MARY ANNE.   *(Flustered.)* Oh. Hi, Tommy. Umm.... JT, this is Tommy Jackson. Tommy, this is....

TOMMY.   "Just terrific" Wells. Yeah, I heard.

JT.   Ah, the boyfriend, yes? Well, it's a rare pleasure to make your acquaintance, young man. You're a very lucky fellow ... *(He starts towards Tommy, hand outstretched but stops when the boy shifts his gun.)* ... but I guess you know that.

TOMMY.   *(Laconically.)* I been told.

JT.   Yes, well.

MARY ANNE.   Be nice, Tommy.

TOMMY.   Like you were?

MARY ANNE.   We weren't doin' nothin'.

TOMMY.   Not yet, anyways.

JT.   Now, Mr. Jackson, I think there's just a little misunderstanding here ...

TOMMY.   Take another step, Mr. "Just Terrific," and I'm gonna misunderstand a hole the size of a butternut squash in the middle of your chest. *(Mary Anne moves between them.)*

MARY ANNE.   Now dammit, Tommy, you just put that gun up right now, you hear me? Right this minute. Or I ain't never gonna speak to you again, as long as I live! *(He grudgingly obeys.)*

TOMMY.   Well, what's he doin' here, huh? Answer me that!

MARY ANNE.   Well, I'm sure I don't know, Mr. High and

Mighty — why don't you just ask him yourself? You ever think of that? No, I guess not. I guess some people been up the creek and outta town so long that they plum forget their manners. Mr. Wells, would you be good enough to tell this poor, ignorant hillbilly what you'd be doin' in these parts?

JT.   *(Grinning.)* Well now, that'd be a real pleasure, Miss Rowen. Fact of the matter is, I'm here to see your daddy. *(Stunned silence.)*

MARY ANNE.   My pa? *(He consults a small, leatherbound book from his pocket.)*

JT.   Well, if your daddy's a Mr. Jed Rowen of Howsen County, Kentucky, currently living up on Shilling Creek, I guess I am. I'm a storyteller! *(Blackout. Fast country music, violins and mandolin, fading up and then down into general laughter.)*

Scene 2

Lights up to reveal the interior of the Rowen house. JT, Mary Anne, Tommy, Jed Rowen and his wife, Lallie, are all seated around a wooden plank table, the remains of a country dinner in front of them.

JT.   I tell you, Jed, there ain't nothing like a home-cooked meal. Now, you might think a traveling man like myself, eating at some fancy restaurant every day of the week, is a man to be envied. But there are moments, sir, when I'd trade it all, every green bean almondine and French this and French that, for a piece of cob-cured country ham and red-eyed gravy like I had tonight.

LALLIE.   It was all right then?

JT.   All right? Ma'am, the President doesn't eat better'n this in the White House!

LALLIE.   Mare, I'll get the coffee, you clear the men's plates and then get yourself somethin' to eat.

MARY ANNE.   I'm not hungry, Ma.

LALLIE.   What's wrong with you, girl?

MARY ANNE.   Nothin'. Just not hungry.

JED.   Leave the child alone, Lallie. She's too busy feastin' her eyes and fillin' her ears to pay much attention to her belly. *(Tommy laughs.)* Pity one can't say the same for you, Tommy Jackson. *(Tommy shuts up. Both women bustle around.)*

JT.   You sure a mighty fortunate man, Jed.

JED.   How you figure that, JT?

JT.   Because, sir, you got your independence. You're not beholden to any man for anything. Here in the middle of God's country, you're a virtual king. Republican nobility. *(The room suddenly gets very still.)*

JED.   Republican?

JT.   *(Quickly correcting his error.)* Figure of speech, Jed. What I mean to say is, you and the people like you, your neighbors, they're what makes this country great! I take it you served in the "Glorious Cause," sir?

MARY ANNE.   My daddy was a hero — he fought with Quantrill!

JED.   *(Warning.)* Now, Mary Anne ...

MARY ANNE.   Well, you did...!

JT.   Is that a fact?

MARY ANNE.   My daddy saved Quantrill's life!

JT.   Isn't that somethin'!

MARY ANNE.   That was in Lawrence, Kansas. Tell him, daddy ...

JED.   It wasn't really all that much ...

LALLIE.   Go on, Jed ...

TOMMY.   Go on, Mr. Rowen ...

MARY ANNE.   See, they was trapped in this house in Lawrence and the Yankees had set it on fire and ...

JED.   MARY ANNE! *(Beat.)* JT's the story teller here; you gonna put the poor fella outta work.

JT.   What was he like, Quantrill? I mean, you hear so many different things.

LALLIE.   He was a real gentleman. That's what Jed always said — isn't that right, Jed? *(Beat.)*

JED.   Well ... I guess he was a lot of different things to different people but ... he always treated me square. Maybe, Mr.

JT, you'd like a drop of somethin' a mite stronger than coffee, to settle your stomach?

JT. Well, sir, I'm not ordinarily a drinkin' man, but as this is a special occasion, I'd be honored.

JED. Mare, you get down that ole mason jar and a couple of glasses.

LALLIE. Now, Jed, you know your stomach can't take it.

JED. *(Warning.)* Lallie ...

LALLIE. You go ahead, but don't you be wakin'me up in the middle of the night with them terrible dreams of yours!

JED. I said, I know what I'm doin', woman! *(Lallie give him a withering look as Mary Anne returns with mugs and the jar. Jed looks for a compromise.)* Well, hell, get me a pitcher of buttermilk then. *(Lallie smiles and exits, returning quickly with a pitcher. Jed pours a clear liquid out of the jar into two mugs. Then, sorrowfully, he pours buttermilk into one of the half-filled mugs.)* Terrible thing to do to good corn liquor. *(Looking at JT.)* I don't suppose you'd care to ...

JT. *(Straight-faced.)* Ordinarily yes, but I'm tryin' to cut back on the buttermilk.

JED. So was I.

JT. To your health.

JED. Mud in your eye. *(They drink.)*

JT. Oh Lord, that is elixer of the Gods. Pure liquid Kentucky.

JED. Heaven in a mason jar.

TOMMY. Mr. Rowen, you 'spect I might have some?

JED. Well, sure, Tommy, help yourself boy. *(To JT with a wink as Tommy reaches over.)* ... to the *buttermilk!* *(General laughter at Tommy's embarrassment.)*

JT. Well, I want to thank you good folks for havin' me in like this, but I know there's nothin' free in this life, so I reckon it's time to sing for my supper, as it were. *(Murmurs of approval and enthusiasm.)*

JED. Mr. JT, afore you get to spinnin' us a yarn, maybe you could say a word or two 'bout what's goin' on out in the world.

JT. Well, sir, we got us a new President, of course — fella

named Grover Cleveland.

JED. Cleveland? Who's he?

JT. Democrat.

LALLIE. Praise be to God!

JED. A Democrat! Lord, we waited long enough for that! Lallie, pour us another round — this is cause for celebration!

TOMMY. Where's he from?

JT. New York.

JED. New York? New York?! Hell, I ain't drinkin' to no *Yankee* Democrat! What they gonna hand us next — Christian Sodomites?

LALLIE. Jed!

TOMMY. What's a sodomite?

LALLIE. Never you mind!

JED. Read your Bible, boy.

TOMMY. Is that the fella who's so helpful and all?

MARY ANNE. That's Samaritan.

JT. Well, I got one piece of news I think you'll like. Ulysses S. Grant died four weeks ago.

TOMMY. Dead!?

JED. Well, I'll be damned!

LALLIE. Very likely, Jed Rowen — you and Tommy Jackson both for your blasphemous ways!

JED. Lallie, as much sin as there is in eastern Kentucky, I don't think the Lord'll notice some bad language.

LALLIE. "Not a sparrow shall fall but what he won't see it."

JED. ENOUGH! Tommy, pour everybody some corn liquor and I think we'll skip the buttermilk this round! *Now*, JT, maybe you'd favor us all with that story you promised.

JT. Well, sir, it'd be a priviledge. *(Through out JT's speech, the other characters feel free to comment and respond: Jed and Lallie with quiet pleasure, Mary Anne with enthusiasm, and Tommy with growing envy and resentment.)* I knew a feller once, luckiest man in the world! I remember him and me once went coon huntin'. Had a terrible time! Lost a dog, most of our shells, and when we finally did tree this old coon up a Sycamore, couldn't get a decent shot at the critter. Well, by this time it was so dark you couldn't see your hand in front of your face.

TOMMY. Well that was pretty dumb, goin' huntin' with no moon out.

MARY ANNE. Be quiet!

JED. Let the man finish his story.

JT. Anyway, we turned around to go home real dejected-like, when all of a sudden the clouds cleared the moon — which was full, of course — to reveal a sight that'd freeze your blood.

MARY ANNE. What?

JT. There in front of us was a big old mama grizzly bear and her cub! Now, my friend only had one shell left in his gun, and I had nothin' a'tall, so we turned to run but there behind us was the biggest rattlesnake I ever seen! We was trapped! I fell to my knees sayin' a prayer, and as I looked up, I remember seein' this huge old flock of geese flyin' over us. Then my friend shot the grizzly bear.

Well, sir, there was a terrible explosion as his gun blew up in his face! Anybody else'd be dead or blind at least. But my friend was so lucky, this is what happened: the bullet kilt the she bear dead; a piece of that stock kilt the rattlesnake and skinned him at the same time; and that old barrel flew up and knocked the lead goose so cold he fell into the river. Well, 'course all the other geese followed him — must've been about a hunnert — right into the river and drowned themselves! Well, I commenced to skinnin' the bear while my friend waded the river to collect all the geese. Took him half an hour and when he stepped out of that creek, wouldn't you know it, he found about fifty pounds of fish stuck in his boots!

We gathered up the bear, the fish, the geese, and the rattlesnake and was just about to start off when that coon we'd been huntin' fell out of the tree stone dead at our feet. Seems in all the ruckus, that baby grizzly had climbed up the same tree to hide, scarin' that coon to death!

You talk about luck — well I guess that friend of mine was full of it! *(General applause.)*

TOMMY. Well, somebody was sure full of somethin'.

JED. Now, what's that supposed to mean?

TOMMY.   What do you think?

JED.   Keep a civil tongue in your head, boy.

JT.   I'm sure the child don't mean any harm, Jed. You know how kids are at that age, liable to say all kinds of stupid things. Puts me in mind of a story I once heard about a couple of kids usta live over in Perry County. Seems there was these two families, the Montages and the Caplets, and they'd been a-feudin' long as anyone could remember.

Now, the Caplets had a daughter name of Juliet, though everybody called her "Jewel," I guess 'cause she was so pretty. Anyway, she'd been promised to this Thomas fellow, about whom the nicest thing you could say was, he'd a few chairs missin' from his attic. Problem was, Jewel was in love with this other fellow she'd just met, a real nice-lookin' stranger name of Jack. She'd made up her mind that she was goin' to marry him and live in New York City in a big old skyscraper. Unbeknownst to her, Jack was a Montage, and when she found out it like to break her heart. But he said it didn't matter to him, her being a Caplet, so they planned to get married anyway, in secret, and then run off together.

Well, right after the weddin', Jack ran into a whole mess of Caplets and afore you know it, they drew on him and he had no choice but to defend himself. He dropped about five of 'em 'cause he was a crack shot, and then he lit out of town, leavin' a message for Jewel to join up with him in Louisville.

Well, she wanted to, but her daddy was real set on her marryin' this Thomas fellow, even if he was close to bein' an idiot. So Jewel went to see this old witch woman and get some help. This here witch, she give her some herbs which'd put her into a sleep like she was dead or somethin'. The plan was, this witch'd get word to Jack to come back and dig Jewel up after she been buried and then they could sneak off. So Jewel took them herbs and everybody thought she'd died and they buried her just like they'd planned. Only thing wrong was this old witch got a terrible arthritis which kicked up about then and slowed her up somethin' fierce. By the time she got to Lousiville, Jack had already heard that Jewel was *dead* and, crazy with grief, he'd gone back home.

That night he snuck into the graveyard to say goodbye to his sweetheart and then kill himself. Well, who should he stumble into with a shovel in his hand but Thomas! Lord knows what he was doin' there, diggin' up dead bodies, but like I said, he was a strange sort of boy. Well, they started to fight, of course, kickin' and gougin' each other somethin' fierce. In the middle of this, Jewel wakes up and sees Thomas chokin' her Jack to death! She gotta lot of spunk, that girl, and afore you could blink, she picks up a shovel and bashes Tom's head in.

Then she explained everything to Jack, who was real glad to hear she wasn't dead and all, and the two of them run off to New York City where they was real happy! *(Everyone applauds.)*

MARY ANNE.   I like that story!

TOMMY.   You son of a bitch! I'LL KILL YOU! *(He leaps across the table at JT and knocks him to the floor. Jed pulls Tommy off and then throws him across the room. General shouts and confusion.)*

JED.   What the hell get into you, boy!

TOMMY.   I ain't no fool!

JED.   Well, you sure actin' like one!

TOMMY.   I see what's goin' on here! This stranger come dancin' in here with his smiles and his stories and everbody falls all over themselves offerin' him this and that, like he some kind of prodigous son, home from the wars!

MARY ANNE.   *Prodigal.*

TOMMY.   I seen you moonin' over him, makin' big cow eyes! "Oh, I like that story, I dooo!"

JED.   I think you better get outta here, boy.

TOMMY.   I'm goin'! Hell, you couldn't pay me to stay. Maybe I make a fool outta myself like you say, old man. But Mr. Silver Tongue stay here tonight with his stories and I bet Mary Anne make a bigger fool outta you by tomorrow mornin'! *(Tommy starts to leave and as he goes, he reaches for his gun by the door. Jed blocks his way.)* Gimme my gun!

JED.   You cool off. Come back tomorrow, and we'll talk

about it.

TOMMY.   Gimme my gun, god damm it!

JED.   You keep pushin' it, son, and I'm likely to do just that.

TOMMY.   *(Near tears with humiliation.)* Oh, come on, Jed, gimme my gun!

JED.   Or what? You gonna cry, maybe? Stamp your feet and shout? Now get outta here, 'fore I turn you over my knee. Go on. Get!

TOMMY.   I ain't forgettin' this. *(To JT.)* And I ain't forgettin' you. *(He runs off. Jed empties the shells out of the gun onto the floor.)*

JED.   Damn fool kid.

JT.   Mrs. Rowen, I surely wanta apologize for bringin' trouble into your home. I was just havin' a little fun. I didn't mean to hurt anybody.

LALLIE.   Don't you worry your head about it, JT — I never did like that Jackson boy nohow.

JED.   What she means is, she never thought he was good enough for our Mare.

MARY ANNE.   Pa!

LALLIE.   Well, he ain't.

JT.   Well, you gotta problem there, ma'am, 'cause you gonna have to look far and wide to find the right somebody for this young lady. *(Beat.)* Well, it's late, and I best be movin' on.

MARY ANNE.   No!

LALLIE.   Surely you're gonna stay the night here?

JT.   I wish but I got obligations ...

MARY ANNE.   Couldn't you give us just one more story 'fore you go?

JED.   There's an idea, one more story and another wet somethin' to go with it.

JT.   Get thee behind me, Satan! *(Everybody laughs.)* Well ... all right! *(General applause and bustle as people get settled and Jed pours drinks.)* I'd like to dedicate this story to you, Jed and Lallie, for the warmth of your welcome and the graciousness of your hospitality. *(He drinks. Laughs.)* Lord that's good! Well, seems a long time ago, Jesus Christ came down to Kentucky disguised as a poor traveler and walking from door to door askin' for hospitality. Well, sadly, things hadn't improved much since he'd shared Roman hospitality up on that lonely hill in Jerusalem, 'cause everywhere he went, people would curse him and shut their doors in his face.

LALLIE.   Oh Lord.

JT.   Finally, he came to this little old shotgun shack belongin' to an old couple name of Baucis and Philomen. Well, they were tickled pink to have company and they hustled the holy stranger inside and gave him the best seat by the fire. Then Philomen killed their only chicken and roasted him up real fine, while Baucis brought down the last of their 'shine and poured it out for the Lord. It was a simple meal, folks, spiced only with a little salt and that more complex and rarer seasoning, human kindness. Much like another simple meal on top of another hill, in Galilee.

LALLIE.   Uh-huh.

JT.   After the meal, Our Lord revealed Himself in all His glory, and those two folks fell to their knees, their faces bathed in tears. He bade them get up and follow him outside. And then they saw the *miracle*. All the towns around them, full of inhospitable people, had been swallowed up by the earth.

LALLIE.   Praise the Lord.

JT.   The Lord said, "You alone, Baucis and Philomen, have shown kindness to the stranger, and as a reward, you may have one wish which I shall grant." Well, those two old people, they knew what they wanted. Baucis said, "Lord, if it wouldn't be too much trouble, Philomen and I have been sweethearts as long as we can remember and if one of us were to die, it'd sure be hard on the other one. If you wouldn't mind, when the time comes, we'd both like to be called together."

And the Lord smiled and said He reckon'd that'd be possible. Years went by, and then one day Baucis was workin' in the garden, he started to feel dizzy. He turned to Philomen and she saw him and smiled, 'cause she knew their time had come. They reached out to each other for one last hug, and as they did, their hands turned into twigs and they were changed into two big old oak trees standin' side by side for all eternity. And as the wind blows through their leaves, it says one thing over and over, throughout all eternity — and that is, "I love you."

LALLIE. *(Quiet.)* I like that story.

JED. Amen. *(They smile at each other.)*

JT. You know, you folks been so kind to me 'n' all, I'd sure like to be able to do somethin' for you in return. I mean, when you see a family like this one, so close, so full of love for each other 'n' all, it just makes you think: "What if?" *(Beat.)*

JED. What if?

JT. What if, God forbid, somethin' should happen to one of you? I mean we can't all be as lucky as Baucis and Philomen and count on the Lord callin' us at the same time, can we? And in the unpleasant event of your absence, you'd sure want your wife and child looked after proper now, wouldn't you?

JED. Well, of course.

JT. It's a problem for sure. But one for which, I'm happy to say, there is a solution.

JED. What's that?

JT. I have been empowered by certain parties to purchase the mineral rights from far-sighted Christian gentlemen like yourself. *(Beat.)*

JED. My mineral rights?

JT. Yes sir.

JED. Oh. Well ... uh ... what exactly are we talkin' about here, JT?

JT. Well, "mineral rights" is just a twenty-five cent word for rocks, actually.

JED. Rocks? You mean somebody wants to buy the rocks offa my land?

JT. That's it exactly. The people I represent will pay you *fifty cents an acre* for the right to haul off all "mineral and metallic substances and combinations of the same." In your case, countin' your ... how many acres would you say you have?

JED. Three hundred and fifty-seven acres.

JT. *(Smiling.)* That'd be about one hundred and seventy-nine dollars in cold, hard American cash. *(There is stunned silence.)*

JED. Let me get this straight, JT — I been breakin' my back diggin' rocks outta my damn fields so I could plow for nigh onto forty years, and now there are people willin' to pay me money for the same priviledge?

JT. What can I tell you, Jed, 'cept there's a fool born every day. Here, you read it for yourself, it's all down there in black and white. *(He pulls out a contract from his jacket and hands it to Jed who inspects it awkwardly, too embarrassed to admit he can't read. JT glances over. Then gently.)* Light's kinda bad in here — maybe you'd like me to go over it for you.

JED. Can't do nothin' with these old eyes of mine.

JT. Essentially, this says that for the sum in question, you, the owner, pass over the title to the minerals underlying your land with all the usual and ordinary mining rights. It says all that a lot longer, but that's what it boils down to.

JED. And that's all there is to it?

JT. That's all.

JED. Well, that sounds easy, don't it! Where am I supposed to sign?

JT. Right here. *(JT hands Jed a pen.)*

LALLIE. Jed, I don't feel right about this.

JED. What don't you feel right about, Lallie?

LALLIE. This land been in your family back before anybody can remember, and I don't think you oughta be sellin' it.

JED. You heard him, Lallie — I ain't sellin' the land, I'm just sellin' the mineral rights.

LALLIE. I don't think you oughta be sellin' any part of it, even them rocks.

JT. *(Smiling.)* I understand your feelings ma'am, 'bout the land, and as a mountain boy I share'em, but I don't think any of your family'd begrudge you makin' a livin' off your land. What's important is the *land,* that it *stays* in your family.

LALLIE. That's right but ...

JED. Man's gotta point, Lallie.

JT. And why not make your life a little easier right now, Lallie? You know — get a new stove, maybe. A new dress for your daughter. A new ...

158

LALLIE.   We don't need things. We got everything we need.

JED.   Lallie ...

JT.   I tell you what. I don't usually do this, but you folks been so nice to me 'n' all, maybe I could see my way to say ... sixty cents an acre. *(Beat.)*

JED.   *(Smiling.)* Seventy-five cents.

LALLIE.   Jed!

MARY ANNE.   Daddy!

JED.   Hush up, now! JT and I are talkin' business now, and he knows as well as I do, you can't let your personal feelin's get in the way of business — can you JT?

JT.   *(Smiling evenly.)* No sir, that's a fact. *(Beat.)* Seventy-five, huh? Well ... I reckon I might could see my way to seventy-five.

JED.   Good enough for me.

LALLIE.   It ain't right, Jed — ain't enough money in the world gonna ...

JT.   Jed, if your wife doesn't want you to do this maybe we oughta just forget the whole thing ...

JED.   I make the decisions for this family, JT, and I SAY THAT'S FINE! *(Beat.)* Now, where do I sign?

JT.   Right here. *(Jed picks up the pen and scrutinizes the document again.)*

JED.   Just outta curiosity, JT, what exactly are those "usual and ordinary mining rights" you were talking about?

JT.   *(Picking his way carefully.)* That means they can excavate for the minerals ... uh, build a road here and there, if necessary — long as they don't disturb you, of course. Use some of the local water ...

JED.   Hold it right there! You never said anything before about cuttin' across my land or taking my water!

LALLIE.   Uh-huh.

JT.   Look, Jed, I promise you, I swear to God, you'll hardly know they're there. They gonna be real careful with your land.

JED.   You want my mineral rights, that's one thing. But I just can't see my way to all that other stuff. Roads and water — no sir! *(Beat.)* 'Less you're willin' to go a whole 'nother quarter an acre.

JT.   What?!

JED.   A dollar an acre and she's yours!

JT.   Hell, Jed, you can practically *buy* land in these part for that!

JED.   Then you do it! 'Course I thought you wanted the mineral rights to a *particular* piece of land. *Mine.*

JT.   You tryin' to cut my throat, Jed?!

JED.   *(Innocently.)* Why no, JT — but you did start out by sayin' how you wanted to do me and mine a favor. *(Beat. Both men are breathing a little hard. JT finally manages a smile.)*

JT.   Jed Rowen, I hope you won't take this the wrong way if I tell you I ain't never met anybody like you. You, sir, are one tough son of a bitch.

JED.   *(Smiling.)* I'd consider that a compliment. *(Beat.)* We doin' business?

JT.   Yeah, we're doin' business.

JED.   Dollar an acre?

JT.   Dollar an acre.

JED.   Where do I sign? *(Jed picks up the pen and then puts it down again.)*

JT.   I ain't goin' any higher, Jed!

JED.   *(Embarrassed.)* Ain't the money, JT. I don't know how to sign my name.

JT.   *(Relieved.)* All you do is touch the pen and make your mark. An X or whatever. *(Jed signs.)* And here's a bank draft for ...

JED.   Three hundred and fifty-seven dollars!

JT.   Now, you just take this draft to the bank — any bank, anywhere. That little paper's as good as gold. *(Jed examines the paper with great respect. JT leans over the table.)* I'm gonna ask you a favor, Jed, man to man. I'd appreciate it if you wouldn't mention this price to your neighbors — least not till after I been around and had a crack at 'em. Make my job a little easier, you know?

JED.   I understand, JT. *(With a wink.)* When it come to business, everybody got his own lookout.

JT.   Ain't that the truth. *(Beat.)* Well, I sure want to thank you folks for your hospitality but I better be goin'.

MARY ANNE.   Can't you stay the night, JT?

JED.   Sure wouldn't be any trouble.

JT.   No, I better be movin'.

JED.   Suit yourself.

JT.   Could use some direction gettin' back to the road, though.

MARY ANNE.   I'll take him, Pa.

JED.   All right, she'll see you down there. I'd do it myself, but I'd probably get us both lost! *(They laugh.)*

JT.   Thanks again for everything, Lallie. I'll dream of your red-eye gravy.

LALLIE.   You're welcome.

JT.   Jed? Take care of yourself, sir.

JED.   Don't you worry 'bout me.

JT.   No, sir, I guess I won't. *(JT and Jed laugh.)*

JED.   Mary Anne. It ain't all *that* far down there. Don't you be too long gettin' back.

MARY ANNE.   I won't, Daddy. *(Mary Anne and JT walk out of the scene and into the woods. Night sounds and shadows surround them.)*

Scene 3

MARY ANNE.   Where you goin' next?

JT.   Oh, just down the road a piece.

MARY ANNE.   You think you ever come back through here?

JT.   Not likely.

MARY ANNE.   Lucky you.

JT.   Seems like a real pretty place to me, Mary Anne.

MARY ANNE.   It's *borin'*. It's always the same. I'd love to do what you do — travel around, meet folks, see new places.

JT.   Maybe my life isn't quite as glamorous as you might think.

MARY ANNE.   No?

JT.   No.

MARY ANNE.   I don't know. *(She stops.)* Wanta trade?

JT.   (*Laughs.*) No. (*Beat.*) Come on, Mary Anne, let's get goin'.

MARY ANNE.   Couldn't we just stop for a minute? Keep walkin' like this we get to that old road in no time.

JT.   Well ... maybe just a minute. (*They sit.*)

MARY ANNE.   Sure is a mighty fine moon tonight.

JT.   Pretty.

MARY ANNE.   Sometimes I get so restless on a night like this, I get up, sneak outta the house, and walk through the woods all by myself. Feels like I'm swimmin' through the moonlight, like a big old lake.

JT.   Long time ago, all this was under water, you know.

MARY ANNE.   When was that?

JT.   Thousands and thousands of years ago.

MARY ANNE.   What happened?

JT.   Somebody pulled the plug.

MARY ANNE.   (*Laughs.*) No, really!

JT.   Nobody knows. Things change, that's all. One time there was an ocean, now there isn't. One time there weren't any mountains here, now there are. (*Beat.*) 'Course, these aren't really mountains, you know?

MARY ANNE.   No?

JT.   This is the Cumberland Plateau. Big, flat-topped rise of land. It's the water, year after year, thousands of years, cutting canyons and gulleys, just makes it seem like mountains.

MARY ANNE.   Gosh.

JT.   Ain't nothin' what it really seems. Not even mountains. (*Beat.*) Let's get goin'. (*She doesn't move.*) I can't take you with me, Mary Anne.

MARY ANNE.   Why not?

JT.   'Cause.... Because this is where you belong, swimming in this damn Kentucky moonlight, on these mountains that ain't mountains. Now let's go.

MARY ANNE.   I ain't showin' you where the road is 'less you kiss me first.

JT.   What?! You really are your father's daughter!

MARY ANNE.   One kiss — what'd it hurt?

JT.   Nothing. Except I couldn't promise you there'd be only

162

the one.

MARY ANNE.   That'd be all right too. *(He kneels in front of her.)*

JT.   You sure this is what you want?

MARY ANNE.   Just kiss me, JT. *(He does.)*

JT.   It won't change my mind.

MARY ANNE.   I know. *(She kisses him again and then slides down to the ground, pulling him with her. Tommy enters with a drawn knife. JT sees him and half gets up.)*

TOMMY.   I said I wouldn't forget you. *(Tommy throws himself at JT, who flips him over. Tommy slashes at JT, cutting him on the shoulder. JT grabs him and they both go down. Tommy comes up on top. He kneels over JT and tries to push the knife into his face. JT holds him off but is clearly weakening.)*

JT.   Help me! Help me! *(Mary Anne, who has watched the whole thing in mute horror, now comes to life. She kicks Tommy hard in the side. He rolls over and loses the knife. JT begins to kick and pummel the boy savagely. He winds up over Tommy, smashing the boy's head into the ground.)*

MARY ANNE.   Stop it! Stop it! You're gonna kill him! Stop it! *(She pushes JT off Tommy, who is bloody and unconscious. JT holds his cut arm, somewhat in shock.)*

JT.   The son of a bitch cut me!

MARY ANNE.   You coulda kilt him!

JT.   He came at me with a *goddamn knife!* Ohh, the little son of a bitch cut me!

MARY ANNE.   Lemme see.

JT.   Son of a bitch!

MARY ANNE.   It ain't bad. *(He pulls away from her angrily.)*

JT.   Son of a bitch! *(Beat.)* You saved my life.

MARY ANNE.   I guess.

JT.   How come?!

MARY ANNE.   I need a reason?

JT.   HOW COME?!

MARY ANNE.   *(Simply.)* I love you. *(Beat.)*

JT.   This doesn't change anything. I can't take you with me.

MARY ANNE.   I know.

JT.   Will you stop being so goddamn understanding about

everything! Goddamn hillbillies! *(Getting hysterical.)* I could cut your hearts out with a rusty razor but as long as I smiled and told another story, you'd just sit there happy as pigs in shit! Oh Lord, I can't do this no more. I can't do this. *(He is sobbing now, his head in her lap.)*

MARY ANNE. Can't do what?

JT. Everything I ever told you, it's all lies! All of it! *(Laughs.)* Your poor old pa, thinking he's slick as goose shit — *a dollar an acre!* What a joke! There he is, sitting on top of maybe fifteen, twenty thousand *tons* of coal an acre!

MARY ANNE. What's coal?

JT. Oh, nothin', little hillbilly, just "rocks," that's all. Millions of dollars worth of "rocks" which your daddy just sold me for a lousy buck! *Millions!* Oh, he's slick, he is, the poor dumb son of a bitch!

MARY ANNE. You're lyin'!

JT. That ain't even the worst of it! You ain't seen what they do. "I swear, Jed, I promise they be real careful with your land." Oh yes sir, they careful — careful not to miss a trick. First they come in here and cut down all your trees ...

MARY ANNE. No!

JT. Listen to me, god damn it! First, they cut down *all* your trees. Then they cut into the land, deep — start huntin' those deep veins, digging'em out in their deep mines, dumping the crap they can't use in your streams, your wells, your fields, whatever! And when they finished, after they squeezed out every nickel, they just move on. Leaving your land colder and deader'n that moon up there.

MARY ANNE. It ain't so!

JT. The hell it ain't!

MARY ANNE. If that's true, how can you do it? How can you do that to your own people? You a hillbilly just like my daddy, just like me!

JT. I ain't no hillbilly!

MARY ANNE. You said you was a boy off the creek, just like ...

JT. That was a long time ago! Now I'm whoever I say I am. I'm JT Wells and I invent myself new every day, just like the stories I tell!

MARY ANNE.   Don't matter what you call yourself — you still one of us, that's the truth!

JT.   *Truth?* Hell, woman, there ain't no such thing. All there is, is *stories!*

MARY ANNE.   *(Frightened and unsure why.)* What're you sayin'?

JT.   Sure. Everybody got his stories! Your *daddy* got his stories. Civil War hero, right? Rode with that "gentleman" Quantrill, right? Shit! Quantrill was a thief and a murderer, and when he died folks danced in the streets!

MARY ANNE.   My daddy was a hero!

JT.   'Course he was! And he's the son of heroes, right? Pioneer stock! That ain't the truth! He's the son of thieves, who came here and slaughtered the Indians and took their land!

MARY ANNE.   We bought this land from the Indians under that oak tree fair and square!

JT.   Well, sure you did! And the people I work for, those Standard Oil people, they bought this land "fair and square" too. And you think they'll sleep any worse at night than your pa does? When they come in here, maybe they'll cut the heart out of that old oak you love so much ...

MARY ANNE.   NO!

JT.   ... and they'll ship it off to New York, where somebody'll cut it into a fine banker's desk and swivel-back chair for Mr. Rockefeller himself! You think when he sits his skinny ass down on that polished surface he gonna be thinkin' about some poor hillbilly girl whose heart got broke in the process?! You won't be part of *his story,* Mary Anne! And when I finish my job for him, I won't be part of his story either. See, he'll give some money to a school or something, and grateful people will call him a hero, a great man, a Real *Christian!* And *that* story is the one that'll survive — he'll see to that. While the other story, the one where he's just a thief, that'll fade away. That's your *"truth."*

MARY ANNE.   That ain't ... you're wrong ... it ain't just stories...!

JT.   That's how somebody like me can do what he does! I

just tell people the stories they want to hear. I say what people want me to say and I am whatever they want me to be.

MARY ANNE.   Then what's left?

JT.   Of what?

MARY ANNE.   At the end of the day, when you're by yourself — who are you? *(He shrugs.)* Why'd you kiss me back there? *(Beat. And then right in her face.)*

JT.   Tell me what you want to hear, and I'll tell you why I kissed you. *(She slaps him. Beat. Tommy moans and moves slightly.)* Take your boyfriend home, little hillbilly. At least he fights for what he believes in ... thinks he believes in. At least he thinks he believes in something. Take him home and marry him and live happily ever after. *(JT staggers up. He pulls Jed's contract out of his pocket and puts it in her hand.)* Here. I owe you one. Tear it up. Tell Jed to tear his bank note up, too. *(JT exits. Mary Anne sobs and moves to Tommy. The lights fade down on her while they come up in a single spot on the Adult Mary Anne. Again, she contemplates her younger self while she speaks to the audience.)*

EPILOGUE

MARY ANNE. I told my pa what JT said ... and Pa said it was a lie. That JT was lyin'. That he'd beat JT in the deal and that JT was just tryin' to get out of it now, tryin' to get his money back. I asked Pa about Quantrill and Kansas and he said I'd just have to make my own mind up about that. That I could believe him, believe my own daddy, or I could believe this stranger. And if I chose JT — well, here was the contract and I could tear that up too.

I didn't tear it up. I didn't want to believe JT, and so I chose not to. Like he said, I guess, people believe what they want to believe. And he was right, of course. Probably the only time in his life, JT Wells told the truth and he wasn't believed. And people say God ain't got a sense of humor.

They came a couple of years later, just like he said they would, and they cut down all of the trees, includin' my oak. I was right about it holdin' up the sky 'cause when they chopped it down, everythin' fell in: moon and stars 'n all. Spring's different now. Without the trees, you get no color; no green explosion. And you got nothin' to hold the land down neither. What you get is just a whole lotta rain, movin' a whole lotta mud. I try to tell my boy, Joshua, what it was like, so he'll know, so it won't be forgotten but he just looks at me and laughs. "Mama's tellin' stories again," he says. *(Pause.)*

Maybe I am.
(Lights fade slowly out.)

END OF PLAY

PROPERTY LIST

Shotgun (TOMMY)
Dinnerware
Drinking mugs (MARY ANNE)
Mason jar (MARY ANNE)
Pitcher (LALLIE)
Contract (JT)
Pen (JT)
Bank draft (JT)
Knife (TOMMY)

SOUND EFFECTS

Creek
Night sounds

FIRE IN THE HOLE

"Watch the rocks, they're fallin' daily
Careless miners always fail
Keep your hand upon the dollar
And your eye upon the scale."

— from the song "A Miner's Life"

CHARACTERS

MARY ANNE ROWEN JACKSON, age forty-nine

JOSHUA ROWEN JACKSON, age ten, Mary Anne's son

TOMMY JACKSON, age fifty, Joshua's father

DOCTOR

MACKIE, a miner

ANDREW TALBERT WINSTON, a mine boss

SILUS, a miner

ABE STEINMAN, a union organizer

MOTHER JONES, a union organizer

CASSIUS BIGGS, a miner and bootlegger

SURETA BIGGS, Cassius's wife

PREACHER

LUCY, a miner's wife

A MAN in the forest

MINERS, TOWNSPEOPLE, ETC.

NARRATOR

Fire in the Hole.

Thirty years later. The year is 1920. Howsen County, Kentucky. In and around the Blue Star Mine and camp.

Fire in the Hole.

FIRE IN THE HOLE

1920. The set is now darker and dirtier looking, almost as if a healthy outer layer of skin had been ripped off and some essential "essence" had been bled out of it. There is no hint of the forest that once stood here. The ground is barren and covered with slate and mud. Looming over it all is a huge metal structure, the coal tipple. A large painted sign hangs on the tipple. It reads: "BLUE STAR MINING CO." Scattered around the stage are faded, rusty tin signs saying: "Dig Coal," "Dig More Coal," "The Success of the War depends on YOU," "Support our Boys Over There," "Democracy needs Coal." etc.

Scene 1

A pool of light comes up on Mary Anne Rowen Jackson, the narrator of Play Six. She stands, even as we remember her, facing the audience.

MARY ANNE.   We lost the land when I was twenty and moved into a coal company camp, where Tommy found work in the mines. I stood on my porch that first day and looked down at my new home: dust and noise and flame. Like some old preacher's vision of hell. *(Ezekiel appears briefly in a tight spot. Quietly.)*

EZEKIEL.   A place of unquenchable fire ... a place of misery and pain ... a place of memory and remorse. *(The spot on Ezekiel fades out.)*

MARY ANNE.   Durin' the day I swept and mopped the coal

dust out of the house but ever night, while I slept, it crept back in with the shadows, like my daddy's bad dreams, and ever mornin' I started all over again. And always there was that smell: like you'd took a corn-shuck mattress, soaked it in piss, covered it with garbage and coal and set it on fire.

JOSHUA.   Mama? *(A pool of light comes up on Joshua Rowen Jackson, ten years old, lying in bed with a fever. Mary Anne walks over to where he lies, and looks out again at the audience.)*

MARY ANNE.   We had five kids, five sons, and ever rainy season for four years the fever came and took one of my boys. He's the last, my Joshua. I sit with him now as he burns and he sweats and I hold his hand and do what every grievin' mother has done since the beginnin' of time: I lie.

JOSHUA.   Mama?! *(Mary Anne stares at the audience.)*

MARY ANNE.   Ssshhhh, Joshua. It's gonna be all right. Doctor comin' soon, gonna fix you up fine. Sssshhhhh. *(The lights crossfade to three men — Tommy Jackson, Cassius Biggs, and Mackie — crouched in a mine shaft facing a wall. Immediately we hear the sound of water dripping and the sound of metal cutting into mineral. Tommy finishes hand augering a hole in the wall. He forces powder charges into the hole and then turns to Cassius.)*

TOMMY.   Hand me a deadman. *(Cassius and Mackie nervously pass him the earthen plugs. Tommy hesitates.)*

CASSIUS.   What's the matter, Tommy?

TOMMY.   We're cuttin' these goddamn pillars too fine. *(A terrible groan of shifting timber and mineral rolls through the mine. The men freeze.)*

MACKIE.   Jesus Christ on a cross.

TOMMY.   Fuck it. *(The men finish packing the hole with powder and fuses. They scuttle back from the wall. Tommy strikes a match, and as he puts it to the fuse he yells out:)* Fire in the hole! Fire in the hole! *(The miners huddle, their eyes almost glowing in the dark. As the lit fuse reaches the wall the following events happen in rapid succession: Mackie's nerves snap. He picks himself up and starts to run down the gallery.)* Mackie!

MACKIE.   We gotta get outta here. We gotta get outta! *(Tommy starts after Mackie but is pulled down by Cassius. There is the sound of an enormous explosion magnified by the narrow mining galleries followed by a slate fall. Joshua sits bolt upright in bed and screams. His scream turns into the ear-shattering blast of a steam whistle mounted on the coal tipple. Lights slam up on the mine. Dust. Confusion. Tommy runs up to the wall of slag and broken timbers that now stands where Mackie fled. He digs at it with his bare hands. Cassius joins him.)*

TOMMY.   Mackie! MACKIE!

CASSIUS.   MACKIE!

TOMMY.   Some help! We need some help here! *(Other men arrive, some dazed and bleeding, but all focused on helping those who are trapped.)* I need some tools here, dammit! Get a doctor! You two get some timbers and start shorin' this line up for we all get killed!

CASSIUS.   MACKIE! MACKIEEEEEE! *(The men are silent. Cassius listens, his face to the wall of slag. He turns to the others and shakes his head. Nothing.)*

TOMMY.   Okay, let's dig. LET'S DIG! *(Crossfade to Jackson house. Mary Anne sits next to the bed. The Doctor enters.)*

DOCTOR.   Got here as fast as I could — they had a slate fall.

MARY ANNE.   Who's hurt?

DOCTOR.   Mr. Winston wouldn't even let me go down there. Said they ain't got to any of'em yet, and when they do, they gonna need a shovel more'n they need a doctor.

MARY ANNE.   You din't hear no names?

DOCTOR.   I told ya, I don't know! If I did, I'm not supposed to say, nothin'. *(Beat.)* Tommy's okay. *(She nods.)* Hell, he eats coal for breakfast, Tommy does. He'll be all right. How's Joshua?

MARY ANNE.   The same.

DOCTOR.   Let me take a look. *(While the Doctor examines Joshua, there is a knock on the door. Mary Anne hesitates.)* Tommy's all right, I tell ya. Go on, get it. *(She opens the door to reveal Abe Steinman, a tall intense man carrying a small satchel.)*

MARY ANNE.   Yes?

ABE.   'Lo, my name's Abe Steinman. I was lookin' for a place to stay.

MARY ANNE.   Can't help ya.

ABE. Willin' to pay, of course.

MARY ANNE. Sorry.

ABE. Boy, if ole Joseph and Mary had come through eastern Kentucky, Jesus mighta never been born!

MARY ANNE. If Jesus been born in eastern Kentucky they'da nailed him up a lot sooner.

ABE. And the Company probly charge Him for the nails! I pay cash. In advance.

MARY ANNE. I'll have to talk to my husband ...

JOSHUA. Mammmmaaa!

DOCTOR. Mary Anne! *(She hurries back into the room. Abe hesitates, then follows. Joshua is thrashing about in delirium.)* Hold'im down or he'll hurt himself. Hold'im! *(Crossfade to mine. The men have been digging furiously but are making little progress. There is another long, low rumble as the earth shifts. They all stop. Andrew Talbert Winston appears.)*

ANDREW. I want every man outta this gallery now — we're shuttin' it down. *(Nobody moves.)* Let's go!

TOMMY. We got people under there, Mr. Winston.

ANDREW. You hear anything?

CASSIUS. No sir.

ANDREW. Then leave'em be. Let's go! *(He exits. The miners begin to follow him but Tommy returns to work.)*

SILUS. We done the best we could, Tommy.

TOMMY. You say the same thing if that was you under that wall, Silus? *(The men leave. Cassius remains. Tommy starts digging again.)*

CASSIUS. Come on, Tommy.

TOMMY. Git the fuck outta here, Cassius. Go on! LEAVE ME ALONE! *(Cassius exits. Tommy flails away at the wall with his shovel, smashing the blade against the rock. Exhausted, he finally drops it. He hugs the wall.)* Mackie? Hey, Mackie? "We done the best we could." Must be a great comfort to ya. *(Crossfade to Jackson house. The Doctor is packing his bag. He sets a small bottle on the table.)*

DOCTOR. I did the best I could. Give'm a spoonful of that if he gets restless again. It'll help'im sleep.

MARY ANNE. What's wrong with my boy?

DOCTOR. Fever.

MARY ANNE.   I can see that. How come?

DOCTOR. Hard to say.

ABE.   He run a rose-colored rash?

MARY ANNE.   All over his chest.

ABE.   Sounds like typhoid, don't it?

DOCTOR. You a doctor?

ABE.   No sir, just seen a lotta dead babies in my time.

DOCTOR. Well, if you know typhoid, than you know you can't do nothin'.

ABE.   I reckon. 'Course if the Company'd built better privys, people wouldn't wind up doin' their business in their drinkin' water. Might make a difference, don'tcha think?

DOCTOR. Yeah, well, privys don't mine no coal.

ABE.   Yeah. 'Course neither do dead babies.

DOCTOR. *(To Mary Anne.)* Fifty cents.

MARY ANNE.   I can't pay you nothin' right now, but if you could just float us for another coupla weeks or so ...

DOCTOR. Hell, Mary Anne, you ain't hardly paid nothin' on what you owe me for last year! *(He takes the bottle off the table and puts it in his pocket. She pulls the Rowen watch out of her apron.)*

MARY ANNE.   Here! How 'bout this? *(He examines it.)*

DOCTOR. Don't work none.

MARY ANNE.   It's gold. It don't have to work.

DOCTOR. Five dollars for it.

MARY ANNE.   You come back if he needs it?

ABE.   How much does she owe? *(Both look at him.)*

DOCTOR. Eight dollars.

ABE.   Here. *(He puts eight dollars on the table. Mary Anne picks it up before the Doctor can.)*

MARY ANNE.   We don't take no charity here.

ABE.   Ain't offerin' any. As your boarder, I'm just payin' you a coupla weeks in advance.

MARY ANNE.   I ain't said you could stay yet.

ABE.   I know.

MARY ANNE.   That's up to my husband.

ABE.   I'm willin' to take a chance. How 'bout you?

179

MARY ANNE. He says yes, this is rent. He says no, you just lost a bet.

ABE. You're on. *(She takes back her watch and pays the Doctor who then starts to leave.)*

MARY ANNE. I want my medicine. *(The Doctor puts it on the table and exits. She picks up the bottle.)*

JOSHUA. Mama?

MARY ANNE. I'm here, baby. *(Beat.)* He gonna die, inne? Maybe he better off — ain't nothin' here I'd wish on any child of mine.

ABE. How long since he had the rash?

MARY ANNE. 'Bout two weeks.

ABE. If his fever breaks soon, he'll pull through. *(Tommy walks in.)*

MARY ANNE. Tommy.

TOMMY. I'm okay. How's Joshua?

MARY ANNE. Burnin' up. Doctor says there's nothin' he can do. *(Tommy sits beside his son.)*

TOMMY. Ain't that the truth. *(To Abe.)* You from the Company?

MARY ANNE. Tommy, this is Abe Steinman — he's lookin' to board here.

TOMMY. We don't take no boarders.

ABE. Why don't I just step outside and let y'all talk about it. *(He stands out on the porch.)*

MARY ANNE. It ain't charity, Tommy — he be payin' us for room and food ...

TOMMY. I can carry my family ...

MARY ANNE. Can ya?

TOMMY. I'm doin' the best I can, Mare!

MARY ANNE. I know that, Tommy, but we just too far behind. I walk in the store, I see how they look at me. I couldn't pay the doctor today — he was just gonna walk off with Joshua's medicine. *(Beat.)* I don't like it anymore'n you do, Tommy, but I don't see no other way do you?

TOMMY. I'm gonna go clean up. *(He exits to the porch. While he talks to Abe he washes his face and hands in a bucket of water.)* Two fifty a week plus meals. My wife'll do your laundry for a quarter a week more.

ABE. Fair enough.

TOMMY. In advance.

ABE. I already paid your wife. *(Tommy glances at the house.)*

TOMMY. That a fact? *(Beat.)* So, you lookin' to hire on at Blue Star?

ABE. If they'll take me.

TOMMY. Oh, they can always use another slate picker I reckon.

ABE. *(Smiling.)* Actually, I was figurin' to hire on as a miner.

TOMMY. A miner? Well, they hired worse I guess.

ABE. Blue Star a good company?

TOMMY. All the same, ain't they?

ABE. You spoke the truth there, brother. *(Tommy just looks at him.)*

TOMMY. Steinman. You a Jew?

ABE. Make a difference to ya?

TOMMY. Hell, I work with niggers. Coal don't care; neither do I. *(Tommy throws the bucket of water on the ground and exits into the house. Steamwhistle.)*

Scene 2

Tipple Office.

Tommy and Abe stand facing Andrew.

ANDREW. You ever been to West Virginia? Colorado?

ABE. "Hell and Repeat?" No sir, I ain't been there.

ANDREW. Blue Star don't need no troublemakers.

ABE. No sir.

ANDREW. You know this man, Jackson?

TOMMY. No sir. Not exactly. He's family on my mother's side. Second cousins or somethin'. *(Andrew turns back to Abe.)*

ANDREW. You load your ten a day, six day a week, keep your head down and your nose clean, and we'll do just fine.

Make trouble and I'll tear your balls off. We on the scrip system here, Company money only. You get paid on Saturdays and we got everything you need at the Company store. And the Company whorehouse. Happy to write you down you find yourself short. Questions?

ABE.   When do I start?

ANDREW.   Week from tomorrow. *(Abe and Tommy start to leave.)* Jackson? *(Abe steps "outside" and waits. Beat. Andrew looks through some papers.)* Company can't write you no more credit. Food, coal, medicine, funeral expenses — hell, you owe me for everythin' ...

TOMMY.   Yes sir. We took in this boarder, that should help some ...

ANDREW.   You mean your mother's "cousin"? *(Laughs.)* You people! You really think you can teach your ole granny to suck eggs?

TOMMY.   My boy, Joshua, should be 'bout ready to start work. He's old enough.

ANDREW.   I don't think another slatepicker's gonna dig you outta this hole you in, Jackson. Mind you, if it were up to me ... but ya just can't let your personal feelin's get in the way of business, can ya?

TOMMY.   No sir. *(Beat.)*

ANDREW.   Hell, I don't know, mebbe we can work somethin' out. I can always use a smart fella like yourself down in the mines. I pay real well for certain kinds of information.

TOMMY.   Information?

ANDREW.   You know what I'm talkin' about. You think about it. *(He dismisses Tommy. Then.)* Tommy? Everybody got his own lookout. If I was you, I'd look out for my family. *(Tommy leaves. Lights down on office. Abe catches up with Tommy.)*

ABE.   That Winston fella, he's a piece of work, ain't he?

TOMMY.   He had'im a brother over in Carolton, was kilt last year inna strike. He been shittin' himself ever since.

ABE.   Sounds to me like maybe they kilt the wrong brother.

TOMMY.   Where you say you from?

ABE.   I didn't, exactly.

TOMMY.   Well, if you was.

ABE.   West Virginia.

TOMMY.   That ain't what you told Mr. Winston.

ABE.   No, I guess I lied. *(Beat.)*

TOMMY.   I heard a bunch of people got kilt up there in West Virginia, near Paint Creek.

ABE.   Yeah? I heard they got themselves a Union. Listen, thanks for helpin' me out there, "cousin."

TOMMY.   Look, let's you and me get somethin' straight here. I ain't your brother, your cousin, or your friend. If you was on fire I wouldn't take the time to piss on you. Right now my family needs the money and you can stay as long as you can pay. When you can't pay or when we don't need the money, you're gone.

ABE.   Look, I'm just tryin' to ...

TOMMY.   Don't say nothin'. Don't tell me nothin'. I don't wanta know. *(Tommy exits. Steam whistle.)*

Scene 3

Night. Mary Anne sits on the side of the bed sponging Joshua's face with a cloth. She sings "Farther Along."* Abe watches. He joins in softly and Mary Anne stops immediately.

MARY ANNE.   Ain't you got nothin' better to do?

ABE.   Not really.

JOSHUA.   No! Noooo! *(Joshua sits upright with the force of his delirium. Mary Anne struggles to hold him down.)*

MARY ANNE.   It's all right, baby. I'm here. Mama's here. Ssshhhh. *(Abe comes over and helps hold Joshua.)*

ABE.   'Stead of just wipin' him down, if you was to wet them rags of yours in cold water and hold'em on his neck and on his wrists like this, it'll help'im more. It'll cool his blood down. *(She hesitates.)* Go on, I'll watch'im. *(She exits. Abe com-*

* See Special Note on Music on copyright page.

183

forts/restrains Joshua.) That's right, boy, you fight it. Fight it hard. That's right. *(She returns.)*

MARY ANNE.   I'll take'im. *(Abe sits back in his chair.)*

ABE.   You might boil his drinkin' water from now on, if you'd a mind to.

MARY ANNE.   Boil it?

ABE.   It's in the water, what's makin'im sick.

JOSHUA.   Mama.

MARY ANNE.   Right here, son. I'm right here.

ABE.   It's a good name, Joshua — onna my favorites. "And the sun stood still in the sky and the walls came a tumblin' down."

MARY ANNE.   Yeah, well, last time I looked Jericho was still standin'. *(Beat.)* He had him four brothers all die of the same thing.

ABE.   I'm sorry.

MARY ANNE.   Yeah. Well, "sorry" don't mean spit, do it?

ABE.   No ma'am. Had me a friend usta say the same thing. Said, "Abe, if I had me a bullet for ever time some sob sister was 'sorry' there'd be a lotta dead folks lyin' around." You remind me a little bit of her. Mary Jones is her name, though most folks just call her Mother. Mother Jones? She lost her whole family to a fever. *(Spot comes up on Mother Jones. She sings "Farther Along"* quietly as she rocks an infant.)* This was down in Memphis. Terrible yella fever come along. The rich folks all lit outta town, of course, and the hospitals and the churches closed up, and so the poor folks was just stuck there. Well, she sat there, all alone in her house with her poor family, through days and nights of grief. Nobody came, nobody ...

MARY ANNE.   Don't you never shut up?! *(Spot out on Mother Jones.)*

ABE.   *(Genial.)* There you go — she usta say the same thing, "Lord, Abe, you gotta bad case of mouth on you!"

MARY ANNE.   What d'you want?

ABE.   Nothin'.

MARY ANNE.   You want somethin' here, don'tcha? Don't tell

---

* See Special Note on Music on copyright page.

me you don't.

ABE. I'm just makin' talk, that's all.

MARY ANNE. Don't lie to me! You ain't no miner. You one of them organizers, ain't ya? *(Beat.)*

ABE. Yes ma'am.

MARY ANNE. Don't you bring no trouble on my house.

ABE. You tell me to and I'll go right now.

MARY ANNE. You bring trouble in here and I'll make you wish the Company had caught ya. We didn't need the money I'd throw you out right now. *(Tommy enters, drunk.)*

TOMMY. What's goin on in here?! *(Joshua sits up in bed.)*

JOSHUA. Mama.

MARY ANNE. Joshua?

ABE. His fever's broke. *(Steam whistle.)*

Scene 4

Lights down on the house and up on a bar. An animated all-male crowd spills onto the stage cheering a brutal fight between two of its members. It ends. The victor, Tommy, staggers over and sits down, a little drunk. When the noise settles, Abe sits down next to him with two beers.

ABE. Here. This one's on me. *(Tommy considers, takes the drink.)* Gotta mighty sweet hook there. Yever fight for money?

TOMMY. I dig coal for money. I just fight for fun.

ABE. Sure like to watch a man do what he does well. Your dancin' partner back there, what's his crime?

TOMMY. He looked like you.

ABE. And you didn't think the poor bastard suffered enough already? *(Tommy grins.)* I hear, as good as you are inna fight, you even better in the mines.

TOMMY. That a fact.

ABE. Everybody 'round here says you wanta know somethin' about coal mining, you talk to Mr. Jackson. 'Course that got me to thinkin' — how come a man like that, with that kinda knowledge, why don't the Company make him a mine engineer, *foreman* at least. Don't make sense, do it?

TOMMY.   That's just the way things is.

ABE.   But do they hafta stay that way, you reckon? Maybe we just been beatin' up on the wrong people. 'Course that's what the Company wants us to do, I guess. They probly figure long as we too busy beatin' the shit outta each other ...

TOMMY.   Thanks for the drink. *(Tommy exits. Abe watches. Steam whistle.)*

Scene 5

Exterior Rowen house. Abe sits in the sun sewing a pair of pants. Mary Anne enters with a basket of beans. She stands watching him.

ABE.   How's Joshua?

MARY ANNE.   Good. It's all I can do to keep him in bed now. Gonna hafta tie'im down, I reckon. *(She sits, snaps beans. Beat.)*

What? What're you grinnin' at?

MARY ANNE.   I hope you move a shovel better'n you work a needle.

ABE.   Well, it's the effort that counts.

MARY ANNE.   Not if your pants fall down. *(Joshua enters.)*

JOSHUA.   Hi.

MARY ANNE.   What're you doin' outta bed? Get back in there.

JOSHUA.   I'm tired of bein' in bed — I wanta be out here with y'all!

MARY ANNE.   Okay, but just for a little while. And when I say "scoot," you get your bottom back in there! Here. You sit here in the sun — I'll get you a blanket.

JOSHUA.   I don't need no blanket.

MARY ANNE.   You want to go back to bed right now?

JOSHUA.   No ma'am.

186

MARY ANNE.   All right then. *(She exits.)*

ABE.   Hey, Joshua, I'm Abe. You 'member me?

JOSHUA.   Sorta. You ain't from New York, are ya?

ABE.   No.

JOSHUA.   I think I got you kinda mixed up in my momma's stories. When I'm sick, she always tells me stories 'bout things.

ABE.   Like what?

JOSHUA.   Old times, I guess, 'fore the mines. People livin' in big old oak trees — somethin' like that. It's all kinda jumbled up. *(Mary Anne returns.)*

MARY ANNE.   Here, drink this water and then wrap yourself up good.

JOSHUA.   This tastes funny.

MARY ANNE.   That's 'cause I boiled it.

JOSHUA.   Well, I don't like it.

MARY ANNE.   You wanta be better, don'tcha? Then you drink it up. *(Beat.)* That Mother Jones person you was talkin' about ... what ever happened to her?

ABE.   Well, first time I met her was in West Virginny, 'bout seven years ago. *(Spot up on Mother Jones.)*

MOTHER JONES.   Abraham. That's a good name, onna my favorites in the Bible. Abraham and Isaac. They still offerin' up our boys in these hills, Abe, and we here to put a stop to it.

ABE.   Lord, she's a fiercesome woman — don't take back water from nobody! We was organizin' Paint Creek back then and these gun thugs was threatenin' us ...

MOTHER JONES.   You muzzle that damn mug of yours up. I ain't afraid of ninety-nine hundred of you! I would clean you up just like a sewer rat!

JOSHUA.   She really said that?

MARY ANNE.   Abe ...

ABE.   I was right there, those gun thugs no further from me'n you are now.

MARY ANNE.   Git inside, Joshua.

JOSHUA.   I wanta hear the rest of the story ...

MARY ANNE.   INSIDE! *(Joshua goes inside. Spot on Mother Jones out.)* I warned you, don't you be bringin' no trouble into my house.

187

ABE.   Seems to me whatever troubles you got was here a long time 'fore I showed up.

MARY ANNE.   Well, then I'll just clean up my own mess, thank you very much.

ABE.   Mary Anne ...

MARY ANNE.   I don't need no stranger to come in here and ...

ABE.   You ain't by yourself, you know? You ain't the only one hurtin' ...

MARY ANNE.   What d'you know about it? Nothin'! You don't know nothin' 'bout me or my life!

ABE.   I know what I see — a good woman, tryin' to keep her head above water ...

MARY ANNE.   There ain't nothin' good about me! *(Beat.)*

ABE.   Why do you say that?

MARY ANNE.   Look at my family. Look how we live. Five kids, buried four of 'em — what the hell kind of mother is that.

ABE.   That ain't your fault.

MARY ANNE.   Whose fault is it?

ABE.   Them bastards up on the hill.

MARY ANNE.   And you think you gonna just waltz in here and tell us alla buncha stories and they're gonna start singing hymns and passin' out baked biscuits!

ABE.   That wasn't no story I was tellin' your boy! Paint Creek really happened — I was there. That was the truth.

MARY ANNE.   Truth? Hell, I may be nothin' but a dumb hillbilly but even I know there ain't no such thing as truth.

ABE.   If you believe that, how do you get through the day?

MARY ANNE.   *(Fiercely.)* Habit!

ABE.   Now, who's tellin' stories? That's dirt under your feet, Mary Anne, and stars over your head, and it don't matter what anybody told you 'bout them, you know they're real, you know they're the truth.

MARY ANNE.   They tore my stars down a long time ago. Stars and moon and all!

ABE.   That's just what they want you to believe.

MARY ANNE.   I cain't, Abe! Cain't you see.... I cain't! *(Steam whistle.)*

Scene 6

Abe whittles a piece of wood. Joshua enters.

JOSHUA.   Whatcha makin'?

ABE.   Don't know exactly. Figure the wood'll tell me when it's ready.

JOSHUA.   You talk to a piece a wood? *(Abe shrugs.)* My daddy says you're crazy.

ABE.   Your mama ain't too wild 'bout me either. What d'you think?

JOSHUA.   Make up my own mind, I guess. You gonna work with my daddy in the mines?

ABE.   You bet.

JOSHUA.   Me too. When I'm old enough.

ABE.   How old are ya?

JOSHUA.   Twelve. Next April. You didn't finish your story the other day.

ABE.   No, I guess I didn't. Where was I? *(Mary Anne enters and stands listening.)*

JOSHUA.   You and Mother Jones was face-off with them gun thugs.

ABE.   Right. Well, Mother Jones just stared'em down, cool as ice, ... *(Abe and then Joshua see Mary Anne. Beat.)*

MARY ANNE.   Joshua.

JOSHUA.   Yes'm? *(Beat.)*

MARY ANNE.   When you finish up out here, you come in, get somethin' to eat. *(She exits. Abe smiles.)*

ABE.   Well, Mother Jones just stared'em down, cool as ice, and then marched into that town. The folks was all scared, of course, but she wasn't gonna have no part of that. *(Spot up on Mother Jones. People gather around Abe/Joshua making them part of the group she is addressing.)*

MOTHER JONES.   Boys, when I got in town today you were afraid to look at me, like a bunch a damn cowards. Well, I

189

been in jail more'n once and I expect to go again and if you are too cowardly to fight, I'll fight by myself! You oughta be ashamed of yourselves, actually to the Lord you ought, just to see one old woman who is not afraid of all those damn blood hounds.

JOSHUA. Damn.

ABE. Then, after she'd pour'd in the powder, she lit the match.

MOTHER JONES. The time is here! If you want the Union you have got that right, but don't beg the masters! Don't beg'em! And don't fear their bullets. How many guards have they got? Shoot, we could take on a whole army and still clean the whole bunch out!

ABE. Fire in the hole!

MOTHER JONES. UNION! *(The crowd surges off stage shouting Union. Spot out on Mother Jones.)*

ABE. And we marched up there and the guards ran before us like yella dogs, just like she said they would, and we got us a Union.

JOSHUA. Damn! I'da sure like to seen that.

ABE. Hold on, I think I'm hearin' somethin'. *(He "listens" to the piece of wood.)* It says, "I'm a whistle." *(He blows on it.)*

JOSHUA. Whatcha gonna do with that when you're done?

ABE. Can you read? *(Joshua nods. Abe pulls a pamphlet out of his pocket, tosses it to Joshua.)* Read this. Out loud. I carve better to a good speech. *(In a halting manner, Joshua begins to read.)*

JOSHUA. "I say to you that the next ..."

ABE. "Generation."

JOSHUA. "... will not charge us for what we have done, they will charge and ..."

ABE. "Condemn."

JOSHUA. "us for what we have left undone. Your children will be free. Freedom or Death."

ABE. Okay. Now gimme that last line again, and put a little somethin' behind it. Like you was talkin' to a whole crowd of folks.

JOSHUA. "Your children will be free. Freedom or Death!"

ABE.   Yeah, that's the way. *(Tommy enters.)* Lord, your boy here's smart as a whip, Tommy — he reads real good. Give 'im that first part, Joshua.

JOSHUA.   "The next generation will not charge us for what we have done, they will charge and condemn us for what we have left undone...." *(Tommy tears the pamphlet out of Joshua's hands. Blackout.)*

Scene 7

The Jackson house. The Preacher enters.

PREACHER.   Greetings, Brother Jackson. You wanted to see me?

TOMMY.   Yes sir — I gotta problem here. My boy's of age, wantin' to go into the mines but ... uh ... I can't seem to lay my hands on his birth certificate.

PREACHER.   Uh-huh. What d'you figure happen to the old one? *(Beat.)* Git burnt up inna fire or somethin'?

TOMMY.   Somethin' like that.

PREACHER.   Damn fires. How old is he?

TOMMY.   Fourteen.

PREACHER.   Surprizin' how many kids around here turn fourteen all of a sudden. Okay, I can make you a new one but there's a lotta paperwork involved, you know, lotta expenses ... *(Mary Anne, Joshua and Abe enter.)*

TOMMY.   How much?

PREACHER.   Three dollars.

TOMMY.   I'll be honest with ya — I only got a dollar in cash on me. I was hopin' I could pay off the rest.

MARY ANNE.   Tommy, what's goin' on in here?

PREACHER.   Well, I don't know — I probly gotta make a special trip down to Morgan ...

MARY ANNE.   Tommy?

PREACHER.   You gotta file birth certificates at the County courthouse.

191

TOMMY.   Maybe I could scrape together a dollar fifty ...

MARY ANNE.   What're you doin', Tommy?

PREACHER.   Cash, not scrip, right?

MARY ANNE.   Tommy?!

TOMMY.   What?! What do you want!

MARY ANNE.   He's too young.

TOMMY.   How soon can you get it?

PREACHER.   Tomorrow.

MARY ANNE.   He got him a birth certificate, he don't need him no new one! Here! I'll show ya! *(She goes into the back and rummages desperately through papers.)*

PREACHER.   Dollar fifty's fine.

TOMMY.   I want it tomorrow. *(He hands the Preacher the money as Mary Anne returns.)*

PREACHER.   Bless you, Mr. Jackson. *(He exits.)*

MARY ANNE.   Here, see! He got him one. Here...! *(Tommy grabs it out of her hand and tears it up.)*

TOMMY.   Well, he ain't got him no goddamn certificate now! *(Beat.)* Don't you ever shame me like that again.

MARY ANNE.   You can't do this to him.

TOMMY.   You said it yourself, Mare — we just too far behind.

MARY ANNE.   We can make it — I can make it work! We got what Abe brings in ...

TOMMY.   We don't need him. This family don't need no charity from that sort!

MARY ANNE.   What're you up to, Tommy? What're you tryin' to do?

TOMMY.   I'm doin' what I shoulda done a long time ago.

MARY ANNE.   This ain't about Joshua.

TOMMY.   You right about that, missy.

MARY ANNE.   I see what you're doin', Tommy, God help ya ... Joshua, you go in the other room!

TOMMY.   Joshua, you stay where you are! We'll settle this right here. Joshua, you wanta be a miner don'tcha, like your daddy? Tell your mama. Tell her!

JOSHUA.   Sure, I guess.

TOMMY.   That settles it, then.

192

MARY ANNE.   He can do better!

TOMMY.   Better'n what? Go on, say it — better'n what!

MARY ANNE.   Better'n minin'.

TOMMY.   What you mean is better'n me!

MARY ANNE.   That's right — better'n you! *(Tommy knocks her to the ground. Joshua lunges at Tommy, who pushes him away.)*

JOSHUA.   Leave her alone! *(Abe pulls Joshua off and stands between him and Tommy.)*

TOMMY.   I want you outta this house. You here when I come back, I'll kill ya. *(Beat.)*

ABE.   Okay. I'll go. But you and me both know I ain't really the problem here. *(Abe goes into the back. Tommy exits. Joshua goes over to his mother. She pushes him away and sits.)*

MARY ANNE.   I'm okay. *(Abe returns with his suitcase. Beat. Mother Jones appears in a dim light.)*

ABE.   Don't suppose you know anybody needs a border?

MARY ANNE.   I'll ask around. *(Beat.)* I'm sorry, Abe.

ABE.   Hey, you ain't got nothin' to apologize for — not to nobody.

MARY ANNE.   What'm I gonna do now?

ABE.   This ain't the end of nothin', Mary Anne.

MARY ANNE.   No?

ABE.   Like Mother Jones usta say:

MOTHER JONES.   War ain't over till we say it is.

ABE.   When the Comp'nies come in here and took this land away from you, it took'em years. They was real patient and they never let up, and that's how you gotta be. Take care of your mama, boy — she's somethin' special. *(He exits. Mother Jones stands behind Mary Anne and holds her. Joshua blows on the wooden whistle which melts into the steam whistle.)*

Scene 8

At the Coal Tipple.

Tommy and the miners enter. Joshua and Mary Anne walk down to meet them. We are at the entrance to the Tipple where men wait to enter the mine.

MINER #1. That your boy, Jackson?

MINER #2. Kinda small, ain't he? Mebbe you better throw'im back till he's keeper size!

MINER #3. New slate picker?

TOMMY. No sir, he's a miner!

MINER #1. A miner!

MINER #2. Fresh blood!

TOMMY. Boy ain't got no blood in him atall. Got coal dust in his veins, same as allus!

CROWD. That's right!/Good to see ya, boy!/God bless ya! *(Andrew steps forward and the crowd quiets.)*

ANDREW. How old's that boy, Jackson?

TOMMY. Fourteen.

ANDREW. Right. Got your affidavit?

TOMMY. Right here.

ANDREW. Well, hell — if you can't take the word of a man of God, who can you trust? Let's go to work! *(The crowd roars its approval and moves into the driftmouth.)*

JOSHUA. Hey, Abe!

ABE. Hey yourself, Joshua. Looks like I'm on your crew.

TOMMY. Lucky me. *(The men take their places in empty coal cars for the mantrip to the main heading. Joshua calls out to Mary Anne.)*

JOSHUA. See you when we see you! *(The lights telescope down on Mary Anne as she watches the car carry Joshua into the darkness. Blackout. Steam whistle.)*

Scene 9

The coal mine. Midday. Tommy and Joshua sit eating lunch.

TOMMY. You cold? *(Joshua ignores him.)* Next time you do what I tell ya — take your coat off when you work, put it on when you sit. *(Tommy tears his sandwich in half and offers it to Joshua.)* Here. Go on, I'm full already.

JOSHUA. I ain't hungry.

TOMMY. Jist gonna go to waste? *(Joshua takes it and eats.)* You make your daddy proud today, boy. 'Nother year or two, ain't gonna be nobody able to keep up with you.

JOSHUA. Yeah?

TOMMY. You bet. *(Beat.)* I know your momma and me, we don't always see eye to eye on everythin', but ... we still family, you know? Ain't nothin' more important than your blood. *(Beat. Joshua sneezes. Tommy grins.)* Bug dust. Gonna killus all, one day. *(He coughs.)* Funny thing is, I like it. I like minin' — bug dust'n all. Your mama ain't never understood that.

JOSHUA. She's scared.

TOMMY. Yeah, she don't like these mines much, that's a fact. Her family ...

JOSHUA. The Rowens?

TOMMY. ... they usta own a lotta this land 'round here.

JOSHUA. You mean it's true, all them stories she tells?

TOMMY. Well, you gotta take mosta them stories of your mama's with a grain of salt, but yeah, her people was somethin' once. 'Course they always usta look down on us Jacksons — figured we was just dumb white trash. Then her smart daddy sold the land to the Company and pretty soon we wuz all in the same boat. Guess he wasn't so smart that day! Your mama was really somethin' in them days, Joshua; purtiest thing I ever seen. Losin' that land just about broke her heart. Didn't mean nothin' to me. Hell, I'd give all these damn mountains and all the coal in'em for her. She's all I ever wanted. *(Abe enters.)*

195

ABE.   Car's here — let's round it over. *(There is a loud rumble and the men freeze.)* What the hell...?

TOMMY.   Get down! GET DOWN! *(Blackout, and then a tremendous explosion roars through the mine, followed by several frantic blasts of the steam whistle. Crossfade to Andrew who yells to a group of unseen subordinates.)*

ANDREW.   Gotta coal bump in Number Five, I want it all shut down, the whole thing! Every goddamn gallery and tunnel! *(Around the stage men call out.)*

MINERS.   Cooooaaaalllll bump! Coal bump! Coal Bump! Coaaalll bump! *(Crossfade to mine.)*

TOMMY.   Joshuaaaaaaaa!

JOSHUA.   Daddy! Daddy!

ABE.   Over here, Tommy! Joshua! Over here! *(Crossfade to porch of Jackson house. Mary Anne huddles nervously with Lucy.)*

MARY ANNE.   What'd they say? How many?

LUCY.   Nobody knows. They won't let nobody down there.

MARY ANNE.   Oh sweet Jesus. Lord have mercy. *(Crossfade back to mine.)*

ANDREW.   Get me a doctor down here! And stretchers! All the timber you can carry! I want all those men outta there now! Move it!

ABE.   This way! *(Crossfade to porch as the men stagger out of the mine, coughing and choking.)*

LUCY.   Here they come! *(All the women now stand on their porches, crying, praying, and calling to one another. The men begin to march, carrying their dead and wounded on homemade stretchers. The men stop and put one body down. The black woman on the porch, Sureta, comes and sobs fiercely over it. Lights close down around her isolating her in a tight spot. As the men exit, Tommy/ Joshua/Abe peel off to meet Mary Anne.)*

JOSHUA.   Mama!

MARY ANNE.   Joshua! Joshua! Oh, baby, you all right?

TOMMY.   He's okay, he's okay. We're all okay.

MARY ANNE.   No, Tommy, we ain't. *(A second spot comes up isolating Andrew.)*

ANDREW.   I gotta partial list here of the men who're still missin':

MARY ANNE.   He ain't goin' back down there. You neither.

ANDREW.   E.O. Boone.

ABE.   Your men don't work, Mary Anne, how you gonna eat?

ANDREW.   Bob Jenkins.

TOMMY.   He's goin' back, we're all goin' back. We always go back!

ANDREW.   Doug Slocum.

ABE.   What's the cost, Tommy?

ANDREW.   Ward Mayo.

ABE.   How many friends you lose down there today?

ANDREW.   Gus Hurley.

ABE.   You think it gonna be any different tomorrow?

ANDREW.   Jack Nolan.

ABE.   What happened down there?

ANDREW.   Frank Dawkins.

MARY ANNE.   *(Gently.)* What happened, Tommy?

TOMMY.   Coal bump.

ANDREW.   Everett Hayes.

JOSHUA.   What's a coal bump?

ANDREW.   Chad Mosely.

MARY ANNE.   Tell'im Tommy.

ANDREW.   Bob Fox.

TOMMY.   Company cut the pillars too fine ... just picked away so much coal that there weren't nothin' left to hold up the mountain.

ANDREW.   Tom Lynch.

ABE.   Why's a Company do that?

TOMMY.   'Cause it's cheaper.

ANDREW.   C.C. Edwards.

MARY ANNE.   It's gotta stop Tommy.

ANDREW.   Sam Berry.

ABE.   Any way we could stop this, Tommy?

TOMMY.   What d'you think?!

ANDREW.   Carl Top.

ABE.   I think Blue Star thinks a ton of coal is worth more'n Tommy Jackson and his boy put together. What d'you think?

ANDREW. Willie Baker.

MARY ANNE. What d'you think we ought to do, Tommy?

ANDREW. Earl Weiss.

ABE. What do you think we ought to do about that?

TOMMY. You son of a bitch! What do you know? You ain't from around here! You don't know nothin' about here!

ANDREW. Sam Waylon.

ABE. I been inna hundred coal camps and this one ain't any different.

ANDREW. Tom Allen.

ABE. You ain't alone in this.

ANDREW. Frank Wayland.

ABE. Don't fight me, Tommy.

TOMMY. Leave me alone!

ANDREW. Carl Knotts.

ABE. You fight me, you fight her, you fight everbody but them. Why don't you fight them!?

TOMMY. I DON'T KNOW HOW! (*Beat. Spot out on Andrew and Sureta.*)

ABE. I know how. (*Beat.*)

TOMMY. Whatta we gotta do?

ABE. Organize the men and then pull'em out. Nobody goes back.

MARY ANNE. Then what?

ABE. They'll bring in scabs, try to replace you. Them we can't organize we chase off.

TOMMY. And them we can't chase off?

ABE. We kill'em. (*Beat.*) We gonna need guns.

TOMMY. Ain't that what the Union does?

ABE. The Operators got this county locked up tighter'n a flea's ass — I can't ship no guns in. But I got money. You got somebody local who ain't too particular 'bout who he sells to and we'll just buy'em.

TOMMY. They's a miner does some bootleggin', s'posed to run guns on the side — army surplus.

ABE. Set it up. (*Beat.*) What's the problem?

TOMMY. He's a nigger.

ABE. Coal don't care, why should you? (*Mary Anne hands*

Abe the Rowen family watch.)
MARY ANNE.   Here. Anybody shoots at my family, they
oughta be able to shoot back. You buy us some damn guns!
(Beat.)
ABE.   Tommy?
TOMMY.   I'll set it up for tonight. *(Steam whistle.)*

Scene 10

*The woods. Night. Standing beside an old wagon is Cassius
Biggs. He is a powerfully built black man in his thirties. He
carries a revolver stuck in the waistband of his pants. His
wife, Sureta, sits on the wagon.*

Tommy walks up, Abe behind him.

CASSIUS.   Evenin'.
TOMMY.   Got somebody wants to meet ya.
ABE.   Mr. Biggs. Evenin' ma'am.
SURETA.   Evenin'.
ABE.   My name's Steinman. Abe Steinman, and I was hopin'
we could do some business.
CASSIUS.   White mule or pickhandle?
ABE.   Pickhandle?
CASSIUS.   Dago homebrew outta raisens — kinda sweet but
gotta wicked kick. White mule's your more traditional sugartop
corn brew — draws an honest bead and guaranteed to knock
you into the middle of next week. White mule or pickhandle?
ABE.   I was thinkin' Springfields. Jorgensons would be all
right too, but I got a sentimental attachment to Springfields
over in France.
CASSIUS.   Somebody havin' some fun with you, mister, I
don't sell no rifles — I sell liquor.
TOMMY.   Oh, come on, Cassius ...
ABE.   No, I think we got the right man. *(Beat.)*
CASSIUS.   You really fight over there in France?

ABE.   Still got the mud between my toes to prove it.

CASSIUS.   I signed on to do my part and fight for freedom and democracy. That was the story, anyways. Only they wouldn't let me fight with you white boys. They figured we colored was only good for diggin' latrines. Paris was nice though. I could walk anywhere, have a drink anyplace. Felt a lot like that freedom I was supposed to be fightin' for — felt like a man, felt good. But get back to here and everythin' still nigger this and nigger that.

ABE.   The Union's color-blind.

CASSIUS.   So's justice, ain't she?

ABE.   *(Smiling.)* No, she's just plain blind. Deaf and dumb sometimes too.

CASSIUS.   Justice in Howsen county's a buncha gun thugs in a automobile, white sheets over their heads.

ABE.   Somebody oughta do somethin' about that.

CASSIUS.   "Woulda," "shoulda" and "oughta" — three of the saddest words they is. You know, six of them twenty-three miners was kilt, was colored. Sureta's brother was one of 'em.

ABE.   Sorry for your loss, ma'am. We had us a strong Union, this sorta thing wouldn't happen.

SURETA.   They gonna bury my brother separate from the white miners. *(Beat.)*

ABE.   Ain't that like the Comp'ny — keep us apart in death as well as life? It don't have to be that way.

CASSIUS.   That the way you see it, Tommy? *(Beat.)* Don't nothin' change.

ABE.   Only for them people too scared to take a chance. Look, Cassius, I ain't gonna pretend that we don't need them rifles of yours, 'cause we do. But whatever else you may think you've known in this life, the Union is different.

CASSIUS.   Different? What you gonna sell me next? The Lord gonna rise up?

ABE.   Jesus was a workin' man, you know.

CASSIUS.   And look what they done to him.

ABE.   He didn't have no rifles. With or without the rifles, Cassius, we'd be proud to have ya. You know where to find us. *(Beat. Abe and Tommy walk away. Cassius lights up.)*

CASSIUS.   What?

SURETA.   Seem like a decent man.

CASSIUS.   'Cause he called me "mister" and tipped his hat to you? They always nice when they need us. He's a Jew lookin' to buy somethin'

SURETA.   Seem different to me. Maybe.

CASSIUS.   Maybe the sun gonna rise in the *West* tomorrow but I wouldn't be layin' no money on it, Sureta. It ain't none of our business.

SURETA.   Uh-huh.

CASSIUS.   White people wanta kill each other, I say more power to'em — it's just one less for us to worry about! I ain't sayin' that's right, I'm just sayin' that's how things is. I wish they was different.

SURETA.   "Woulda," "shoulda," and "oughta" — three of the saddest words they is.

CASSIUS.   Joinin' the damn Union ain't gonna bring your brother back!

SURETA.   No, it ain't! But I got a fool husband who goes down into them mines ever day and a ten-year-old boy who wants to be just like his daddy, and if joinin' the Union keep them alive, that'd be enough for me. *(Beat. Cassius holds her.)*

CASSIUS.   Lord, what'd I do to get stuck with you.

SURETA.   You just a lucky man, Cassius Biggs. You are a lucky man.

Scene 11

Night. A tent city set up outside the Town. There is a fire. Mary Anne stands in a pool of light.

MARY ANNE.   And so Cassius and Sureta joined us. *(Cassius and Sureta enter and sit.)* And Silus and Lucy ... *(Silus and Lucy enter.)* and the word spread like a fever, and every man and woman in that camp joined us ... *(All the other actors enter. Music starts; there is singing and laughing.)* ... and the mines shut down and the steam whistle went rusty. We moved into a holler near the tracks and people put up tents or just slept out in the open, like a big church meetin'. And at night, I lay on my back lookin' up at the sky and I put the moon and the stars back up again, one by one. *(Mary Anne joins the group as they begin singing "A Miner's Life,"* led by Abe.)*

"A miner's life is like a sailor's
'Board a ship to cross the waves
Every day his life's in danger,
Yet he ventures, being brave.

Watch the rocks, they're fallin' daily
Careless miners always fail
Keep you hand upon the dollar
And your eye upon the scale.

(Chorus.)
Union miners stand together
Heed no operator's tale
Keep your hand upon the dollar
And your eye upon the scale!"

(The song finishes. An instrumental begins as Abe crosses to where Joshua is sitting by himself and squats down beside him.)

ABE.   Don't feel like singin' tonight? *(Joshua shrugs.)* What ya thinkin' on?

JOSHUA.   I'm scared.

ABE.   Yeah? *(Tommy stands nearby, listening.)*

JOSHUA.   We gonna win, ain't we? *(Abe hesitates.)*

ABE.   You look around you, Joshua — look at all these people together like one big family. You feel the power in that? *(Beat.)* Well, family just ain't your own kin, now, Joshua. It's everybody there is — everybody there ever was, everybody there ever will be. That's Union. *(Beat.)*

TOMMY.   Joshua, you s'pose to be in bed.

JOSHUA.   Oh, daddy, I'm just ...

TOMMY.   Get yourself in that tent right now and go to

---

* See music at back of text.

202

sleep. Go on!

JOSHUA. G'night, Abe. 'Night daddy.. *(He exits.)*

TOMMY. You didn't answer his question, did ya? We gonna win? *(Beat.)*

ABE. If not this time, then the next.

TOMMY. That's real easy for you to say, innit?

ABE. I'm scared, too, Tommy, but I ain't gonna quit.

TOMMY. Hell, your courage don't cost you nothin', Abe. You ain't got nothin' to lose.

ABE. I wouldn't say that.

TOMMY. This strike don't work, you ain't gonna have to bury your family, are ya? *(The sound of a train approaching.)*

ABE. They usually load those trains this time of night?

TOMMY. No.

ABE. *(Screaming.)* Silus, douse that light! Get down! Everybody get down! *(Silus leaps up from the circle and throws a blanket over the fire. The train is very close now. As it's whistle blows, a machine gun opens up and rakes the camp. People scatter, falling and screaming. Abe throws himself at Tommy and knocks him to the ground. Chaos. The train passes. Mary Anne runs in.)*

MARY ANNE. Tommy?

TOMMY. Joshua okay?!

MARY ANNE. I thought he was with you!

TOMMY. In the tent. Stay with 'im! *(She exits U.S.)*

MARY ANNE. Joshua! *(Abe and Tommy are joined by Cassius, Silus and the other miners.)*

ABE. How bad?

SILUS. *(Shaking his head.)* Armored train with a goddamn machine gun!

ABE. How many we got hurt!

SILUS. Two down, at least one dead.

MINER #2. How the hell we gonna fight that!

MINER #1. They gonna kill us all!

CASSIUS. Abe, you get me a couple of men with picks and shovels and I'll take care of that damn train.

TOMMY. Picks and shovels against machine guns?!

CASSIUS. You can't run a train without tracks, Tommy.

ABE. Easy.

MINER #2.   We need guns, real guns! I ain't gonna fight no machine gun with some damn squirrel rifle.

CASSIUS.   We're gettin' guns.

TOMMY.   When?

CASSIUS.   Saturday night.

ABE.   All right. Silus, you and Tommy make sure everybody's okay and then post some more guards. Cassius, let's you and I go wreck us a train. *(The men disperse leaving Tommy alone on stage. The lights change as Andrew appears.)*

Scene 12

The Tipple Office.

ANDREW.   Whatd'ya want, Jackson?

TOMMY.   I want my family safe; I want my job back.

ANDREW.   There's a strike on, Tommy, didn't you notice?

TOMMY.   Strike wasn't my idea ...

ANDREW.   Whose idea was it?

TOMMY.   Look, I just want my job back. That's all.

ANDREW.   I'm afraid it ain't gonna be that easy. *(Beat.)*

TOMMY.   I don't wanta hurt nobody else.

ANDREW.   Me neither. I think this whole thing was justa local problem got blown outta shape by a buncha outsiders. Take them people outta the picture and things get a lot more reasonable. These agitators come in here, talkin' that talk, promisin' you people this and that and pie in the sky. I heard'em — sure, butter wouldn't melt in their mouths. Meanwhile, you lost your job, they eatin' ya outta house and home and probly puttin' a pair of horns on you in the bargain. And then, when push comes to shove, they just gonna walk away, leavin' you holdin' the bag. You been suckered, Tommy. I got the fuckin' army comin' in.

TOMMY.   The army?

ANDREW.   You think that little railroad visit last night was

204

somethin', wait'll they roll those tanks in here. *(Beat.)* This is a waste of time. Russ!

TOMMY.   Everybody gets their job back.

ANDREW.   I can't promise that ...

TOMMY.   That's the deal! Everybody gets their job back.

ANDREW.   I need a name.

TOMMY.   I don't want nobody to get hurt.

ANDREW.   I need a name and a place.

TOMMY.   Your word, nobody gets hurt. *(Beat.)*

ANDREW.   Okay. *(Beat.)*

TOMMY.   Cassius Biggs.

ANDREW.   He the only one? *(Tommy hesitates.)*

TOMMY.   Abe Steinman.

ANDREW.   I need a place.

TOMMY.   Up on the Shilling, where the old Treaty Oak usta stand; we s'posed to buy some guns.

ANDREW.   When?

TOMMY.   Tomorrow night.

ANDREW.   Tomorrow night. *(Andrew exits. The lights fade down isolating Tommy. A quiet whistle from off stage. The lights shift. We are in the woods near the Treaty Oak. Cassius and Abe join Tommy. Everyone is nervous, tense.)*

CASSIUS.   This is my show, gentlemen. Everbody does exactly what I tell'em to. Everbody got that? You got that Tommy?

TOMMY.   I got it. *(Again, the quiet whistle. Cassius whistles back. A man walks out of the woods.)*

MAN.   Evening.

CASSIUS.   Where's Carver?

MAN.   Couldn't make it.

ABE.   Problems?

CASSIUS.   This ain't who I usually deal with.

MAN.   Guns is guns, gentlemen. And cash is cash. If you got one, I got a shitload of the other.

CASSIUS.   I don't like this. Let's go.

ABE.   Let's see what he's got.

CASSIUS.   Abe! *(The Man pulls a pistol out of his coat as other men, also armed, step out of the shadows. Abe grabs the pistol, and as he and the Man fall to the ground, the gun goes off. In the confusion, Cassius escapes. Abe is subdued. Andrew steps out of the darkness.)*

ANDREW.   Where's Biggs?

MAN.   He got away.

ANDREW.   All right, you're free, Jackson — now get the fuck out of here. *(Tommy turns to Abe. Beat.)*

TOMMY.   Abe...? *(Beat. Abe just stares at Tommy.)*

ANDREW.   I want him on his knees. *(The Man hands his revolver to Andrew as Abe is forced to kneel.)*

TOMMY.   There wasn't s'posed to be no killin'. That was the deal.

ANDREW.   Any last words?

ABE.   They say over in Carolton, 'fore he died, your brother wept like a woman and pissed himself. *(Andrew shoots Abe in the back of the head. The men exit. Tommy stares down at Abe's body. Tommy reaches down and touches the corpse. He hesitates and then pulls the watch out of Abe's vest, and looks at it. Joshua comes out of the shadows. Tommy sees him. Beat.)*

TOMMY.   Joshua?

JOSHUA.   You kilt him. *(Tommy pockets the watch.)*

TOMMY.   What're you.... You s'pose to ...

JOSHUA.   I heard'im.

TOMMY.   No.

JOSHUA.   I heard what he said.

TOMMY.   They lied to me.

JOSHUA.   You killed him! *(Joshua starts to run away. Tommy grabs him.)*

TOMMY.   Look here. Look at me! *(He pins Joshua's arms.)* We was gonna lose the strike. You hear me? They was bringin' in the *army!* They woulda kilt us all, you and your mama both, and I wasn't gonna let that happen!

JOSHUA.   No!

TOMMY.   I love you, Joshua. You hear me?

JOSHUA.   *(Crying.)* No. *(Tommy rocks him in his arms.)*

TOMMY.   I love you. I know. I know, it's hard. But that's just the way it gotta be. *(He rocks Joshua in his arms. Lights shift. Cassius, Mary Anne and all the miners enter. Tommy and Joshua rise and join them. It is morning in the tent city. The group stands silent and suspicious.)*

SURETA.   Somebody sold us out. *(Beat.)*

TOMMY.   I got hit in the head with an axe handle or somethin' — they musta figured I was dead. Prob'ly woulda been if Joshua hadn't found me, brought me back. *(Beat.)*

CASSIUS.   Only a few of us knew the particulars 'bout the deal. *(Beat.)*

TOMMY.   Yeah. You, for one. But who saw you come back to camp after we got jumped, Cassius?

CASSIUS.   Meanin'?

TOMMY.   Kinda odd, don't you think?

SILUS.   Now hold on a minute.

TOMMY.   They were his rifles. And now he's got our money *and* his rifles. Plus whatever them Pinkertons paid him.

CASSIUS.   You son of a bitch! *(Cassius jumps at Tommy and they struggle as Silus pulls out a pistol and fires it.)*

SILUS.   That's enough! *(The men are pulled apart. Joshua steps forward.)*

JOSHUA.   He's lyin'. *(Beat.)* They kilt Abe. I saw it. They let my daddy go.

TOMMY.   What're you sayin' boy?

JOSHUA.   We buried Abe together. He made me promise not to say nothin'. *(Beat.)*

MARY ANNE.   Tommy?

TOMMY.   He's lyin'. *(Joshua crosses to his father and pulls the watch out of his pocket.)*

JOSHUA.   How'd you get this?

MARY ANNE.   Tommy. *(Beat.)*

TOMMY.   They're bringin' in the army. *(The crowd murmurs.)* That's right, the army! We was all gonna get kilt — and for what? I talked to 'em 'bout gettin' our jobs back.

SURETA.   You didn't have no right to make a deal for us.

TOMMY.   I gotta right to protect my family. Cain't nobody tell me different. *(Mary Anne walks over to Tommy and faces him.)*

MARY ANNE.   I 'member when you was courtin' me, how mean my folks was to you and how you just stood there and took it 'cause you loved me, and even my daddy had to admit, "That Tommy Jackson, he ain't no quitter." And I thought, no, he ain't. When they tore my stars down, I'da give up right then but you wouldn't let me. I didn't love you but I thought, "They can tear these mountains apart, but Tommy Jackson won't quit on me."

I know you loved our boys, and I loved you for that. I put up with the drinkin' and you hittin' me 'cause I knew you grieved in your heart like I did and I reckon I didn't think I deserved any better. You wasn't never kind, Tommy, and you weren't never wise, but I never thought you was a quitter.

And then you quit on me.

My name is Rowen. Mary Anne Rowen. I got one son, Joshua Rowen, and this man is a stranger to me. *(Beat. All the men save Cassius gather around Tommy.)*

TOMMY.   Joshua? *(The men drag Tommy off.)* Jooooooossss-hhhhhuuuuaaa! *(Beat.)*

CASSIUS.   I'm prepared to fight Andrew and his gun thugs, with or without rifles, but I ain't ready to fight the whole damn U.S. army. Strike's over. *(Cassius leaves and the women huddle disconsolately. Light shift.)*

JOSHUA.   What we gonna do, Ma?

MARY ANNE.   I don't know.

JOSHUA.   We ain't gonna give up, are we?

MARY ANNE.   I don't know! *(Mary Anne moves away from the group. Joshua follows but at a distance.)*

SURETA.   *(Bitterly.)* Well, I guess we could always pray for a miracle.

WOMAN.   Like what?

SURETA.   For a plague of frogs and locusts ...

LUCY.   For the water in the Shilling to turn to blood ...

SURETA.   And for the Angel of Death to come flyin' in low over Blue Star ...

WOMAN.   ... and carry off ever last one of them goddamn guards! *(Beat.)*

MARY ANNE.   No. *(The women turn to Mary Anne and then she screams.)* Nooooooooooooooooooooooooooooooooooo!!!!! *(Silence. The women stare at Mary Anne, unnerved.)*

JOSHUA. Mama?

MARY ANNE. I come too far for this! Get up. I give up too much! Get up. What are you doin' sittin' there? Get up!

SURETA. What're you think you gonna do without the men, Mary Anne? The men give up!

MARY ANNE. I think if we always waited for the men to do somethin' we still be livin' in caves.

LUCY. What about the army?!

MARY ANNE. They wouldn't've called them in less they was scared. You hear me! We scare them!

WOMAN. It's hard!

MARY ANNE. What's hard — dyin'?! I'll tell you what's hard: Waitin' for that knock on the door and some long face from the Company sayin' they're sorry, ma'am, but there's been an accident — that's hard. Watchin' your son go down into the dark mine in the mornin' and not knowin' whether you'll ever see him again — that's hard. Buryin' a baby you just.... I buried four children in this ground, you hear me, four babies, and I didn't have no choice about it but I got a choice now *and I ain't buryin' another one!* They can bring in a hundred goddamn armies and it can't be nothin' worse than what we've known. It won't never stop unless we say it stops, and I say it stops now. Right now. Right here. *(Beat.)* Stand up! *(Mary Anne hits the set. Again. Sureta joins her, establishing a rhythm. The other women join them, beating the set, the scaffolding, with their hands, their shoes, sticks, pots and pans — whatever they have. The men join them one by one, hitting the set with axe handles and the rhythm builds under and through Joshua's speech as the light shifts. There is a single spot up on Joshua.)*

JOSHUA. And my momma rolled the rock off their hearts and pulled them back into life and we marched, all the women and me, banging pots and pans and singing songs until the men, shamefaced, joined us. And then we marched in thousands outta that camp, holding hands, and the earth trembled under my feet and the sun stood still in the sky and Abe and Mother Jones danced together and we marched on that coal tipple and they threw down their guns in fear and fled before us like Pharoh's army before the ocean! I felt sorry for'em all! Hell, I even felt sorry for Mr. Winston that day! *(The drumming stops abruptly. Lights shift as Andrew and armed guards appear. Beat.)*

ANDREW. I want you people off this property. *(Beat.)*

MARY ANNE. We want us a Union, cash wages 'stead of scrip, and we want to see them gun thugs of Blue Star on the first train outta here. *(Beat.)*

ANDREW. I'll give you ten minutes to clear the tipple. *(Beat.)*

MARY ANNE. We only gonna need five. *(She gestures, and Sureta and Lucy carry out a case of dynamite. Joshua follows with a burning carbide lamp. Mary Anne puts the list of demands on top of the case.)* We don't get us a contract, we gonna blow your operation to hell. *(Beat.)*

ANDREW. You're not serious.

MARY ANNE. Joshua? *(Joshua puts the burning lamp <u>on</u> the case. Beat.)*

ANDREW. I sign this today, it won't mean nothin' tomorrow. *(Beat.)*

MARY ANNE. That's all right. You change your mind, we can always change ours. *(Beat. Andrew walks over stiffly and scrawls his signature on the paper. He exits. People smile and look at each other. And then chaos erupts. The successful strikers are cheering and crying and hugging each other. More music. People start singing "Step by Step."*)*

ALL. "Step by step the longest march
 Can be won, can be won.
 Many stones can build an arch
 Singly none, singly none."

(The crowd freezes as they continue to hum the song. Mary Anne crosses to Joshua who has stood apart from all the festivities.)

MARY ANNE. You all right, honey?

JOSHUA. I guess. *(She hugs Joshua.)*

MARY ANNE. Me too. Don't know whether I'm comin' or goin'.

* See music at back of text.

JOSHUA.   (Crying.) I miss my daddy.

MARY ANNE.   (Fiercely.) Hush now! You can't be thinkin'
about him no more! Hmm? Not ever agin. The Union gonna
be your daddy now. And your mama and your brothers and
your sisters. That's the truth, and you hold onto that. You
remember what we done here and what it cost, and you tell
the people, Joshua! You tell'em the story and don't you leave
nothin' out! You make'em *remember!* (Relenting.) Sssshhhh, baby.
I know. I know. But there ain't no need to feel lonely,
Joshua, not ever again! Just look around you, Joshua, look at
all your family! Ain't union grand! *Ain't union grand! (The
crowd comes back to life and finishes their song.)*

ALL.   "And by Union what we will
    Can be accomplished still!"

*(The crowd begins to chant "Union" as two men hoist Joshua up on
their shoulders. Mary Anne backs US as the chant builds to a roar
and then suddenly freezes. The lights come down in twin spots on
Joshua and Mary Anne. Joshua looks directly at the audience.)*

JOSHUA.   I'm what you call a "born again" — once in
Christ by a coal-company preacher in the muddy waters of the
Shillin' and once in the Union in a river of blood. *(Mary
Anne stands at the highest part of the stage, framed between Abe and
Mother Jones. She raises her arms to Joshua — a blessing, a com-
mandment — and shouts to the world.)*

MARY ANNE.   UNION! *(Blackout.)*

END OF PLAY

PROPERTY LIST

Matches
Small satchel (ABE)
Doctor's bag (DOCTOR)
Small bottle (DOCTOR)
Rowen watch (MARY ANNE)
8 dollars (ABE)
Shovel (TOMMY)
Bucket of water (TOMMY)
2 beers (ABE)
Sewing material (ABE)
1 pair of pants for sewing (ABE)
Basket of beans (MARY ANNE)
Wood piece (ABE)
Whittle knife (ABE)
Pamphlet (ABE)
Birth certificate (MARY ANNE)
$1.50 (TOMMY)
Wooden whistle (ABE)
Sandwiches (TOMMY, JOSHUA)
Homemade stretchers
Revolver (1920) (CASSIUS)
Blanket (SILUS)
Pistol (1920) (MAN, SILUS)
Sticks
Pots
Pans
Axes
Case of dynamite (MARY ANNE)
Carbide lamp (lit) (JOSHUA)
List (MARY ANNE)
Pen (ANDREW)

SOUND EFFECTS

Water dripping
Metal cutting into mineral re: coal mining (1920)
Mine shaft groan (shifting of timbers, etc.)
Mine explosion
Slate falling
Loud steam whistle
Rumble in mine
Train approaching and passing (1920)
Train whistle (1920)
Machine-gun fire (1920)
Pistol shot (1920)

WHICH SIDE
ARE YOU ON?

‹❦›

*"Which side are you on, Brother,
which side are you on?"*

— Florence Reese

CHARACTERS

JOSHUA ROWEN, age forty-four, president of United Mine Workers, District 16

MARGARET ROWEN, Joshua's wife

SCOTTY ROWEN, Joshua's son

JAMES TALBERT WINSTON, age forty-three, owner of Blue Star Mining Company

FRANKLIN BIGGS, age forty-four, a successful businessman, owner of Biggs & Son Liquor.

LANA TOLLER, Joshua's secretary

STUCKY, head of security, District 16

RAY BLANKO, sheriff of Howsen County

CALVIN HAYES, a District #16 Local President

MIKE, a District #16 Local President

CHUCK, a District #16 Local President

GREG, a District #16 Local President

RICK, a District #16 Local President

BOB SMALLEY, a security guard at the Blue Star mine.

UNEMPLOYED MINERS AND THEIR FAMILIES

PARTY GUESTS

MEN IN THE BAR

PHOTOGRAPHERS AND PRESS

NARRATOR

Which Side Are You On?

It is thirty-four years later, November, 1954. Howsen County, Kentucky, in and around the UMW Union Hall near the Blue Star mine.

Which Side Are You On?

WHICH SIDE ARE YOU ON?

Hanging in the shadows of the background upstage, like dusty ghosts, are the strike banners from the end of Play #7. Behind them, and still looming over the set, is the Coal Tipple. It is early November, 1954, in Howsen County.

Scene 1

Darkness. The stage is filled with men and women. Standing on the highest point of the set upstage is Joshua Rowen, now a large, charismatic man in his mid-forties. A large crowd of unemployed miners, their families, and TV and news reporters face him. They react throughout.

JOSHUA. I'm not gonna stand up here and tell you people somethin' that ain't so just to make ya feel good. Too many of you men have had to make that long walk home with a pink slip in your hands and face the wife and kids.
MAN #1. Get'em to open up the gates!
JOSHUA. There ain't no question what with the coal slump and the layoffs that these are hard times in Howsen county ...
MAN #2. This ain't puttin' no food on my table!
JOSHUA. ... but if we all stick together and tough it out, we'll get through this. *(Man #2 and his family stalk off. The crowd yells after them. Joshua struggles to hold the crowd.)* I remember another hard time around here, some thirty years ago. We'd gone out on strike for the first time and we didn't worry so much about whether we were ever gonna get our jobs back ... we worried about whether the Company was

gonna murder us while we slept. I was ten years old and I don't mind tellin' you I was scared. And then one night, this organizer said somethin' to me that I have never forgotten. He said, "Joshua, family ain't just your own kin now. It's everybody there is; everybody there ever was; everybody there ever will be. That's your family now. That's *Union*." We'll get through this, 'cause we got each other. We got the Union. Union! Union! Union! *(The crowd begins to chant with him, louder and louder. The chant freezes and the crowd clears the stage leaving Joshua isolated in his spot and revealing Margaret Rowen, Joshua's wife, in an armchair C.)*

Scene 2

The Rowen house. Margaret has fallen asleep, glass in hand, in front of the TV set. It's broadcast day finished, the television plays "The Star Spangled Banner." Scott Rowen walks onstage, dressed in a Marine uniform and carrying a duffel bag. Beat. Scotty turns off the TV. He takes the glass out of her hand and puts it on the table.

MARGARET.   Joshua? *(The spot on Joshua fades out.)*

SCOTTY.   No, momma, it's me.

MARGARET.   Scotty? Is that you, baby? Oh, Scotty! *(She gets up and hugs him fiercely.)* Let me look at ya! Aren't you a sight for sore eyes. Scotty, Scotty, Scotty. Why, honey, you're so thin, you're nothin' but skin and bones. Didn't they feed you over there? Here, let me get ya somethin' to eat ...

SCOTTY.   That's okay, momma, I ain't hungry ...

MARGARET.   I can just scramble you some eggs or somethin', it's no problem   ...

SCOTTY.   No, really, I gotta sandwich at the bus station ...

MARGARET.   That's not eatin'. We oughta have a drink, that's what! That's what we oughta do, we oughta celebrate! I hadda glass here somewheres ...

SCOTTY.   That's okay, momma ...

MARGARET.   You're not gonna make me drink alone now, are you? Not on your homecomin'! *(She pours two drinks.)* That's better. "Hail to the conquering hero!" Oh my, this place is such a mess. Look at me; who's talkin', right?

SCOTTY.   You look fine, Momma. You look beautiful.

MARGARET.   Lord love you for a liar. We didn't expect you back till tomorrow.

SCOTTY.   They cut me loose twenty-four hours early ...

MARGARET.   ... Nothin's ready. I was gettin' your room all painted ...

SCOTTY.   That's okay, I'll just sleep down here on the couch ...

MARGARET.   Well, you'll have to fight your father for that honor ... I'm so restless these nights. 'Sides, he gets in so late, usually ...

SCOTTY.   Where is dad?

MARGARET.   Oh, makin' a speech somewhere's. You know, "Union business." What else is new, huh? Now, I don't want talk about your daddy, I wanta talk about you. How are you? Really.

SCOTTY.   I'm fine. Really.

MARGARET.   The news is always full of such terrible stories. Last month, *LIFE* magazine had a whole series of pictures on Korea. Awful. Just awful. It's around here somewheres. Lemme see ...

SCOTTY.   Momma ...

MARGARET.   He's probably taken'em to the office or somethin'. It just makes me so mad when he does that ...

SCOTTY.   I don't need to see any pictures! *(Beat.)*

MARGARET.   Sure. I was just ...

SCOTTY.   I know.

MARGARET.   I mean if you don't wanta talk about it ...

SCOTTY.   ... I don't wanta talk about it.

MARGARET.   Okay. But if you do ...

SCOTTY.   If I do, I'll let you know.

MARGARET.   Okay. Josh says, you're gonna go to work down there ...

SCOTTY.   District Field Rep ...

MARGARET. You wanta another drink?

SCOTTY. That's okay ...

MARGARET. I'm so glad you're here, son. That's all that matters! *(She hugs him again. Light shifts. Spot holds on Scotty as Margaret exits and the company enters.)*

Scene 3

It is one night later. The Union Hall for District #16. A crowd of men and women enter singing, "For He's a Jolly Good Fellow." Present are James, Franklin, Ray, Lana, Stucky, Calvin, Jefferson and various guests. Scotty stands between Joshua and Margaret. Applause. Joshua gestures for quiet.

JOSHUA. Margaret and I wanta thank you all, from the bottom of our hearts, for bein' here tonight to help celebrate Scotty's return. We haven't had a lot to celebrate around here recently but ...

CALVIN. You got that right.

JOSHUA. ... but I think we can all agree on this one thing, and that is, Scotty, you done us proud! And now, Scotty has decided to take his place alongside me here in the UMW! So, how about a big welcome for the new Field Representative for District #16, Scotty Rowen! *(Applause. Joshua takes the gold watch out of his pocket.)* There's somebody who couldn't be here tonight, although I'm sure she's here in spirit: my mother, the "Mother Jones of Howsen County," Mary Anne Rowen. Y'all know this watch. You know the story of how it was all she had left from her daddy and how she sold it to buy the guns that made this Union possible. And you know that I have carried it next to my heart since the day she died — but now I think it's time to pass the torch.

SCOTTY. Dad ...

JOSHUA. No, I think you should have it. Please. 'Sides, you're gonna need somethin to keep you on time, 'cause if the Field Rep keeps the men waitin', they'll have you for breakfast: somewhere between the grits and the bituminous coal operators! *(Laughter. Applause.)* Speaking of the BCOA, James Talbert Winston, the owner of the Blue Star mines. James...?

JAMES.   Usually when I get invited to a Union function, it winds up costin' me a lot of money but I wouldn't have missed tonight for anything in the world. This country owes you a debt of gratitude, Scotty, for fighting the good fight against Communism over there in Korea. We're proud of you, boy.

JOSHUA.   I got an old family friend here, Franklin Biggs! Come on, Franklin. Come on...! *(Franklin, an expensively, if conservatively, dressed black businessman, steps forward.)*

FRANKLIN.   Scotty, it seems just like yesterday that you and my Jefferson were runnin' around and gettin' into trouble and here you are, back from the service and Jefferson, he's just goin' in, and I think ... Josh, where the hell did the time go? *(Laughter. He pulls out a pint flask.)* Anyway. Scotty, here's a little somethin', a taste of Biggs and Son "original recipe" to welcome you home. Welcome home, Scotty! *(Applause.)*

JOSHUA.   Now, how 'bout we hear from the guest of honor?

CROWD.   Speech! Speech! Speech! etc.

SCOTTY.   I wanta thank you all ... 'cept you, Stucky! *(The crowd laughs.)* But especially my dad and my mom, for this great party. I know I got big shoes to fill but I'm not afraid of a little hard work. I'm lookin' forward to workin' for the United Mine Workers of America, the greatest labor organization in the history of the world, and I intend to do the best damn job I can! *(Applause.)*

JOSHUA.   Hey, Lana, haven't we got some cake or somethin'?

LANA.   Comin' up!

JOSHUA.   Ladies and Gentlemen, the smokin' lamp is lit! *(Joshua hugs Scotty.)* I'm so damn proud of you.

SCOTTY.   Thanks, dad.

JOSHUA.   Stucky! Get this man a drink will ya?

STUCKY.   Yes sir! *(Lana comes in with a cake with candles. The*

group begins to clap rythmically. Scotty blows out the candles. Cheers.
As Joshua passes by Lana, his hand sweeps casually down her back.
Scotty notices. He looks away. The lights fade down to a single spot
on Joshua.)

Scene 4

The Union Hall, one night later. Josh is alone onstage, con-
tract in hand as he talks on the phone.

JOSHUA.   I am doin' the best I can ... I will talk to the local companies but.... Listen, you people in Washington have
gotta cut us some slack on this contract or the rank and file
is gonna go apeshit! We're in a real bad position here. *(Un-*
seen by Joshua, Lana enters the room.) You can't just dump this
problem on the districts and then walk away! Fine. *(Joshua*
hangs up in disgust. He goes back to poring over the contract.)
LANA.   Hey.
JOSHUA.   Hey.
LANA.   Still no help from the National?
JOSHUA.   I'm beatin' my head against a wall. I just keep
thinkin' there's gotta be somethin' else.
LANA.   Well, killin' yourself in the process won't make any-
body but them operators happy. You'll figure somethin' out.
JOSHUA.   Keep tellin' me that.
LANA.   I got you a sandwich and some coffee from that new
place in Morgan.
JOSHUA.   What happened to Jack's?
LANA.   Outta business.
JOSHUA.   Everything's changin', innit?
LANA.   Not everything. Good luck with your meetin'.
JOSHUA.   It's probably gonna go late but when it's over, if
you wouldn't mind the comp'ny?
LANA.   I'll leave the porch light on.
JOSHUA.   Thanks. *(They kiss.)*
LANA.   Josh. It's a good thing ... what you're doin' for

Franklin.

JOSHUA.   No problem.

LANA.   We both know that ain't true. Thanks. *(As she exits James comes in.)* Evenin'. *(He nods. Watches her leave.)*

JAMES.   Attractive girl.

JOSHUA.   Cut the crap, James. Let's just get to it.

JAMES.   You gotta complaint about the contract?

JOSHUA.   You're gonna have big problems with these layoffs.

JAMES.   We all had to give a little, Joshua, and it seems to me, all things considered, that you fellas did pretty well: little salary increase, even got yourself that coal royalty. You been talkin' about buildin' a hospital here in Howsen County for years. With those royalties now you can do it.

JOSHUA.   That's just sugar coatin'.

JAMES.   The National agreed to this contract, Joshua.

JOSHUA.   Yeah? Well, when I'm the one who has to sell it to the rank and file, and there's no tellin' what they'll do.

JAMES.   The number of layoffs in that contract is non-negotiable.

JOSHUA.   Nothing is non-negotiable. I want a thirty percent reduction in the layoffs and I want'em staggered out over the length of the contract. *(James laughs and begins to sing.)*

JAMES.   "Beautiful dreamer, wake unto me ..." *(Franklin walks in. Beat.)*

FRANKLIN.   'Evenin' Joshua. Mr. Winston.

JAMES.   You expectin' "company," Joshua?

JOSHUA.   Franklin's people are pretty worried about these layoffs too.

FRANKLIN.   These layoffs always seem to be kinda "selective," Mr. Winston, you know what I mean? So, my people got together 'n asked me to step forward here, try to work somethin' out.

JOSHUA.   I explained to Franklin that who gets laid off is management's call and that maybe he oughta speak to you about it ... 'fore things get outta hand.

JAMES.   You're very generous with my time, Joshua. I can't help you, Mr. Biggs. Much as I'd like to. It's not that I have anything against the colored but let's face it, the men are happier workin' with their own kind. I'm just respectin' the wishes of the community here.

FRANKLIN.   Yes sir, community is sure important, I know that. You take my community now; people on the Eastside are hurtin' real bad, gettin' so's I don't know what they might do. *(Beat.)*

JAMES.   Is this supposed to be a threat of some kind?

FRANKLIN.   No sir, I wouldn't dream of that.

JOSHUA.   What Franklin and I are sayin' is, we can't guarantee you labor peace ... not the way this thing stands right now. You could be lookin' at wildcat strikes in every local in the district ... wouldn't be a damn thing we could do about it.

FRANKLIN.   So, I'm just wonderin', when you get down to it, how important are those "wishes of the community?" Really. *(Beat.)*

JAMES.   Well, everything's relative of course.

FRANKLIN.   I was sure we could work somethin' out.

JAMES.   I haven't agreed to anything yet.

FRANKLIN.   I just want the same thing Joshua wants ...

JOSHUA.   ... we want the layoffs reduced and staggered out ...

FRANKLIN.   ... but I want 'em on *seniority,* not color.

JAMES.   I could maybe ... reduce the layoffs by ten percent; staggered out over the first year of the contract. On Seniority.

JOSHUA.   Thirty percent.

JAMES.   I can't do any better'n ten.

JOSHUA.   Twenty. Over the whole contract.

JAMES.   Fifteen, over two years but I get your word, both of you: no walkouts, no slowdowns, and no *wildcat strikes.* The coal never stops.

JOSHUA.   All right.

FRANKLIN.   So, we all in agreement then?

JAMES.   I'm gonna need one more thing. I'm gonna need a little more leeway from the District on this safety issue.

JOSHUA.   You were supposed to hose down your mines two weeks ago.

JAMES.   I cannot stop production right now.

JOSHUA.   You got a dust problem, James, and we're in the middle of the fuckin' explosion season for Christ sakes.

JAMES.   And I'm in the middle of contract negotiations with the TVA and if they think I can't deliver, they'll go somewhere else and we'll all be outta work!

JOSHUA.   I've given you way too much slack as is; safety is not on the table.

JAMES.   "Nothin' is non-negotiable."

JOSHUA.   Forget it.

JAMES.   I just need another six weeks, Joshua.

JOSHUA.   I am not gonna endanger my men!

JAMES.   No, you're just gonna put'em all outta work! Forget it, Franklin, forget the whole damn thing!

FRANKLIN.   All right, let's all just hold on a minute! Now there's gotta be some middle ground here.

JAMES.   Hey, I'm not the problem; I'm ready to deal. *(Franklin pulls Joshua aside.)*

FRANKLIN.   Come on, Josh, there's gotta be some way to make this thing work.

JOSHUA.   You got people down there, Franklin; you willin' to take that risk?

FRANKLIN.   What choice've we got?

JAMES.   Six weeks. What's that in the great scheme of things? Gimme those piddlin' six weeks and you guarantee your membership, all your membership, a job for the next three years. *(Beat.)*

JOSHUA.   I'll give you three weeks, that's it.

JAMES.   Oh, come on, Joshua, you know I can't ...

JOSHUA.   That's it!

JAMES.   Okay.

JOSHUA.   But I want extra ventilation equipment in those mines *this* week.

JAMES.   It's on order from Louisville; soon as I get it, it goes in.

JOSHUA.   It goes in this week if you have to rent a flatbed from U-Haul and drive it down here yourself. This week!

JAMES.   Okay.

JOSHUA. I'm not done. That land of yours between County Roads 27 and 35 just outside of Morgan? Blue Star's gonna *donate* a hundred-and-fifty-acre parcel for that hospital.

JAMES. A hundred and fifty ... you're not serious?!

JOSHUA. I thought you were ready to deal, James? Come on, I'll make you a goddman deal.

FRANKLIN. Come on.

JAMES. "Come on," my ass. It's no skin off your nose, is it!

JOSHUA. Franklin, I'm gonna start a fundraising drive for the endowment and I wanta see a ten thousand dollar contribution from Biggs and Son.

FRANKLIN. Ten thousand!

JAMES. "Come on," Franklin!

FRANKLIN. This hospital gonna be open to the Eastside?

JOSHUA. All the people of Howsen County.

JAMES. Well, hell, Joshua, while you're playin' Abe Lincoln why don't you put the colored in our schools!

FRANKLIN. Don't worry, Jim, my people are too smart to think that Fourteenth Amendment stuff applies to Howsen County!

JOSHUA. We have a deal or are you two gonna refight the Civil War? *(Beat.)*

JAMES. Okay.

FRANKLIN. Fine. *(Scotty walks in.)*

SCOTTY. Dad?

JOSHUA. Hey, Scotty ...

JAMES. Hi.

FRANKLIN. Hey, Scot.

JOSHUA. What's up?

SCOTTY. I didn't know if I'd see you in the mornin' so I thought maybe, we'd get a drink or somethin'.

JOSHUA. I can't right now ... how 'bout tomorrow night?

SCOTTY. I'm gonna be in Perry and Breathitt the next coupla days. Remember?

JOSHUA. Right. How 'bout next week? Tuesday night?

SCOTTY. OK. Sure. Sorry to interrupt.

JOSHUA. No problem. Give'em hell, son! *(Scotty exits. James turns to Joshua.)*

JAMES.   I'm gonna assume our conversation this evenin' was private. You pretty much thinkin' along those lines, Joshua? *(Joshua stares cooly back at James. Franklin steps in quickly.)*
FRANKLIN.   I think we all understand each other.
JOSHUA.   I'll take this contract to the Local Presidents in two weeks. If they think the men'll go for it now, fine. But if they don't; all bets are off. *(Lights shift. Joshua is left in a spot as he crosses towards Margaret.)*

Scene 5

Rowen back porch. Several nights later. Night. Margaret is seated, glass in hand. Joshua walks up.

JOSHUA.   You're up late. *(No answer.)* What're you doin' out here, Margaret, you'll catch your death o' cold.
MARGARET.   How'd your speech go?
JOSHUA.   You really wanta know? *(Beat.)* It went okay. All anybody wants to hear about is the new contract.
MARGARET.   I do wish you luck, you know. I know how important it is to you.
JOSHUA.   Thanks. *(He sits.)*
MARGARET.   I was sittin' here thinkin' about the first time I ever heard you speak. You remember? You were organizin' the men at my daddy's operation. My God, you were like some ... prophet outta the old Testament ... only a lot better lookin'. I watched you talk to that crowd and every person there thought you were talkin' to him alone. I didn't think you'd even noticed me. And then the second time I saw you was the day my daddy signed a union contract. And as you were leavin', you winked at me and said, "I'll be back for you, Maggie." *(Beat.)*
JOSHUA.   That was a long time ago, Margaret. *(He gets up and starts to leave.)*
MARGARET.   Josh? When did you stop callin' me "Maggie?" *(Beat.)*

JOSHUA. I don't know.

MARGARET. I couldn't remember either. *(Beat.)* You and me, Josh ... we are what we are. But Scotty, he really needs somethin' to believe in right now. Try not to disappoint'im too much, will you? *(Margaret exits. Light shift. Spot on Joshua as he crosses into the bar area.)*

Scene 6

One week later. A bar. A juke box plays in the background. Scotty waves to Joshua.

SCOTTY. Dad?

JOSHUA. Sorry I'm late. *(Scotty hands him a beer.)*

SCOTTY. Beer okay?

JOSHUA. Better'n okay.

MEN AT BAR. Hey Josh.

JOSHUA. Hey fellas, how ya doin'?

GREG. When we gonna see that new contract, Josh?

JOSHUA. Soon enough, Greg. No point in borrowin' trouble now, is there? *(Josh turns back to Scotty.)* You gonna let me pay for that, aren't ya?

SCOTTY. No.

JOSHUA. Okay. I'll get the next round then. So, how you doin'?

SCOTTY. I was wonderin' what kinda plans there were for all of us to get together for the holiday.

JOSHUA. I don't know about Thanksgivin' ...

SCOTTY. ... we haven't spent that much time together since I got back.

JOSHUA. I know, I'm sorry, but I gotta see how this contract plays out. I may have to go up to Washington, kick some ass ...

SCOTTY. ... I think it'd mean a lot to momma.

JOSHUA. I think Margaret'll understand.

SCOTTY. Are you and mom okay?

JOSHUA. Scotty, what's between your momma and me is

230

just that, all right? *(Beat.)* So, how's the job workin' out? What do you hear out there?

SCOTTY. Dad, I'm findin' a lotta stuff here that doesn't seem to add up. *(Beat.)*

JOSHUA. Like what?

SCOTTY. Well, for one thing, I got all these calls from guys about their pensions. Sam Jaspar, Steve Collins, Bob Colt ...

JOSHUA. Oh, that's probably just some bureaucratic fuck–up ...

SCOTTY. Dad, I gotta whole list here, it goes District-wide.

JOSHUA. Look, Scotty, don't worry about it.

SCOTTY. What do you mean, "don't worry about it," this is my job!

JOSHUA. Your job is to collect grievances and report'em to the District President. All right? You've done it.

SCOTTY. Dad, *Silus Howard got turned down.* Silus. He marched on the tipple with you and gramma Mary Anne. He was there. And they told him he been "outta the mines too long" for a pension. What the hell is goin' on? *(Beat. Joshua pulls Scotty aside.)*

JOSHUA. Okay, I'll tell you, but this doesn't go any further'n here. The truth is ... the pension plan is underfunded. The National had to tighten up the require-ments or watch the whole thing fold.

SCOTTY. You mean they're trimmin' the rolls?

JOSHUA. That's right.

SCOTTY. Why didn't you tell me that up front?

JOSHUA. Look ... it's a complicated situation and most of the men aren't gonna understand it.

SCOTTY. So don't tell'em?

JOSHUA. Scotty, I run this district but I don't call the shots. I have to do a lotta things I don't like 'cause that's what the National wants. I'm just followin' orders here.

SCOTTY. I thought I left all that "followin' orders" stuff back in Korea. What's Silus Howard, dad, just an "acceptable casualty?"

JOSHUA. Look, Scotty, you're makin' this sound a lot worse'n ...

SCOTTY.   It's the same goddamn thing! One time over there I got ordered to take this village, see, and I knew it was a mistake but I went ahead anyway 'cause those were my orders and so I marched my men in there and they fuckin' cut us to pieces! *(Beat.)*
JOSHUA.   You were just doin' your job, Scotty.
SCOTTY.   Two days later, they ordered us to pull out. The men just looked at me like.... What was the point, dad? What *is* the point? Why'd you make me field rep if you don't want me to *look after my men?*
JOSHUA.   I made you field rep 'cause I thought I could depend on you.
SCOTTY.   "Depend on" or just rubber stamp?
JOSHUA.   Look, Scotty, we meet with the Local Presidents in one week; Just help me get this contract through, okay? That'll settle us for the next three years and maybe by then, the recession'll be over and we can fix all these things. Make it right. Okay?
SCOTTY.   I don't know if I can do that.
JOSHUA.   Please, Scotty, stay with me, all right? I need you. Christ Almighty, you got doubts okay, but don't just up and quit on me!
SCOTTY.   I just need you to tell me the truth, dad; that's all. Whatever it is.
JOSHUA.   OK.
SCOTTY.   Okay. *(Joshua raises his glass.)*
JOSHUA.   Here's to better days. And a new contract. To the Rowens! *(Lights shift. Scotty exits. Joshua remains in a spot. Lana enters.)*

Scene 7

The Union Hall. One week later.

LANA.   We hear back from any of the other districts?
JOSHUA.   Birmingham turned the contract down flat.
LANA.   Oh, Christ.

JOSHUA. I hear they're already walkin' off the job in West Virginia.

LANA. They must be goin' crazy up in Washington.

JOSHUA. Oh yeah, now they wanta talk to me. Now that this district's all that stands between them and forty thousand national guardsmen. What've you been hearin' in Morgan?

LANA. People are scared. Angry.

JOSHUA. The fuckin' National's just been to the well once too often. I tried to tell'em that, you heard me. I tried to tell'em. Fuck it. What time is it?

LANA. Almost ten.

JOSHUA. You seen Scotty today?

LANA. This mornin'.

JOSHUA. He seem okay to you?

LANA. How do you mean?

JOSHUA. I don't know, I just ... I don't know. Where the hell is everybody?

LANA. They oughta be here inna coupla minutes. *(Scotty enters.)*

SCOTTY. Dad.

JOSHUA. Hey, Scotty.

SCOTTY. They're comin' back now.

JOSHUA. What's the feelin' out there?

SCOTTY. Gonna be a tough sell.

JOSHUA. Tell me somethin' I don't know. You ready?

SCOTTY. Let's do it. *(Stucky enters.)*

STUCKY. I think we're all here, Mr. Rowen.

JOSHUA. Send'em in.

STUCKY. All right! All right, let's go fellas. *(The local presidents enter; some sit, some stand. Their mood is grim. Joshua stands.)*

JOSHUA. Okay, we're in order. The new contract. I think we all know what we're dealin' with here. We got us a salary increase and a coal royalty. That royalty, in combination with local donations, should build us a hospital here in Howsen County. That's the good news. The bad news is there'll be a lot more layoffs. Believe me, we are doin' a lot better than most of the other districts. I have been squeezin' concessions outta local operators till my hands are raw. Now, I know it's not a great contract, but we could've done a lot worse and that's what we need to make clear to the men.

CALVIN. We all appreciate what you done, Josh, but these layoffs are just too damn much. *(Murmurs of agreement.)* I don't see how we can recommend this.

JOSHUA. Look, Calvin, we got an industry-wide recession here 'n we pushed the BCOA as far as we could. The National knows what it's doin'.

CHUCK. I'm with Calvin; this layoff business is bullshit! Membership ain't gonna take too much more of this, I mean it ...

JOSHUA. Hey, Chuck, we're all on the same team here, all right?

CHUCK. They fired my brother last week, Josh. Twenty-eight years in the mines and they just threw his ass out! Dave didn't get nothin'; he don't know nothin' but coal. What's he s'posed to do now? Huh? What're we s'posed to tell our people, Josh?

JOSHUA. Look, the market'll come back, just like it always has, and when it does, there'll still be a UMW here to look after the miners' interests and that's the important thing.

CALVIN. And what're the men s'posed to do in the meantime? Like Chuck was sayin' about his brother. The National's just turnin' its back on them ...

JOSHUA. Wait a minute, Calvin, nobody's turnin' ...

CALVIN. When the National says "layoffs" it's just words to them, numbers onna page, but what it comes down to is people like Dave and his family. Chuck's right, what's he gonna do now? There ain't no other kinda work around here.

JOSHUA. Look, you've had your say, Calvin, more'n your say, and we've all heard you. Now it's time to close ranks 'n move on. The National is aware of the problem and they'll take care of it. *(Calvin sits down.)*

CALVIN. Well, let's hope they do a better job with this'n they do with safety.

SCOTTY. You gotta problem at Blue Star?

JOSHUA. ... Let's go, fellas ...

CALVIN. ... I been complainin' about the dust down there

for months ...

JOSHUA.   ... We're wanderin' here ...

CALVIN.   ... Whole operation's dry as a box of matches ...

JOSHUA.   ... That's enough, Calvin ...

SCOTTY.   ... Who'd you talk to...?

CALVIN.   ... Joshua said he'd take care of it personally ...

JOSHUA.   ... Let's get back to the contract! *(Scotty stands up.)*

SCOTTY.   Why didn't you tell me this?

JOSHUA.   Because it's bein' taken care of.

SCOTTY.   You heard Calvin, it's not bein' taken care of. Why didn't you tell me!

JOSHUA.   Because I didn't want a three hour argument about it. *(Scotty starts to leave.)* Where do you think you're goin'?

SCOTTY.   I'm gonna go down to Blue Star and pull those men out right now.

JOSHUA.   The hell you are.

SCOTTY.   Come on, Calvin.

JOSHUA.   Sit down, Calvin! Now you listen to me, Scotty, I gave my word that there would be no wildcat strikes. You pull those men out and you will kill this contract.

SCOTTY.   I don't give a fuck about this contract!

JOSHUA.   Now you listen to me, goddammit...!

MIKE.   ... All right, let's all just hold on a minute ...

JOSHUA.   ... there is more at stake here than a goddamn piece of paper!

SCOTTY.   You're right about that. Let's go, Calvin.

MIKE.   Hey, wait a minute, Scotty!

JOSHUA.   Sit down, the both of you!

SCOTTY.   I can't, Dad! Now, why won't you come with me and help pull those men out?!

JOSHUA.   Scotty, you are either with us or against us.

SCOTTY.   I'm gonna go take care of my men. *(Scotty and Calvin exit.)*

JOSHUA.   You walk outta here, you turn your back on this Union, and I swear to God, I will cut you out of it like a boil! *(Beat.)*

GREG.   Jesus, Josh.

JOSHUA.   All right, let's not panic here.

MIKE.   What're we gonna do if they wildcat?

JOSHUA.   It's not gonna come to that.

GREG.   How do you know?!

JOSHUA.   *Because I won't let it!* I'll deal with Blue Star and there won't be no goddamn walkout. Now, let's us get this contract out to the rank and file before anybody else gets crazy! The Union needs this contract, fellas, and we need it a lot worse'n anybody knows. The truth is, we're a fuckin' house of cards right now and if this District goes, all the rest'll fall. The Union needs our support; now, which side are we on? Are we gonna get behind it?! *(The men look at one another warily.)*

MIKE.   I'll do what I can, Josh.

CHUCK.   Hell, we'll all do what we can but if those men walk out, our men are like to join'em. *(The men exit, sullen and subdued.)*

STUCKY.   You okay, Mr. Rowen?

JOSHUA.   Get me a drink.

STUCKY.   Yes sir.

LANA.   Mebbe you oughta slow down a little.

JOSHUA.   I need a drink, Lana, not a lecture! Get James Talbert Winston on the phone. *(She goes to the phone. Dials.)* A wildcat strike at Blue Star. Jesus.

STUCKY.   Here's your drink, Mr. Rowen.

JOSHUA.   He doesn't know what he's doin'.

LANA.   Mr. Winston, please.... I'm calling for Joshua Rowen ... uh, huh ...

JOSHUA.   Is he there? *(She shakes her head.)* No message.

LANA.   No. No thank you. *(She hangs up.)* He just left. She didn't know where to.

JOSHUA.   Great. Just great!

LANA.   You're gonna need Franklin.

JOSHUA.   Get'im on the phone. Scotty's gonna fuck up the whole thing.

STUCKY.   You want me to do somethin' here, Mr. Rowen?

JOSHUA.   Go down to Blue Star and see how serious they

236

really are about this. Stucky! I don't want to give anybody down there an excuse to make trouble. Don't start nothin'; just find out what's goin' on. *(Stucky exits.)*

LANA. Franklin? It's Lana Toller for Joshua Rowen.

JOSHUA. Gimme that. Franklin? You better get over to the Union hall; we gotta problem. I'll explain when you get here. *(He hangs up.)*

LANA. What do you think's gonna happen?

JOSHUA. I don't know.

LANA. Josh, what Calvin said, is that true?

JOSHUA. What are you sayin' to me, Lana?

LANA. I have friends down there ... I'm askin' you, did you know there was a problem at Blue Star? *(Beat.)*

JOSHUA. I didn't have anything else to trade'em. *(Beat.)*

LANA. What have you done, Joshua.

JOSHUA. You think James Talbert Winston was gonna help us outta the goodness of his heart? *This is how things get done.*

LANA. It don't have to be that way.

JOSHUA. No? Franklin was right there, and he didn't like it any better'n I did but what choice did we have?

LANA. There must've been somethin' else.

JOSHUA. What do you know about it, Lana? Nothin'! *(Beat.)*

LANA. No, you're right, I guess not. *(She picks up her coat and heads for the door.)*

JOSHUA. Where the hell do you think you're goin'?

LANA. I don't know what I was thinkin', Josh. I know, I thought I was part of somethin' here ...

JOSHUA. Look, Lana ...

LANA. I'm not talkin' about us, Josh, I'm talkin' about you. This place. This was s'posed to be somethin' different and now I think, what have we been doin' all this time? I can't do this, Josh. I'm sorry. I won't. *(She leaves. Beat. Joshua gets a drink. James enters with Sheriff Ray.)*

JAMES. Joshua?

JOSHUA. You heard about the walkout?

JAMES. Security called me as soon as they got to the mine.

RAY. Hey, Josh.

JOSHUA. *(Re: the Sheriff.)* I see you came loaded for bear.

JAMES. I'm not gonna take any chances, here. We had a deal, Joshua. You agreed to it.

JOSHUA. I know.

JAMES. Then call this off!

JOSHUA. I can't.

JAMES. Look, are you in charge of this district or not?! Put that damn local in trusteeship and I'll bring in a new crew. I will not permit this, Joshua; the National won't permit this.

JOSHUA. The National won't care if you "voluntarily" close your mine.

JAMES. If I what?!

JOSHUA. Shut it down and Calvin and Scotty haven't got a cause. Shut it down and hose it, like you should've done a month ago.

JAMES. I can't stop now! I close it or they close it, it doesn't make any goddamn difference, I'm outta business! *(Stucky enters.)*

STUCKY. I didn't see Calvin, Mr. Rowen, but I talked to Scotty up at the gate. They're all comin' out, startin' at midnight.

JAMES. Great.

STUCKY. Mr. Rowen. Scotty said to be sure and tell you that once the men come up, they're not leavin'. They're gonna *occupy the tipple* and make sure no other crews go down there.

JAMES. Jesus fuckin' Christ. Ray, get your men ready ...

JOSHUA. Ray! Nobody leaves, Stucky. Shut it down, James! You go down there in force, it'll be a fuckin' bloodbath.

JAMES. Well they shoulda thought of that before. Now, that's private property and I want those men outta there! I'll meet you down at the gate in five minutes.

JOSHUA. I'm not goin'. *(Beat.)* Scotty's right.

JAMES. With you or without you, Joshua, it doesn't make a damn bit a difference to me. *(Suddenly there is a tremendous explosion nearby. One of the windows shatters under the force of the blast. A lound horn begins to wail.)*

JOSHUA. Get down! RAY. Jesus! JAMES. What the hell?!

JAMES. Goddamn it, you see that?! They fuckin' bombed my operation! *(Ray has pulled his gun out and is looking cau-*

tiously through the shattered window.)

JOSHUA.   Shut up, James, until we figure out what the hell is goin' on! Go get your 'mergency generator runnin'. *(James exits. Joshua picks up the phone.)* Phone's dead. Ray, get on your car radio and get an ambulance and the fire department down there. Stucky, see if you can find out what's goin' on; give Ray whatever he needs. *(Ray and Stucky exit. Joshua looks through the window. There are muffled explosions in the distance.)* Jesus God have mercy. *(Beat. Franklin enters.)*

FRANKLIN.   I got here as quick as I could. What the hell's goin' on?

JOSHUA.   We don't know for sure. Scotty was leadin' a walkout. There was some kinda explosion.

FRANKLIN.   Where is Scotty?

JOSHUA.   Stucky saw'im up at the gate; he should be okay.

FRANKLIN.   What're we gonna do, Josh? *(Outside, a gasoline generator starts up. Stucky staggers in, carrying a badly wounded man in his arms.)*

JOSHUA.   Christ almight! Sit'im down there. Franklin, hand me that first aid kit.

STUCKY.   The explosion was down in onna the workin' galleries.

JOSHUA.   Where'd you find'im?

STUCKY.   'Bout fifty yards this side of the mantrap. Figure he musta been thrown twenty, mebbe thirty feet. *(The man is burned along one side of his body, and he is bleeding from both his ears and his mouth. He moans.)*

JOSHUA.   Easy now, easy. Breath this. *(He shoves smelling salts under his nose. The man jerks upright.)* Did you see what happened? *(No response.)* Did you see what happened?

FRANKLIN.   He can't hear you, Josh. *(The man pats his breast pocket. Joshua pulls out a piece of paper.)*

JOSHUA.   He's gotta sign-in sheet. Least we know who's down there. *(Joshua turns the list over and scribbles a note. He shows his written question to the man and hands him the pen.)* Did you see what happened? *(The man tries to write.)*

STUCKY.   They gotta hose goin' down there, Mr. Rowen, but we might just as well piss on it for all the good it'll do.

JOSHUA. *(To Stucky.)* Ok. Get out there and get ready for the rescue crews. I'll be out inna minute. Stucky? *(He pulls Stucky aside.)* Make sure my boy's okay, huh? Keep an eye out for'em. *(Stucky exits. James enters.)*

JAMES. God. That's Bob Smalley; he's onna my mine guards. Is he gonna be okay?

JOSHUA. I think so. Stucky went to get some help. He hadda crew list on him, so at least we'll know how many are missin'.

JAMES. I coulda told you that; nightshift in Gallery Seventeen is twenty-two men. Could he tell you what happened?

JOSHUA. *(To Franklin.)* All we got is a note. Can you read it? *(Franklin looks at Bob's scrawl.)*

FRANKLIN. It just says, "dust." *(Stunned silence.)*

JOSHUA. *(To James.)* You son of a bitch. *(Sheriff Ray enters.)*

RAY. Mr. Winston, emergency crew's are on their way; should be here inna coupla minutes. I'm gonna wait for'em up here and then guide'em on down.

JAMES. That's good, Ray.

RAY. We also gotta news crew from Channel Seven here, chompin' at the bit ...

JAMES. A news crew!

RAY. ... I can keep'em up the road apiece for a while but when the rest of'em get here, somebody's gonna have to talk to'em.

JOSHUA. Well, send'em on down, Ray. *(Ray starts to leave.)*

JAMES. Wait a minute, Ray!

JOSHUA. What're you gonna do, James, pretend you don't have a problem down there?! Go on, Ray, go get'em!

RAY. Mr. Winston?

JAMES. Ten minutes, Ray, and then you let'em go as far as here.

RAY. You got it. *(Ray leaves.)*

JAMES. Okay, Joshua, you got all the answers, what do you think we oughta say to these people?

JOSHUA. What do you mean, "we?" You're gonna tell'em the truth; you had a dust problem and you didn't take care of it.

JAMES.   Don't you forget Joshua, you are in this every bit as deep as I am!

JOSHUA.   It was your operation!

JAMES.   And they were your men! You coulda pulled'em out anytime!

JOSHUA.   You are *not* gonna lay this on the Union!

JAMES.   I am not gonna be the fall guy, here, Joshua. If I go, I am gonna take the Union with me, THE WHOLE DAMN THING! *(Beat. Joshua walks away. James gestures towards Bob.)* We shouldn't be talkin' 'bout this in front of him.

FRANKLIN.   He can't hear you; his eardrums are bust.

JAMES.   And how about you, Franklin, how are your eardrums?

FRANKLIN.   You don't have to worry about me, James; we're all in this together now.

JAMES.   That's all I'm sayin', Joshua. We're all in this together, so we might as well be smart about it. *(Stucky enters.)*

STUCKY.   Mr. Rowen, Sheriff said to tell you he'd appreciate it if you could meet the rescue crews down at the mine. Also, that another news crew arrived and they're all gettin' pretty restless; somebody's gotta talk to'em. What do you want me to say?

JOSHUA.   Tell'em I'll be out there inna few minutes. Help this guy over to the Medics, will you, Stucky? *(Stucky helps Bob out. Franklin glances at the crew list while Joshua gets a drink.)*

JAMES.   What do you wanta do, Joshua?

JOSHUA.   Just shut up for a minute! *(Joshua downs the drink.)*

FRANKLIN.   Josh. Scotty's name is on here.

JOSHUA.   What?

FRANKLIN.   He's down in there with'em.

JOSHUA.   Lemme see. *(Beat.)* Why did he go back? *(Beat. Margaret enters.)*

MARGARET.   Joshua? *(Joshua is still stunned. He looks at her in disbelief.)*

JOSHUA.   What are you doin' here?

MARGARET.   What happened? The phone's been ringin' off the hook all night ... people askin' about you and Scotty ... then drivin' over, I heard the explosion ... hell, everybody in

Howsen County heard it. Are you all right? *(Beat.)*

JOSHUA.   There's nothin' you can do here, Margaret.

MARGARET.   Are you okay, Joshua? What is goin' on out there?

JOSHUA.   Margaret ... please ... go home, we'll handle this.

MARGARET.   Is that what you fellas are doin'; you "handlin' it?" You got things under control? Where's Scotty? *(Beat.)* Where's Scotty? What is it? What aren't you tellin' me? *(Beat.)*

JOSHUA.   Scotty was down at the mine. *(Beat.)*

MARGARET.   What was he doin' there? *(Beat.)*

JOSHUA.   He was takin' the men out. *(Beat.)*

MARGARET.   Why? *(Beat.)*

JOSHUA.   It was unsafe.

MARGARET.   Why were they down there? *(Joshua moves towards her, as if to embrace her.)* Don't touch me! No. Don't ... touch. What did you do, Josh?

FRANKLIN.   ... Margaret, nobody knew this was gonna happen ...

MARGARET.   ... What did you do...?

JAMES.   ... It was an accident, Margaret ...

MARGARET.   ... You killed him ...

JOSHUA.   ... No ...

FRANKLIN.   ... That ain't fair, Margaret ...

MARGARET.   *(Crying.)* SHUT UP! All of you, just shut up! God, I am so sick of you all! Where's my Scotty, Josh? Where is he? *(Margaret exits. Beat.)*

JAMES.   Josh?

FRANKLIN.   I'm sorry, Joshua.

JAMES.   Jesus, I'm so sorry.

JOSHUA.   *(To James.)* I can't do this ...

JAMES.   Look ... Joshua ... you're right, you shouldn't have to face those guys out there right now. You let me go talk to'em, okay? *(Stucky re-enters.)*

STUCKY.   Mr. Rowen, we can't hold'em back much longer.

JAMES.   That's okay, Stucky, I'll come out and make a statement.

STUCKY.   They wanta hear Mr. Rowen.

JAMES.   It's all right, Stucky, Josh 'n I agreed that I would ...

242

STUCKY.   Those are Union men in that mine and their people wanta hear from the leadership! Mr. Rowen? *(Beat.)*
JOSHUA.   Okay, Stucky.
JAMES.   *(Panicked.)* Joshua...?! *(Stucky exits as Sheriff Ray enters.)*
RAY.   Mr. Winston, somebody's gotta talk to 'em now!
JAMES.   I'll just say a few words, Joshua, and then you come out. Okay? *(James turns helplessly to Franklin.)* Franklin...? *(James and Sheriff Ray exit. There is a burst of noise from the Reporters.)*
REPORTERS.   What happened, Mr. Winston? How many men are down there? What's goin' on, Mr. Winston? Over here, sir! What happened?
JAMES.   We don't know a whole lot more'n you people about what happened down in Gallery #17 but rest assured, we are gonna find out.
FRANKLIN.   What're you gonna say, Joshua?
JAMES.   In the meantime, our hearts and our prayers go out to their loved ones.
JOSHUA.   I don't know.
JAMES.   I would like to say that our primary concern at Blue Star has always been the welfare of our men and I think that right now the most important thing is to do everything we can for the men still trapped in that mine.
FRANKLIN.   What're you gonna tell'em?
JAMES.   Now, Joshua Rowen, the President of UMW District #16 will be out here any minute and he will have more to say about that.
FRANKLIN.   Joshua? *(Stucky enters again.)*
STUCKY.   Mr. Rowen? We gotta go, Mr. Rowen. *(Joshua and Stucky step outside. They are immediately surrounded by the Reporters. Joshua comes and stands next to James.)*
REPORTERS.   Mr. Rowen, what happened? Over here, Mr. Rowen! What's the story, Mr. Rowen! This way! Over here! How many men are still in there?! Is there any chance of them bein' alive?! Were there any survivors?! Was this a safe operation, Mr. Rowen?! etc. etc. *(Joshua signals for quiet.)*
JOSHUA.   What happened here ... at Blue Star ... is a tragedy. They'll be an inestigation, I promise, a thorough investigation. But I can say that ... what I can say is ... what I can

243

say is that Blue Star has always been a safe and responsible operation with a good record. What this ... tragedy says to me is that one thing we all know but nobody likes to admit. And that is ... that mining is a dangerous business and ... we just have to live with this. *(James steps forward and pulls out the sign-in sheet.)*

JAMES.   I have a list of names of the missing ... *(As he begins to read, the Reporters freeze and the lights fade down on them. Joshua crosses DC and enters a pool of light.)*

Bob Wayland.

E.O. Baker.

Carl Nolan.

Chad Dawkins.

Gus Mayo.

Thomas Hayes.

C.C. Baker.

Carl Berry.

Willie Allen.

Jack Fox.

Frank Mosely.

Bob Lynch.

Scott Rowen.

(Everyone on stage turns and looks at Joshua. He stares front. Blackout.)

END OF PLAY

PROPERTY LIST

Drinking glass with drink (MARGARET, JOSHUA)
Drinking glasses (MARGARET)
Duffel bag (SCOTTY)
Liquor (MARGARET)
Rowen watch (JOSHUA)
Pint flask (FRANKLIN)
Cake with candles (LANA)
Contract (JOSHUA)
Beer (SCOTTY)
Coat (LANA)
Contracts (LOCAL PRESIDENTS)
Gun (1954) (RAY)
Smelling salts (JOSHUA)
Sign-in sheet (MAN)
Pen (JOSHUA)

SOUND EFFECTS

Mine explosion
Mine horn wailing (1954)
Muffled explosions (distance)
Generator start up (1954)

THE WAR ON
POVERTY

"I sat upon the shore
Fishing with the arid plain behind me
Shall I at least set my lands in order?"

— T.S. Eliot

CHARACTERS

STEVE

FRANK

JAMES TALBERT WINSTON (64)

JOSHUA ROWEN (65)

FRANKLIN BIGGS (65)

NARRATOR

The War on Poverty.

Twenty-one years later. The year is 1975.

The original Rowen homestead near the Shilling creek. The surrounding fields, now abandoned, are mostly broom sedge and hardrock with an occasional young pine tree. It is spring.

The War on Poverty.

THE WAR ON POVERTY

Early spring of 1975. We have returned to the original Rowen homestead near the stump of the Treaty Oak. The Shilling Creek is now full of silt and garbage and abandoned cars, and only occasionally rouses itself in memory of its former glory during one of those torrential thunderstorms that sometimes batter the Plateau. The surrounding fields, heavily timbered and mined and then abandoned, have also accumulated their share of refuse over the years but if you look closely, you can see that the land is slowly regenerating itself. Now it is mostly broom sedge and hardrock, but here and there a young pine asserts itself. It is spring after all, and the land, although bruised and battered, still remembers.

Darkness. The sound of wind. A tight spot comes up on Joshua Rowen. He is a lot less kempt now. His face is lined and unshaven, and his hair is longer and streaked with grey. There is still that tremendous energy about him but it seems to have turned inward.

JOSHUA.   I keep havin' this dream. *(Beat.)* In my dream, I'm crossin' some kind of desert. It's all slate and ashes and dust. I hear Scotty callin' to me and I run after his voice till I come to this river. Somehow I know it's the Shillin' but it ain't nothin' like that pathetic sewer you see out there today. This is deep and wide and fulla fast movin' muddy water. Scotty's on the other side; I can't get to'im. And then I notice he's not alone. He's standin' there with my daddy. I haven't thought about Tommy in years but there he is, got his minin' clothes on, coal dust on his face. I don't realize till I see'im how much I miss'im. And momma's standin' right next to'em, got her arm around him. And then behind them is this whole buncha people I don't know and they're all

251

talkin' to me, yellin' somethin' but I can't hear it; the river's too loud and the wind is blowin' the dust like crazy. I know if I could just hear what they were sayin' I'd know what I was supposed to do. I'm supposed to do somethin', see, but I can't hear it, I can't hear Scotty. *(Beat.)* And then I wake up. *(Spot fades out. Joshua exits. Lights come up on the stage. It is early in the morning, about thirty minutes before sunrise. DC there is a deep hole in the ground, recently dug. Next to it is a small fire and some hand tools. Two men work the area; one in the hole and the other crouching nervously on the edge. The man in the hole stands up suddenly, holding a torn piece of material, covered with dirt.)*

STEVE. Jesus, Frank, I think we hit the jackpot.

FRANK. Whattaya got?

STEVE. Can't tell for sure. Feels like a piece of buckskin.

FRANK. I'm gonna turn on the Coleman.

STEVE. Don't turn on the goddamn light.

FRANK. I can't see shit, Steve. *(Frank lights the Coleman. Steve pulls himself out of the hole. Both men crouch over the piece of buckskin.)*

STEVE. Whatdya think?

FRANK. Buckskin all right. Hand me the brush; get this dirt off it. *(Beat.)* Christ.

STEVE. Look at that beadwork.

FRANK. We got the real thing here, Steve, this is really somethin'!

STEVE. What the hell else is down there? *(A bullet explodes in the dirt behind them.)* Jesus! Let's go! *(They start off. Frank drops the piece of buckskin. He stops.)*

FRANK. I dropped it! *(Another bullet kicks up the dirt at their feet.)*

STEVE. Let's go! *(Both men run off. Beat. Joshua hurries on carrying a rifle. He stops and looks off after the departed men. He looks at the holes they've dug. He looks out at the landscape. Franklin Biggs enters slowly. Always heavy, his muscle has begun to turn to fat. He is sweating heavily, and his face is dark with exertion.)*

FRANKLIN. Jesus, Josh, you coulda killed somebody.

JOSHUA. I just wanted to chase'em off. This is private property; they had no damn business bein' out here.

FRANKLIN. Man, this fog is a bitch. (*Franklin takes out a pill-box and puts a small tablet under his tongue. James calls from off-stage.*)

JAMES. (*Off.*) Joshua?! Franklin?!

FRANKLIN. Over here, James!

JAMES. (*Off.*) Where are you?!

FRANKLIN. This way! (*James Talbert Winston runs on out of breath. He's still a distinguished looking man but there is a tiredness about him that has nothing to do with the distance he has just run. His pants are torn and covered with mud.*)

JAMES. Jesus, do you guys mind waitin' up?! I can't see shit around here.

FRANKLIN. What happened to your pants? (*James pulls out a bottle and drinks.*)

JAMES. Nothin'. (*Franklin laughs.*) I heard shots.

FRANKLIN. Daniel Boone here chased off some poachers.

JOSHUA. They were grave robbers, not poachers.

JAMES. Grave robbers? (*Franklin unfolds a map.*)

JOSHUA. Big local industry these days. Hell, what else is there since the mines shut down.

JAMES. You mean there's real money in that?

JOSHUA. You wanta franchise, James?

FRANKLIN. I don't see nothin' 'bout a cemetery on the map.

JOSHUA. All these mountains is full of bones; everywhere you walk.

FRANKLIN. I can't tell where the hell we are. Any of you guys know?

JAMES. The ass end of nowhere.

FRANKLIN. I'm serious.

JAMES. Lemme see. (*James and Franklin look at the map; Josh stays apart from them.*) I think that must be some part of the Shillin' over there.

FRANKLIN. So Morgan must be that way. Right?

JAMES. Can't be; we came in from over there. (*James points in the opposite direction.*)

FRANKLIN. Josh?

JOSHUA.   Got me.

JAMES.   You mean we're really lost? Jesus fuckin' Christ.

JOSHUA.   Look, 'stead of stumblin' around in the fog, why don't we just wait here till it burns off; we'll figure it out.

JAMES.   Great, that's great. Well, I hope you're satisfied, Joshua. We could've wrapped this whole thing up back in Morgan but no, you insisted we come out here and look over the property.

JOSHUA.   I think we oughta know what we're talkin' about before we sell it, that's all.

JAMES.   Well, we've seen the land now all right, we've *all* seen the land and it's just like I told you, it's a garbage dump. Can we please finish this?

FRANKLIN.   There's no point gettin' sentimental here, Josh ...

JAMES.   The hospital's dead, the court said dispose of the assets, Consolidated wants it, and I say goodbye and God bless.

FRANKLIN.   It's a good price; it'll give the creditors' somethin'....

JOSHUA.   I don't feel right about it.

JAMES.   Oh, Jesus...!

FRANKLIN.   Come on, Josh, this land has been bought and sold a thousand times!

JOSHUA.   Look, I am not gonna be pushed into somethin' here, so just back off! *(Franklin and James look at each other and shrug. They huddle around the fire.)*

JAMES.   Christ, it's cold. Put some more of that wood on the fire, Franklin.

FRANKLIN.   You put it on.

JAMES.   You're closer.

FRANKLIN.   So what?

JAMES.   So, you put it on.

FRANKLIN.   Fuck you.

JOSHUA.   You guys are really somethin'.

JAMES.   Hey! I just asked him to put some wood on the fire 'cause he was closer. Nevermind, I'll do it myself, all right? There. You happy, Franklin? *(Franklin indicates Joshua's gun.)*

FRANKLIN.   What's with the artillary, Josh?

JOSHUA. I heard there was a wolf out here.

FRANKLIN. A wolf?

JAMES. Hell, there hadn't been a wolf in the Cumberland in fifty years.

JOSHUA. Jon Victor swears he saw a wolf over on the North Fork Buckhorn last week.

JAMES. Jon Victor. You could fit that man's brain in a flea's ass and still have room for an acorn.

FRANKLIN. If Jon Victor had a thought, it'd die of loneliness! *(James and Franklin laugh.)*

JOSHUA. I just didn't wanta take any chances, that's all. *(Beat.)* Walkin' over here, did you guys see that big old tree stump on the other side of the Shillin'

JAMES. I couldn't see shit in this fog.

JOSHUA. It was huge; looked like it mighta been some kinda oak. God, it musta really been somethin' here, once. I 'member my momma usta tell me stories about these hills, 'fore the mines came. "Oaktrees like skyscrappers." I usta dream about Spring ... when I was a kid ... green like an ocean. *(Beat.)* Can I have some of that coffee, Franklin? *(Franklin passes Joshua the thermos of coffee.)*

JAMES. How about a splash of juice?

JOSHUA. No thanks. *(Franklin and James share a look.)*

FRANKLIN. You haven't gone religious on us, have you Joshua?

JAMES. He's probably havin' another hallucination or somethin'.

JOSHUA. I quit.

FRANKLIN. You quit?

JAMES. The sound you hear is the crash of alcohol related stocks going bellyup.

JOSHUA. I was spittin' blood 'n my last blackout lasted two weeks. Woke up in a goddamn men's shelter in Cincinatti, no idea how I got there. I was scared shitless. *(Beat.)*

JAMES. Damn, it's as cold as a witch's tit out here.

JOSHUA. Isn't Jefferson s'posed to get released this year?

FRANKLIN. Next March.

JOSHUA. Ten years. That's a long haul.

FRANKLIN. Yeah, well ... welcome to the Marines: "The few. The proud."

JOSHUA. Musta been a buncha guys refused to fight over there, you know? Or just went to Canada or somethin'.

FRANKLIN. Not Marine officers. Not *black* Marine officers.

JAMES. Are you sayin' it was some kind of racial thing?

FRANKLIN. What do you think?

JAMES. Jesus. Everything is race with you people ...

FRANKLIN. Why do you think that is, James?!

JOSHUA. Hey! Hey! HEY! Let's everybody take it easy.

JAMES. I'm easy.

FRANKLIN. Fine.

JAMES. Come on, Joshua, I'm freezing my ass off. Let's close this thing.

JOSHUA. You ever seen any of Consolidated's work?

JAMES. Of course. My god, that "Mountaintop removal mining" is fantastic; gonna be the wave of the future.

JOSHUA. *(Sarcastic.)* "The wave of the future!"

JAMES. You seen it, Franklin? They go in there with those big drag scoops and eat up somethin' like sixty cubic yards of earth at a time.

JOSHUA. Jesus.

JAMES. It would have taken over a hundred men workin' all day to dig that much coal.

FRANKLIN. You gotta admit, Josh, it's pretty amazing.

JOSHUA. You see what they did to Martin County? They leveled that place!

JAMES. Jesus Christ on a cross, Joshua, it's coal mining not gardening!

JOSHUA. Well, that makes it all right then, don't it!

JAMES. Look, this new system is cheaper and a hell of a lot more efficient; you get a hundred percent of the coal and 'stead of a buncha useless mountains, you wind up with flat pastureland.

JOSHUA. Oh, so this is "progress," huh?

JAMES. Well, it's *safer*. Nobody dies choking on coal dust or in an explosion. I'd of thought you of all people would appreciate that! *(Beat.)*

JOSHUA.   Fuck you. *(Joshua gets up and walks away. Franklin angrily walks James in the opposite direction.)*
FRANKLIN.   Jesus, James...!
JAMES.   No, to hell with him! Where does he get off with this holier'n thou atitude?
FRANKLIN.   All right, calm down, James ...
JAMES.   I didn't hear him complainin' about coal when it was payin' his liquor bills!
FRANKLIN.   All right, that's enough! Just give us five minutes here, will ya? *(Franklin crosses back to Joshua.)*
JAMES.   Fine! *(James exits.)*
FRANKLIN.   How come you're makin' this so hard, Josh?
JOSHUA.   I told you, I don't wanta get pushed into somethin' ...
FRANKLIN.   Yeah, okay ...
JOSHUA.   And that fuckin' James...!
FRANKLIN.   He's an asshole, all right, no argument. Come on, Josh, what's goin' on here? *(Beat.)*
JOSHUA.   Last coupla months ... I can't help thinkin' 'bout things; goin' over 'n over'em in my head.
FRANKLIN.   What kinda things?
JOSHUA.   Old stuff. You know.
FRANKLIN.   What?
JOSHUA.   The day we unsealed that mine. The service. That list of names that seemed to go on forever. All those women, all those widows and daughters, standing there in black, like so many crows, lookin' right through me ...
FRANKLIN.   Josh ...
JOSHUA.   Or Stucky handin' me Scotty's watch and then walkin' away, not able to shake my hand or even look me in the face.
FRANKLIN.   *(Gently.)* You can't change nothin' in the past, Josh. You gotta let it go.
JOSHUA.   Oh, we're good at that, aren't we, we're real good at "lettin' it go." Christ, we had somethin' here, Franklin, we hadda community here, you and me, but look at it now. It's just empty house after empty house, leanin' 'gainst each other in the fog like drunks. Morgan's a fuckin' ghost town ... inna

"desert" fulla broom sedge and open graves.

FRANKLIN.   So let Consolidated come in and plow the whole damn thing under. So let'em! What difference does it make now?

JOSHUA.   I wasn't sure till this mornin' and then, walkin' out here, every once in awhile the fog'd move 'n you could see the tops of these mountains and I thought, after they come in here it'll never be the same.

FRANKLIN.   So?

JOSHUA.   It'll be like we never were. It'll be like Cassius and Mary Anne and everything we tried to do, never was. (*Beat.*)

FRANKLIN.   After we get back to Morgan, I'm gonna drive up to that ... concrete tomb where you shouldn't keep a dog and I'm gonna wait for Jefferson, even though I know he ain't ever gonna come out and talk to me, and then I'm gonna go home and that's just the way it is. And that's the difference 'tween you and me, Josh; I know that's the way it is. You're right, things oughta be different. But they ain't. And there ain't nothin' we can do about it.

JOSHUA.   But it wasn't always like that. I remember that first year after the strike, you remember this big meetin' we had in Morgan? I 'member my momma and your daddy, sittin' up on this platform made outta wagons, talkin' to this huge crowd come from all over the Cumberland: men 'n women 'n children. I hadn't never seen so many people before and the mountains behind'em seem to go on forever. And you and me, they made us stand in the back 'cause we could never sit still on them platforms. You remember?

FRANKLIN.   Yeah, I guess.

JOSHUA.   We couldn't have been, what...?

FRANKLIN.   I don't know ...

JOSHUA.   Twelve or thirteen? And we couldn't see over the people's heads, remember? So we climbed up on top of this store. And the roof was hot, so you found us somethin' to sit on ...

FRANKLIN.   A flour sack or somethin' ...

JOSHUA.   That's right. An old flour sack. And we sat there together on this little burlap island, lookin' out over this sea of people like the mountains in bloom in that spring my momma usta tell me about in her dreams, and they were all holdin' hands and swayin' back and forth and it was *all one thing.* All of us and them mountains, and I remember thinkin', there ain't nothin' we can't do! Nothin'! *(Franklin gets up and moves away.)*

FRANKLIN. That was a long time ago, Joshua. *(James returns, holding the buckskin.)*

JAMES. Hey, look what I found.

FRANKLIN. What is it?

JAMES. Piece of buckskin, I think.

FRANKLIN. Lemme see. Man, that's beautiful.

JAMES. Those guys you chased off musta dropped it. Where were they workin' when you saw them?

JOSHUA. Over there. *(James looks down into the hole.)*

JAMES. I don't see anything. *(He gets down on his hands and knees and looks into the hole.)* Wait a minute ... I think there is somethin' here. *(He reaches in and pulls out an old deerskin bundle.)* Jesus Christ. *(The men crowd around.)*

FRANKLIN. Look at the beadwork on that.

JOSHUA. Lemme see. *(James hands him the bundle.)* Looks like stars, don't it; like the milky way. Like all the stars in the sky was sown on that piece of deerhide.

JAMES. What do you think's in there?

FRANKLIN. Gotta be somethin' valuable.

JAMES. Hell, the buckskin alone's a collectors' item.

FRANKLIN. Open it up, Josh. *(Joshua slowly unwraps the bundle. The men crouch around him, next to the open grave. Pause.)*

JOSHUA. It's a baby. *(Beat.)*

JAMES. Damn.

FRANKLIN. Jesus.

JAMES. That thing must be ... what?

JOSHUA. ... two hundred years or more. Ain't been no Indians in the Cumberland for two hundred years.

FRANKLIN. Can't be that old. Look at it, man.

JOSHUA. She's beautiful. Look at her: hair; fingernails.

JAMES. I read about things like this; freak stuff. They dug

some guy out of a peat bog in Europe, couple of thousand years old.

JOSHUA.   The buckskin musta kept the water out. Preserved her. *(James takes the baby back.)*

FRANKLIN.   What do you think we oughta do with it?

JOSHUA.   I don't know.

JAMES.   It's plenty valuable, I know that. There are private collectors who'd pay thousands for something like this.

JOSHUA.   You'd sell her?

FRANKLIN.   Oh man, your taste is all in your mouth.

JOSHUA.   Jesus.

JAMES.   I found it.

JOSHUA.   On hospital land ...

JAMES.   *Was* hospital land. Don't get up on your high horse again with me Joshua.

JOSHUA.   Oh, come on ...

JAMES.   I'm serious, don't start with me.

FRANKLIN.   Fine, James, it's yours!

JOSHUA.   No, it's not! Put her back.

JAMES.   Hell, no.

JOSHUA.   Than I will. Give her here.

JAMES.   No!

JOSHUA.   Give her to me, James.

JAMES.   No, I found it, it's mine.

JOSHUA.   Give her to me!

FRANKLIN.   Come on, Joshua, quit horsing around ...

JOSHUA.   I'm not kiddin'...!

FRANKLIN.   Come on, Joshua, what difference does it make?!

JOSHUA.   IT MAKES A DIFFERENCE! *(Joshua picks up his gun.)* Now give her to me.

FRANKLIN.   Joshua!

JOSHUA.   Don't move, Franklin. *(Beat.)*

JAMES.   Goddamn you. *(Joshua cocks the rifle.)*

JOSHUA.   Do it. Go on, James. Put her down.

FRANKLIN.   Okay. Let's everybody take it easy. Put it down, James. Come on, what does it matter? Come on, James, let him have it! Give it to him and we'll all just go home. All right? *(Beat. James puts the baby down on the ground. He never takes his eyes off Joshua. Joshua picks up the baby.)* Okay, Joshua, put the gun down. *(Joshua lowers the gun but he doesn't put it down.)*

JAMES.   You are outta your fuckin' mind, Joshua; you know that? You know what this is about, don't ya Franklin? It was all my fault, right Joshua? Bullshit! You're just as guilty for what happened as I am, and you are just gonna have to live with it.

JOSHUA.   I'm tryin', James. *(James backs off.)*

JAMES.   We can get this land without you, you know? It'll take a little longer but I can get a court order. *(He exits.)*

JOSHUA.   I know he can make this work without me, Franklin, but he can't do it without you. Don't let him do it.

FRANKLIN.   It ain't gonna make no difference, Joshua.

JOSHUA.   We gotta try, don't we? *(Franklin slowly picks up his things.)*

FRANKLIN.   I'll think about it. *(He exits in the opposite direction of James. Beat. Joshua moves to the grave and kneels down. He carefully re-wraps the baby in her buckskin shroud. He starts to lay her in the grave and then stops.)*

JOSHUA.   It's cold down there, baby. It's so cold. *(He takes off his jacket and wraps it around around her. He pauses. He removes a leather thong from around his neck. Tied to it, is the now battered and tarnished Rowen family gold watch. He holds it up to the sunrise and looks at it. Then he tucks it into the coat wrapped around the infant.*

He lays her in the grave. He shoves the dirt in with his bare hands. Finished burying her, he rocks back on his heels, with his head bowed. As he prays, he begins to weep.

Behind him, and clearly unseen by Joshua, the ground erupts. Pushing up through the soil are the figures of those we have watched live and struggle and die over this ground.

Star rises, reunited with her baby at last. Joe Talbert stands beside his daughter, Rebecca.

Sally Biggs and her son Jessie stand side by side, arms around each other.)

Richard Talbert rises, his Confederate uniform still damp from the muddy waters of the Cumberland. Beside him, is his son, Randall. Jed Rowan stands next to both of them.

Scotty Rowen, crushed miner's cap under one arm, sits next to his unseeing father and drapes an arm over Joshua's shoulders. Joshua rests his head on Scotty's shoulder.

Mary Anne Rowen and Tommy Jackson stand just behind them. She touches both Joshua and Scotty. She smiles.

Long beat.

A wolf howls. Joshua grabs the rifle. He cocks it and stands up slowly. He looks out front and raises the rifle. He stops.)

JOSHUA.   Look at you, you big beautiful son of a bitch. Christ Almighty, look at you. *(The figures behind Joshua watch him without emotion. Joshua laughs. He points the gun into the air and fires it. He yells.)* RUN, YOU SON OF A BITCH! RUN! RUNNNNNNN! *(Joshua stands yelling at the wolf in sheer joy and exultation. The figures watch. Blackout.)*

END OF
THE KENTUCKY CYCLE

PROPERTY LIST

Hand tools
Beaded buckskin piece (STEVE)
Coleman stove (FRANK)
Rifle (1975) (JOSHUA)
Pillbox with pills (FRANKLIN)
Drinking bottle (JAMES)
Map, folded (FRANKLIN)
Thermos of coffee (FRANKLIN)
Deerskin bundle (JAMES)
Rowen watch on leather thong (JOSHUA)

SOUND EFFECTS

Wind

STAR'S LULLABYE

Music by
JAMES RAGLAND

[CHEROKEE INDIAN LYRIC
SPELLED PHONETICALLY]

JAHK NEH GI DUH HA TAHV SHA

TAHK LEE ___ KEE, JAHK NE GI DUH HA

TAHV SHA EE NEE ___ HA KEE.

AH HYON DA QUA LO SKO JA LO

KEE SOHN ___ KEE. OH HI TOE SKI

OH JI GO TEE SKO JA LO SOHN HA KEE.

A MINER'S LIFE

TRADITIONAL

♩ = 124

G   G
A MI-NER'S LIFE IS LIKE A

G   C
SAIL-OR'S 'BOARD A SHIP TO CROSS THE

G   D   G   G
WAVES, EV-'RY DAY HIS LIFE'S IN DAN-GER, STILL HE

A   A/G   A/F#   A/E   D   D/C   D/B   D/A
VEN-TURES BE-ING BRAVE, WATCH THE

G   G
ROCKS, THEY'RE FALL-ING DAI-LY, CARE-LESS

C   G   D
MI-NERS AL-WAYS FAIL. KEEP YOUR

G   G   C   Cm
HANDS U-PON THE DOL-LAR AND YOUR

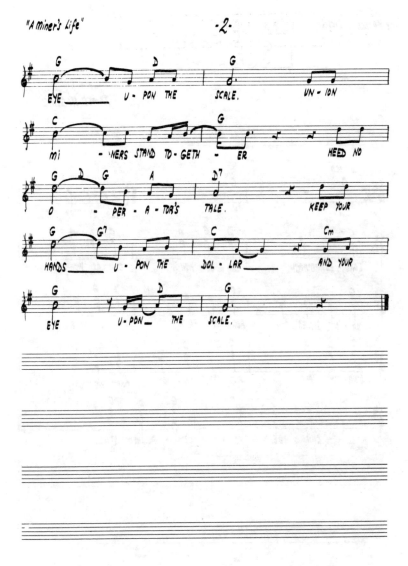

STEP BY STEP

Music by
JAMES RAGLAND

♩ = 120

STEP BY STEP THE LONG-EST MARCH CAN BE WON, CAN BE WON; MA-NY STONES CAN FORM AN ARCH, SING-LY NONE SING-LY NONE. AND BY UN-ION WHAT WE WILL, CAN BE AC-COM-PLISHED STILL.

NEW
PLAYS

THE LIGHTS
by Howard Korder

THE TRIUMPH OF LOVE
by James Magruder

LATER LIFE
by A.R. Gurney

THE LOMAN FAMILY PICNIC
by Donald Margulies

A PERFECT GANESH
by Terrence McNally

SPAIN
by Romulus Linney

Write for information as to availability
DRAMATISTS PLAY SERVICE, Inc.
440 Park Avenue South   New York, N.Y. 10016

NEW
PLAYS

LONELY PLANET
by Steven Dietz

THE AMERICA PLAY
by Suzan-Lori Parks

THE FOURTH WALL
by A.R. Gurney

JULIE JOHNSON
by Wendy Hammond

FOUR DOGS AND A BONE
by John Patrick Shanley

**DESDEMONA, A PLAY ABOUT A
HANDKERCHIEF**
by Paula Vogel

*Write for information as to
availability*
DRAMATISTS PLAY SERVICE, Inc.
440 Park Avenue South   New York, N.Y. 10016